To Mary Maples Dunn
with Compliments & affection,

FHE

CAMBRIDGE STUDIES IN EIGHTEENTH-CENTURY
ENGLISH LITERATURE AND THOUGHT 10

Sentimental Comedy: Theory & Practice

Sentimental comedy is the kind that makes you laugh and cry at the same time, like certain sequences in Charlie Chaplin films. It grew to importance on the London stage of the eighteenth century. Frank H. Ellis's study elaborates a theory of the subgenre based on close study of a wide range of plays in the period. Women, the lower classes, money, and the past are typical objects of sentimental attitudes, some of which are shown to be revolutionary as well as funny. The practice of sentimental comedy is illuminated through an analysis of sentimental attitudes in ten popular plays from 1696 to 1793. An appendix includes the texts of *The School for Lovers* by William Whitehead (1762) and Elizabeth Inchbald's *Every One Has His Fault* (1793).

With its detail concerning eighteenth-century performance and stage production, this book makes a contribution to the current revision of our understanding of sentimentalism. It presents its arguments with a clarity which will open the subject for general readers.

CAMBRIDGE STUDIES IN EIGHTEENTH-CENTURY
ENGLISH LITERATURE AND THOUGHT

The growth in recent years of eighteenth-century studies has prompted the establishment of this series of books devoted to the period. The series is designed to accommodate monographs and critical studies on authors, works, genres and other aspects of literary culture from the later part of the seventeenth century to the end of the eighteenth. Since academic engagement with this field has become an increasingly interdisciplinary enterprise, books will be especially encouraged which in some way stress the cultural context of the literature, or examine it in relation to contemporary art, music, philosophy, historiography, religion, politics, social affairs, and so on.

The mask is the familiar comic mask, but the face behind the mask expresses considerable distress: the perfect emblem for sentimental comedy.

Sentimental Comedy:
Theory & Practice

FRANK H. ELLIS

Mary Augusta Jordan Professor Emeritus, Smith College
Northampton, Massachusetts

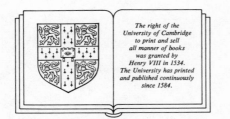

The right of the
University of Cambridge
to print and sell
all manner of books
was granted by
Henry VIII in 1534.
The University has printed
and published continuously
since 1584.

CAMBRIDGE UNIVERSITY PRESS

CAMBRIDGE
NEW YORK   PORT CHESTER   MELBOURNE   SYDNEY

Published by the Press Syndicate of the University of Cambridge
The Pitt Building, Trumpington Street, Cambridge CB2 1RP
40 West 20th Street, New York, NY 10011, USA
10 Stamford Road, Oakleigh, Melbourne 3166, Australia

First published 1991

Printed in Great Britain at the University Press, Cambridge

British Library cataloguing in publication data
Ellis, Frank H.
Sentimental comedy: theory and practice – (Cambridge studies
in eighteenth-century English literature and thought, 10)
1. Drama in English, 1625–1745 – critical studies
I. Title
822.409

Library of Congress cataloguing in publication data
Ellis, Frank H. (Frank Hale), 1916–
Sentimental comedy: theory and practice / Frank H. Ellis.
p.   cm.
Includes index.
ISBN 0–521–39431–7
1. English drama – 18th century – history and criticism.
2. English drama (Comedy) – history and criticism.
3. Sentimentalism in literature.   I. Title.
PR635.S4E4 1991
822′.05230905 – dc20   90–40490   CIP
ISBN 0 521 39431 7 hardback

Peace to thy shade, and may the laurel bloom
With deathless green, O CIBBER, on thy tomb!
Hugh Kelly, *Thespis* (1766)

Contents

Illustrations

The mask is the familiar comic mask, but the face behind the mask expresses considerable distress: the perfect emblem for sentimental comedy. *frontispiece*

1 William Penkethman created the role of Snap, Loveless's servant, in *Love's Last Shift*. His mobile face made him a great success as a clown. Engraving by Edward Harding after a drawing by George Vertue (courtesy of British Museum, Department of Prints and Drawings, Burney, VII 13, No. 27). *page* 29

2 In this bird's-eye view of Windsor Castle, the terraces are on the right, St. George's Chapel is at upper left and Charles II's enclosed tennis court is at center left, Engraving by Johannes Kip after a drawing by Leonard Knyff (courtesy of British Museum, Department of Prints and Drawings, *Nouveau Theatre de la Grande Bretagne*, London, 1724, plate XIV). 37

3 Richard Steele (before he was knighted in April 1715), an engraving by George Vertue after a portrait by Sir James Thornhill (courtesy of the Print Collection, The Lewis Walpole Library, Yale University). 45

4 In a 1786 revival of *The Foundling* at Covent Garden, the comic leads, Young Belmont and his sister Rosetta, were played by the great Joseph Holman at the beginning of his career and an otherwise unknown actress named Ann Warren. Holman's later career took him to New York, Philadelphia, and Charleston. Engraving by John Scott after a drawing by Thomas Stothard (courtesy of British Museum, Department of Prints and Drawings, Burney, IV 126, No. 241). 61

5 Richard Cumberland, an engraving by William Evans after the three-quarter figure by George Romney now in the National Portrait Gallery. Romney painted Cumberland shortly before Cumberland wrote *The West Indian* and before Romney himself

Preface

The "theory" elaborated in the first part of this book is not a hypothetical construct deduced from first principles, but a paradigm derived from inductive study of eighteenth-century printed plays (and manuscript copies in the Larpent Collection).

The plays analyzed in the second part of the book were chosen (1) because they are the plays most frequently called sentimental in the existing literature, (2) because of their inter-connectedness: A is the model for B, B is satirized in C &c., (3) for chronological scope (1696–1793), and most importantly (4) because they illustrate almost all of the ways in which eighteenth-century comedies are sentimental. The surprise came when the paradigm devised to analyze sentimentality in eighteenth-century comedy was found, apparently, to work as well with literature in other languages, other genres, and other epochs.

Sentimental comedy projects on the stage important sociological changes – new values assigned to old objects, from the cosmos to chimney sweeps. Playwrights and audiences alike are exposed to these changes. So particular attention in this study is focussed (1) on the writing of the play as an event in the affective life of the playwright, and (2) on the effect of the play on the first audiences (and readers).

I am grateful to the Trustees of The Huntington Library, Art Collections, and Botanical Garden for an unencumbered semester in that Edenic site. I am also grateful for help received from the following friends, living and dead: L. N. R. Ashley, Fletcher A. Blanchard, Evelyn B. Cannon, George B. Clarke, Blanche Cooney, Eveline Cruickshanks, Joseph N. Donohue, John G. Graiff, Donald Greene, Robert D. Hume, Randy O. Frost, John Loftis, John H. Middendorf, Mary Paul Pollard, Claude Rawson, Elizabeth P. Richardson, John Richetti, Bruce T. Sajdak, Anthony W. Shipps, Claude M. Simpson, Harold Skulsky, George A. Starr, David M. Vieth, and Reginald Williams.

Abbreviations

ABDA *A Biographical Dictionary of Actors, Actresses, &c.*, ed. Philip H. Highfill, Jr. *et al.*, 12 vols. to date, Carbondale and Edwardsville: Southern Illinois University Press, 1973–

A Criticism 1748 *A Criticism of The Foundling, in a Letter to the Author*, London, 1748

Aitken 1889 George A. Aitken, *The Life of Richard Steele*, 2 vols., London, 1889

Apology 1889 Colley Cibber, *An Apology for the Life of Colley Cibber*, ed. Robert W. Lowe, 2 vols., London, 1889

Baker 1812 David Erskine Baker, *Biographia Dramatica*, 3 vols., London, 1812

Bateson 1928 F. W. Bateson, *English Comic Drama 1700–1750*, Oxford: Clarendon, 1928

Bernbaum 1915 Ernest Bernbaum, *The Drama of Sensibility*, Boston: Ginn, 1915

Bevis 1980 Richard Bevis, *The Laughing Tradition. Stage Comedy in Garrick's Day*, Athens: University of Georgia Press, 1980

Boaden 1825 James Boaden, *Memoirs of the Life of John Philip Kemble*, 2 vols. in 1, Philadelphia, 1825

Boaden 1833 James Boaden, *Memoirs of Mrs. Inchbald*, 2 vols., London, 1833

Boswell 1934–50 James Boswell, *The Life of Samuel Johnson, LL.D.*, ed. G. Birbeck Hill and L. F. Powell, 6 vols., Oxford: Clarendon, 1934–50

Boswell 1950 James Boswell, *London Journal*, ed. Frederick A. Pottle, New York: McGraw-Hill, 1950

Branfman 1954 Theodore Branfman, "The psychology of sentimentality," *Psychiatric Quarterly* 28 (1954), 624–34

Broadus 1921 Edmund K. Broadus, *The Laureateship*, Oxford: Clarendon, 1921

Caskey 1927 John H. Caskey, *The Life and Works of Edward Moore*, New Haven: Yale University Press, 1927

Cibber 1753 Theophilus Cibber, *The Lives of the Poets*, 5 vols., London, 1753

Cumberland 1806 Richard Cumberland, *Memoirs of Richard Cumberland Written by Himself*, London, 1806

DNB   *The Dictionary of National Biography*, ed. Sir Leslie Stephen and Sir Sidney Lee, 22 vols., Oxford: Oxford University Press, 1949–50

D'Aubignac 1927   François Hédelin, Abbé d'Aubignac, *La Pratique du théâtre* (1657), ed. Pierre Martino, Algiers: Bastide-Jourdan; Paris: Champion, 1927

Davies 1780   Thomas Davies, *Memoirs of the Life of David Garrick*, 2 vols., London, 1780

Davies 1783–4   Thomas Davies, *Dramatic Miscellanies*, 3 vols., London, 1783–4

Dennis 1943   John Dennis, *The Critical Works*, ed. Edward N. Hooker, 2 vols., Baltimore: Johns Hopkins University Press, 1939–43

Dibdin 1800   Charles Dibdin, *A Complete History of the English Stage*, 5 vols., London, [1800]

Donohue 1970   Joseph W. Donohue, Jr., *Dramatic Character in the English Romantic Age*, Princeton: Princeton University Press, 1970

Dryden 1800   John Dryden, *The Critical and Miscellaneous Prose Works*, ed. Edmond Malone, 3 vols. in 4, London, 1800

ELH   *ELH, A Journal of English Literary History*, 1933–

Fitzgerald 1868   Percy Fitzgerald, *The Life of David Garrick*, 2 vols., London, 1868

Frye 1957   Northrop Frye, *Anatomy of Criticism*, Princeton: Princeton University Press, 1957

Garrick 1831   David Garrick, *The Private Correspondence*, 2 vols., London, 1831

Garrick 1963   David Garrick, *The Letters of David Garrick*, ed. David M. Little *et al.*, 3 vols., Cambridge MA: Harvard University Press, 1963

Gentleman 1770   [Francis Gentleman], *The Dramatic Censor*, 2 vols., London, 1770

Goldsmith 1966   Oliver Goldsmith, *Collected Works*, ed. Arthur Friedman, 5 vols., Oxford: Clarendon, 1966

Grove 1980   *The New Grove Dictionary of Music and Musicians*, ed. Stanley Sadie, 20 vols., London: Macmillan, 1980

Havens 1945   Raymond D. Havens, "The sentimentalism of *The London Merchant*," *ELH* 12 (September 1945), 183–7

Hazlitt 1902–6   William Hazlitt, *Lectures on the English Comic Writers* (1819), in *The Collected Works*, ed. A. R. Waller and A. Glover, 13 vols., London: Dent; New York: McClure, Phillips, 1902–6

Hume 1972   Robert D. Hume, "Goldsmith and Sheridan and the supposed revolution of 'laughing' against 'sentimental' comedy," in *Studies in Change and Revolution. Aspects of English Intellectual History 1640–1800*, ed. Paul J. Korshin, Menston: Scolar, 1972

Hume 1981   Robert D. Hume, "The multifarious forms of eighteenth-century comedy," in *The Stage and the Page. London's "Whole Show" in the*

Eighteenth-Century Theatre, ed. George W. Stone, Berkeley: University of California Press, 1981

Inchbald 1808   The British Theatre, ed. Elizabeth Inchbald, 25 vols., London, 1808

Kames 1779   Henry Home, Lord Kames, Sketches of the History of Man, 3rd. ed., 2 vols., Dublin, 1779

Kenny 1971   The Plays of Richard Steele, ed. Shirley S. Kenny, Oxford: Clarendon, 1971

Koon 1986   Helene Koon, Colley Cibber. A Biography, Lexington: University Press of Kentucky, 1986

Kovach 1986   Thomas A. Kovach, "Lessing, Oliver Goldsmith, and the tradition of sentimental comedy," in Lessing and the Enlightenment, ed. Alexej Ugrinsky, New York: Greenwood, 1986, 43–52

Loftis 1952   John Loftis, Steele at Drury Lane, Berkeley: University of California Press, 1952

Mandel 1968   Seven Comedies by Marivaux, trans. Oscar and Adrienne S. Mandel, Ithaca: Cornell University Press, 1968

Marivaux 1968   Pierre Carlet de Chamblain de Marivaux, Théâtre complet, ed. Frédéric Deloffre, 2 vols., Paris: Garnier, 1968

Moore 1756   Edward Moore, Poems, Fables, and Plays, London, 1756

Murphy 1801   Arthur Murphy, The Life of David Garrick, 2 vols., London, 1801

NCBEL   The New Cambridge Bibliography of English Literature, vol. 2, ed. George Watson, Cambridge: Cambridge University Press, 1971

Nienhuis 1974   Terry R. Nienhuis, "A Critical Study of Edward Moore's Dramatic Works," University of Michigan Ph.D. Dissertation, 1974

O'Leary 1965   Thomas K. O'Leary, "Hugh Kelly: Contributions toward a Critical Biography," Fordham University Ph.D. Dissertation, 1965

Olson 1968   Elder Olson, The Theory of Comedy, Bloomington: Indiana University Press, 1968

PMLA   Publications of the Modern Language Association of America, 1885–

Shaftesbury 1900   Anthony Ashley Cooper, 3rd Earl of Shaftesbury, Characteristics, ed. John M. Robertson, 2 vols., London: Grant Richards, 1900

Sherbo 1957   Arthur Sherbo, English Sentimental Drama, East Lansing: Michigan State University Press, 1957

Smith 1899   Garnett Smith, "The sentimentalists," Macmillan's Magazine 80 (October 1899), 449–58

Steele 1701   Richard Steele, The Christian Hero, London, 1701

Sterne 1928   Laurence Sterne, A Sentimental Journey through France and Italy, London: Oxford University Press, 1928

Taylor 1832   John Taylor, Records of My Life, 2 vols., London, 1832

The London Stage   The London Stage, ed. William B. van Lennep et al., 5 parts in 11 vols., Carbondale: Southern Illinois University Press, 1960–8

Thorndike 1929 Ashley H. Thorndike, *English Comedy*, New York: Macmillan, 1929

Victor 1761–71 Benjamin Victor, *The History of the Theatres of London and Dublin*, 3 vols., London, 1761–71

Walpole 1797 Horace Walpole, "Thoughts on Comedy," in *The Works of Horatio Walpole, Earl of Orford*, 5 vols., London, 1797, II 315–22

Walpole 1937–83 Horace Walpole, *Correspondence*, ed. Wilmarth S. Lewis *et al.*, 48 vols. in 47, New Haven: Yale University Press, 1937–83

Waterhouse 1907 Osborn Waterhouse, "The development of English sentimental comedy in the eighteenth century," *Anglia* 30 (1907): 137–72, 269–304

Whitehead 1774–88 William Whitehead, *Plays and Poems*, ed. William Mason, 3 vols., London and York, 1774–88

Wilkes 1759 Thomas Wilkes, *A General View of the Stage*, London, 1759

Theory

1

Theory

What is sentimental?

Fear without an object, or anxiety, has been studied almost more than any other vagary of the human mind. But pity without an object, or sentimentality, has been studied very little. So Dr. Theodore Branfman's groundbreaking study, "The Psychology of Sentimentality," may be a good place to begin.[1]

One of Dr. Branfman's patients, Miss A., was

a hospital nurse who came into analysis for severe depression, neurotic fears, and alcoholism ... Her first three years of life were unfortunate in that she was repeatedly separated from, and then re-united with, her mother. There was tremendous bitterness toward the mother, consciously focused on pre-puberty and adolescent disagreements ... In the course of her work as a nurse, she had frequent occasion to observe the behavior of parents as they brought an ill child to the hospital and left him there. Whenever these parents would be especially and noticeably affectionate, understanding and loving as they left the child, Miss A. would become flooded with sentimentality – feel tears coming to her eyes, become sad; but (as she reported in her analysis) *not* painfully depressed.

(625–6)

In this scene, the nurse in pediatric service breaking into tears at the sight of loving parents parting from a sick child, Dr. Branfman finds the archetype of sentimentality. He "believes this example to be paradigmatic for the psychology of all sentimental reactions" (626).

Dr. Branfman concludes that Miss A. is saying to herself, "Why didn't my mother ever treat *me* that way," which he understands as a reversal of Edmund Bergler's theory of the magic gesture. The magic gesture, in turn, is defined as a "seemingly senseless act of irrational generosity, devotion, love" (625). Sentimentality is the passive observation of "seemingly senseless acts of irrational generosity, devotion, love." Dr. Branfman emphasizes the importance of passivity in the archetypal scene: "this quality of *passive observation* ... is crucial to the working of the mechanism of sentimentality" (625).

He explains this mechanism in terms of Bergler's five-level model of consciousness:

[1] Branfman 1954.

3

1 Unconscious masochistic enjoyment of self-pity;
2 *Super-ego reproach*: enjoyment of self-pity is wrong;
3 *Primary ego defense*: I want revenge against mother for having mistreated me;
4 *Super-ego reproach*: aggression is wrong;
5 *Final defense of unconscious ego*, "the reaction of sentimentality": I want neither passively to enjoy the feeling of mistreatment, nor actively to exact revenge, "*I am merely observing, passively ... how I should have been treated, but was not.*"

(626)

The sentimental reaction to witnessing actual child abuse would be, "This is the way I should *not* like to have been treated," which Dr. Branfman calls "*negative* wistful observation" (628). Yorick's famous interaction with mad Maria of Moulines is an example of negative wistful observation. If the success of sentimental literature depends, as Dr. Branfman says it does, on "The ability of all human beings to feel ... mistreated" (630), then the future of sentimental literature is immense.

But the word "sentimental" is a refractory term with a marked tendency to slump and if anything useful is to be made of it, it must be shaped up. Existing definitions have not helped. One of the commonest ones, "indulgence of feeling for the feeling's sake,"[2] invites the question, "For what else's sake do we indulge feeling?" Nor are the lexical definitions any help. "An *excessive* degree of emotional excitability and response to experience"[3] invites such questions as "What is a normal degree of emotional excitability" and "How do we measure excessiveness?" Faced with problems like these, sober professors of literature have resorted to metaphor to convey their meaning. Sentimentality is something with a mainspring, or a taproot, or a core, or something like an Irish wake or a "many branching upas tree" the sap of which is deadly poisonous.[4] One writer on sentimental drama simply abandons the attempt to define "sentimental." Another critic calls "The whole concept of sentimental comedy ... a distraction and a red herring."[5]

So what is needed may not be another definition, but a simple analysis of sentimentality. Essential to any understanding of the phenomenon is the fact that sentimentality is "not an entity but a complex of elements," "un ensemble de réactions," "a name for several allied phases of thought which graduate imperceptibly into each other."[6] It is, in other words, a spectrum of

---

2 Smith 1899, 449.
3 *Encyclopedia of Psychology*, ed. H. J. Eysenck *et al.*, 3 vols. (New York: Herder and Herder, 1972) III 205.
4 George B. Rodman, *ELH* 12 (March 1945): 45, 54; Havens 1945, 184.
5 Sherbo 1957, 140; Hume 1981, 12.
6 John H. Smith, *Modern Philology* 46 (1948–9): 23; Paul Van Tieghem, *Edda* 27 (1927): 159; Leslie Stephen, *History of English Thought in the Eighteenth Century*, 2 vols. (London, 1876) II 436. Laughter, an effect that comedy produces, is also a complex of elements, a spectrum ranging from a childish giggle to "das schreckliche Lachen des Menschenhasses" (Lessing, *Minna von Barnhelm* (1767) IV vi; quoted in Kovach 1986, 46.

attitudes reaching from pity for a non-existing object at one extreme to pity for all humanity at the other (see diagram below).

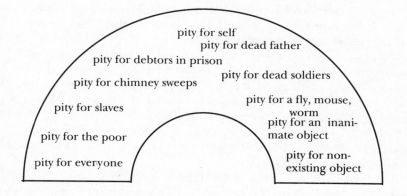

Some examples may make this clearer. In *The Tatler* of 6 June 1710 Steele resolves to "run over all the melancholy circumstances" of the bereavements that have occurred to him in his whole life. He begins with the death of his father, when he was not yet five years old, and recalls his inability to understand why no one would play with him the next day. Then he thinks of dead soldiers, "gallant men ... cut off by the sword," some of whom Richard Steele, captain of the second troop of Life Guards, may have known. And finally he turns to the widows and orphans of the dead soldiers. But these bereaved are not bereavements of Richard Steele. Steele's father, Richard Steele Sr., was a creature of flesh and blood, a successful Dublin attorney with a summer house at Monkstown. The dead soldiers exist as memories. But "the tender and the innocent" bereaved exist for Steele only by inference. And yet, for these figures, hovering on the brink of non-existence, "pity enters with an unmixed softness," Steele says, "and possesses all our souls at once." These examples form a spectrum, moving away from pity for a real object. Pity for a ghost would be an example of pity for a non-existing object: "HAMLET ... poore Ghost."[7]

The opposite end of the spectrum, pity for all humanity, is also represented in Steele's work. In *The Christian Hero* (1701) he talks about "that noble spark of Caelestial Fire, we call Charity or Compassion, which opens our Bosoms

[7] Pity for a ghost (not known to be a ghost) is a feature of folklore motif E215 The Spectre Bridegroom, of which Gottfried Bürger's *Lenore* (1773) is the best-known literary expression (Stith Thompson, *Motif-Index of Folk-Literature*, 2nd ed., 6 vols. (Bloomington: Indiana University Press, 1955–57) II 420; hereafter cited by index number only. Throughout this study it is assumed that the plots of comedies are pieced together from preexistent folklore motifs (*Restoration: Studies in English Literary Culture, 1660–1700*, XI (1987), 94–106).

and extends our Arms to Embrace all Mankind."[8] Out of context this may sound simply like an elaboration of 1 Corinthians 13.2: "though I have all faith ... and have not charity, I am nothing." But it is more than this. As it develops in Steele's work it almost becomes a physical attribute of man: "that Touch within, which Nature gave / For Man to Man."[9] And it came to be called universal benevolence. Although it swirls and eddies from Shaftesbury into *An Essay on Man* (1733–4),[10] universal benevolence remained outside the main current of English thought. Swift, Fielding, Johnson, Goldsmith, Gibbon, Blake, Coleridge, Walter Scott, all ridicule it. The case *for* universal benevolence is argued by Samuel Richardson and Francis Hutcheson. "God Almighty's Creatures act worthy of the Blessings they receive," Pamela rhapsodizes, "when they make, or endeavour to make the whole Creation ... happy." Hutcheson concludes "that there is in human Nature a *disinterested ultimate Desire* of the Happiness of others."[11]

"A *disinterested ultimate Desire* of the Happiness of others" was *not* characteristic of the seventeenth century in England.[12] The dominant attitude then was summarized by an anonymous writer in 1701. "Mankind now adays," he said, "are not so immoderately desirous to serve one another, much less those that have most need." "The Charity of the World ... in this Age," Daniel Defoe added, "indeed runs very low." Thomas Hobbes had even argued that "To ... pitty, is to Dishonour."[13]

Yet within the eighteenth century a whole complex of strange feelings began to find expression:

Pity for a fly caught in a spiderweb:

the fluttering wing

---

[8] Steele 1701. Steele even introduces sentimentality into his translation of Terence's famous sentence, *Homo sum: humani nil a me alienum puto.* Steele makes it, "*I am a Man, and cannot help feeling any Sorrow that can arrive at Man*" (*The Spectator* 6 October 1712).

[9] *The Lying Lover: Or, The Ladies Friendship* (London 1704) Epilogue, sig. a3v.

[10] "To love the public, to study universal good, and to promote the interest of the whole world, as far as lies within our power," said the good Lord Shaftesbury, "is surely the height of goodness, and makes that temper which we call divine" (Shaftesbury 1900, I 27). Pope versified this in *An Essay on Man* IV 369–72:

> Wide and more wide, th'o'erflowings of the mind
> Take ev'ry creature in, of ev'ry kind;
> Earth smiles around, with boundless bounty blest,
> An Heav'n beholds its image in his breast.

[11] *Pamela, or Virtue Rewarded*, 4 vols. (Oxford: Blackwell, 1929) II 170; cited hereafter by volume and page number; *An Inquiry into the Original of our Ideas of Beauty and Virtue*, 4th ed. (London, 1738) 152.

[12] Esmé C. Wingfield-Stratford, *The History of British Civilization*, 2nd ed. (London: Routledge, 1932) 577–8; Max Beloff, *Public Order and Popular Disturbances 1660–1714* (London: Oxford University Press, 1938) 3.

[13] *Bellum Medicinale, or The Present State of Doctors and Apothecaries in London* (London, 1701) 30; *The History of the Union of Great Britain* (Edinburgh, 1709) xxxii; *Leviathan* (London, 1651) I x.

> And shriller sound declare extreme distress,
> And ask the helping hospitable hand;

Pity for a mouse:

> Wee, sleekit, cowrin, tim'rous beastie,
> O, what a panic's in thy breastie;

Pity for a worm:

> I would not enter on my list of friends,
> ... the man
> Who needlessly sets foot upon a worm.

"This is the way I should *not* like to have been treated." Common to these examples[13] is pity for an inadequate or undemanding object. In what is probably its purest form, sentimentality may be pity for a non-existing object, or "pity without an object," "*sadness without any apparent occasion*," in Robert Burton's phrase, or "misery to no purpose," in Samuel Johnson's.[15]

In its simpler forms – pity for a fly, pity for a worm – sentimentality is merely ludicrous, but as it evolved in the eighteenth century to include pity for the poor wretches in debtors' prisons, pity for chimney sweeps, and pity for negro slaves, sentimentality created one of the great advances in western civilization. We are witnesses to this transference when Uncle Toby liberates a fly that had been pestering him at dinner: "Go poor devil, get thee gone," he said, "why should I hurt thee? – This world surely is wide enough to hold both thee and me." Tristram Shandy was an impressionable ten year old at the time and "the lesson of universal good-will then taught and imprinted by my uncle *Toby*," he said, "has never since been worn out of my mind: And tho' I would not depreciate what the study of the *Literae humaniores*, at the university, have done for me in that respect ... yet I often think that I owe one half of my philanthropy to that one accidental impression."[16]

Sentimentality is also responsible, in what may be called the sentimental paradox, for some of the greatest nonsense in modern life: "I have sinned, I may say, from *virtue*,"[17] or, "He killed her because her loved her too much,"

> she was ...
> Perfectly pure and good: I found

---

[14] James Thomson, *Summer* (1727) 278–80; Robert Burns, *To a Mouse* (1785); William Cowper, *The Task* (1785) VI 560–3.

[15] Frye 1957, 37; Burton, *The Anatomy of Melancholy* (London, 1621) Part I, Section I, Member III, Subsection I; Boswell 1934–50, II 94. Lord Kames goes a step further and postulates "an appetite after pain, an inclination to render one's self miserable" (Henry Home, Lord Kames, *Essays on the Principles of Morality and Natural Religion*, 2nd ed. [London, 1758] 9–10).

[16] Laurence Sterne, *The Life and Opinions of Tristram Shandy, Gentleman*, 11 vols. (London, 1760–7) II 79, 80. Ludwig Wittgenstein declares that the aim of philosophy is to liberate flies (*Philosophical Investigations*, trans. G. E. M. Anscombe [New York: Macmillan, 1953] 103).

[17] Sophia Lee, *The Chapter of Accidents: A Comedy* (London, 1780) 15.

A thing to do . . .
And strangled her.[18]

A more recent critic than John Dennis has complained that "There is not even agreement whether sentimentality is a positive or negative quality."[19] The truth must be that it is both. But not even its worst aberrations can conceal the fact that it may represent man's last best hope. "We mistrust sentiment because we value it so highly," Garnett Smith says. When Jonas Hanway wrote *A Sentimental History of Chimney Sweepers* (1785), his purpose was to arouse widespread resentment against a particularly ugly example of child labor. Part of the sentimental outcry came a few years later in the paired chimney sweeper poems of William Blake's *Songs of Innocence and of Experience*. And indeed it was Blake who summarized the tendency of a whole century when he wrote in 1789:

> And all must love the human form,
> In heathen, turk, or jew;
> Where Mercy, Love, & Pity dwell
> There God is dwelling too.[20]

What is comedy?

By the end of the seventeenth century there was little disagreement about what constituted a comedy. Although Samuel Johnson observes that "Comedy has been particularly unpropitious to definers," the definition worked out by a French monk, François Hédelin, Abbé d'Aubignac, and translated into English in 1684, was not disputed:

La *Comédie* servoit à dépeindre les actions du peuple, et l'on n'y voyoit que Débauches de jeunes gens, que Fripponneries d'Esclaves, que Souplesses de femmes sans honneur, qu'Amourettes, Fourbes, Railleries, Mariages et autres accidens de la vie commune.

[The purpose of comedy is to represent the actions of ordinary people, including the debaucheries of the young, the knaveries of servants, the guiles of prostitutes, love affairs, deceptions, jokes, marriages and other accidents of ordinary life.][21]

---

18 Robert Browning, "Porphyria's Lover," *The Monthly Repository* January 1836. The sentimental paradox can be encapsulated in an oxymoron: "cruel generosity," "cruelly kind" (Whitehead, *The School for Lovers* [London, 1762] 62; Kelly, *False Delicacy* [London, 1768] 61).

19 Paul E. Parnell, *PMLA* 78 (1963): 529.

20 Smith 1899, 458; William Blake, *The Complete Writings*, ed. Geoffrey Keynes (London: Nonesuch; New York: Random House, 1957) 117. The phenomenon of sentimentalism in the eighteenth century may be summarized, in a variation of Janet Todd's phrase, as a fortunate "feminization of culture" (*Sensibility, An Introduction*, London and New York: Methuen, 1986, 43).

21 *The Rambler* 28 May 1751; D'Aubignac 1927, 144. For a survey of theories of comedy 1660–1710 see Robert D. Hume, *The Development of English Drama in the Late Seventeenth Century* (Oxford: Clarendon, 1976), 32–62.

Here are all the traditional "actions" of the genre. Any of these, *developed* in a comic tone, that "Frolique and Gay humor" that Samuel Butler talks about, and *ended* happily, might make a comedy.[22]

"The Life, and the very Soul of Comedy," as Dennis says, is "Laughter," and a generation earlier the great Dryden had determined that "the Business of the [comic] Poet is to make you laugh." During the first run of *She Stoops to Conquer* (1773) Goldsmith was eager to learn the verdict of James Northcote, to whom he had given a pass:

GOLDSMITH. Did it make you laugh?
NORTHCOTE. Exceedingly.
GOLDSMITH. Then that is all I require.

What the audience was to laugh *at* were the vices and follies, the errors and disgraces, of ordinary people. Aristotle had supplied a reason why we laugh at comedy. "To be ridiculous," he said, "is a kind of deformity, and the causes of laughter are errors and disgraces not accompanied by pain or injury." Dryden had learned from Hobbes that it is the deformity we laugh at, not physical deformity of course, or even moral deformity. The deformity is social: the folly of old men marrying young women, or of young men marrying the woman of their father's choice, or "the misfortunes which befal young women after the loss of their virginity." Whereas tragedy makes men bigger than life, comedy diminishes: "how little do our Passions make us," Colley Cibber observes. Real distress, "accompanied by pain or injury," is not considered a proper subject for merriment. Murdering a house guest or someone with whom you are involved in a traffic accident is not funny.[23]

Richard Hurd was not the first to claim that plot is less important in comedy than it is in tragedy. Vanbrugh had said "I believe I cou'd shew, that the chief entertainment [in comedy] . . . lies much more in the Characters and the Dialogue, than in the Business and the Event." Vanbrugh does not develop the point but Hurd says explicitly that "a good plot *is not so essential to comedy, as tragedy.*" From Aristotle's discovery that tragedy is an imitation of an action (*mythos*) of a certain kind, Hurd infers that comedy is an imitation of character (*ethos*) of a certain kind, but Hurd (and Vanbrugh) may be wrong. Comedy is an imitation of an action of a different kind. If it is true, as Northrop Frye says, that character in a comedy is a function of plot, "what a character is follows from what he has to do," then plot is clearly the determining factor. Plot determines character. On the other hand, by refining

---

22 Samuel Butler, *Characters and Passages from Note-Books*, ed. A. R. Waller (Cambridge: Cambridge University Press, 1908) 278. A plot that "achieves its happy ending with a self-righteous tone" is not a comedy but a melodrama (Frye 1957, 167).

23 Dennis 1943, II 245; Dryden 1800, I ii, [2]200; James Northcote, *Memoirs of Sir Joshua Reynolds* (Philadelphia: 1817) 148; Aristotle, *De Poetica*, 1449a; Hobbes, *Leviathan* I vi; Frye 1957, 168; Pierre Bayle, *Dictionnaire historique et critique*, trans. Peter Birch *et al.*, 10 vols. (London, 1734–41) I 665; Cibber, *The Careless Husband. A Comedy* (London, 1705) 40.

on the pseudo-Aristotelian *Tractatus Coislinianus*, Frye reduces the comic plot
to a formula: Boy meets girl > Boy wants girl > Blocks occur > Blocks are
removed (comic peripeteia) > Boy gets girl. The boy-wants-girl element can
be very slight – as in Volpone's passing fancy for Celia or Manly's late-
discovered passon for Fedelia – or even non-existent – as in Plautus's *Captivi*.
What remains constant in the plot of comedy is (1) the pattern of Somebody
wants something > Block > Comic peripeteia > Somebody gets something;
and (2) deception, deliberate or accidental. The true muse of comedy may
not be Agnoia, as Bernard Knox has suggested, but Exapatesis, or deception.[24]

By studied misconstruction, of course, anything can be ridiculed, but the
thing that is most frequently ridiculed in comedy is the courtship rites of the
upper middle classes. George Farquhar, the last of the Restoration dramatists, inferred that this was what makes the difference between comedy and
tragedy. "As the Catastrophe of all Tragedies is Death," he said, "so the end
of Comedies is marriage." Nor did his successors, even though writing in a
different idiom, disagree with Farquhar. "The great business of comedy,"
Hugh Kelly said, "consisted in making difficulties for the purpose of removing
them; in distressing poor young lovers; and in rendering a happy marriage the
object of every catastrophe." Richard Cumberland agreed that "The making
or obstructing marriages is the common hinge, on which most comic fables are
contrived to turn."[25] From one age to another, therefore, English comedies
may differ mainly in the degree of frankness with which they approach that
"subject that can only be glanced at indirectly, that is a sort of forbidden
ground to the imagination, except under severe restrictions, which are
constantly broken through," as Hazlitt said.[26]

What is sentimental comedy?

In theory there may be a sentimental attitude about anything. But in the
literature of the eighteenth century the subjects treated sentimentally do not
appear to be numerous. They include the following:

A1   The universe
A2   Man

---

[24] *The Complete Works of Sir John Vanbrugh*, ed. Bonamy Dobrée and Geoffrey Webb, 4 vols.
(London: Nonesuch, 1927–8) I 209; Richard Hurd, "Dissertation on the Provinces of
Dramatic Poetry" (1753), *The Works*, 8 vols. (London, 1811) II 38, 45; Frye 1957, 171; Bernard
Knox in *The Rarer Action. Essays in Honor of Francis Fergusson*, ed. A. Cheuse and R. Koffler (New
Brunswick: Rutgers University Press, 1970) 86.
[25] George Farquhar, *Love and a Bottle. A Comedy*, 2nd ed. (London, n.d.) 47; Kelly, *The School for
Wives. A Comedy* (London, 1774) ii; Richard Cumberland, *The Observer*, 2nd ed., 5 vols.
(London, 1787–91) III 48.
[26] Hazlitt 1902–6, VIII 14, quoted in Waterhouse 1907, 154.

A3   Woman
A4   Parents
A5   Children
A6   The lower orders: servants, peasants, foreigners, the poor
A7   Animals, vegetables, minerals
A8   The emotions
A9   Evil, crime, death
A10 Money
A11 The past; the elsewhere.[27]

The sentimental attitude toward the universe is called cosmic optimism: "If everything which exists be according to a good order, and for the best," as Lord Shaftesbury assures us that it is, "then of necessity there is no such thing as real ill in the universe" and "Whatever is, is RIGHT."[28] No such convenient term exists for the sentimental attitude toward man, the belief that man is naturally good, morally self-sufficient, and universally benevolent. For this attitude the term Pelagian heresy may be appropriated.[29] The unsentimental attitude toward man, illustrated in the Old Testament by Genesis 6.5: "every imagination of the heart of man is only evil, and that continually," and by Article IX of the Thirty-nine Articles: "man ... is of his own nature inclined to evil," was still assumed at the beginning of the eighteenth century to be unquestionable: "The sole End of Religion then is to reform and correct our Evil Natures"; "we *Low-Churchmen* believe that *Christian Principles* ought to correct and subdue nature"; "That Religion is chiefly designed for perfecting the Nature of Man ... is a Truth so plain, that without further arguing about it, All will agree to it."[30] But at exactly the same time Steele began writing about man's "good natural Impulses" and insisting that virtue is "natural to uncorrupted Youth."[31] By mid-century Lord Kames was arguing that virtue is natural to man.[32]

The sentimental attitude toward women, parents, children, the lower orders (as they were called in the eighteenth century), and animals imputes to

[27] Further research, and particularly research into nineteenth-century melodrama and twentieth-century soap opera, may require adjustments to and extensions of the subjects of sentimental comedy. A7 (Animals, vegetables, minerals) may need to be renamed Nature. But eighteenth-century sentimental comedy is not sentimental about Nature as such. It may be necessary to unbundle A9 (Evil, crime, death) and to consider each topic separately, but the three coalesce into a single topic in eighteenth-century sentimental comedy. It is not difficult to imagine topics that may need to be added: Art, Insanity, Religion, Nation, War &c.

[28] Shaftesbury 1900, I 239; Pope, *An Essay on Man* (1733–34) I 294.

[29] Pelagius was a Welsh(?) monk who went to Rome about 405 to propagate his beliefs that Adam's fall did not involve his posterity and that man can achieve salvation without the intervention of divine grace.

[30] Simon Clement, *Faults on both Sides* (London, 1710) 51; John Toland, *The Memorial of the State of England* (London, 1705) 99; Gilbert Burnet, *The Abridgment of the History of the Reformation of the Church of England* (London, 1705) sig. A4v.

[31] *The Spectator* 28 April 1711; *The Tatler* 24 November 1709.   [32] Kames 1779, II 277, 291.

them a higher position in the scale of being than that traditionally or empirically assigned to them. "I don't know how to express my self," says the hero of *The Lying Lover* (1704), "but a Woman methinks is a Being between us and Angels."[33] "Why is it," William Cowper asks, "that the women are . . . in all the most important points superior to the men?" Woman is endowed with a moral or psychological superiority, a finer sensibility than man's: "Woman is a more glorious, honourable and excellent creature than Man," "Possessed of peculiar delicacy, and sensibility," "Women feel the pleasure arising from the contemplation of a beautiful scene more acutely than men." It is this attribute that Goldsmith ridicules in *She Stoops to Conquer* (1773). Marlow, who feels at ease only in the company of street-walkers, calls, "a modest woman . . . the most tremendous object of the whole creation."[34] And it is this freak of eighteenth-century thought that has become a political movement in the twentieth century.

Parents are similarly upgraded. The non-sentimental attitude toward parents is illustrated by Samuel Johnson's confession that he never believed a word his father told him. "I always thought that he spoke *ex officio*," he said. In Cibber's *Love's Last Shift* (1696) it is illustrated by the following exchange:

> AMANDA. . . . He was a Father to me.
>
> HILLARIA. He was better than some Fathers to you; for he dyed, just when you had Occasion for his Estate.
>
> NARCISSA. I have an old Father, and the Duce take me, I think he only lives to hinder me of my Occasions.
>
> (I i 317–21)

This contrasts sharply with sentimental passages in Shadwell's *The Squire of Alsatia* (1688), which Steele imitates in *The Conscious Lovers*:

> BELFOND, JR. [*to his foster father*]: I beg your consent [to marry Isabella], for I will die before I Marry without it.
>
> SIR EDWARD. Dear *Ned*, thou hast it.[35]

Children are upgraded on the model of Addison's dictum: "*L'enfant dit*

[33] Steele, *The Lying Lover: Or, The Ladies Friendship* (London, 1704) 3; cf. "the sentimental novel tends to invert the existing hierarchy, and to assert that the whole constellation of feeling and behavior . . . regarded as feminine is not the mere equal of the masculine one, but preferable to it in all essential respects" (George A. Starr, *L'Egalité* 9 (1984): 128–9).

[34] William Cowper to Mrs. King, 21 October 1791, *The Letters and Prose Writings*, ed. James King and Charles Ryskamp, 5 vols. (Oxford: Clarendon, 1979–86) III 577; James Hodges, *Essays on Several Subjects* (London, 1710) 71; David Carey, *Craig Phadric, Visions of Sensibility, with Legendary Tales, and Occasional Pieces* (Inverness, 1811) 142; Goldsmith 1966, V 130.

[35] Boswell 1950, 284. Changing attitudes toward parents in English comedy of 1660–1720 is the subject of a study by Elisabeth Mignon, *Crabbed Age and Youth. The Old Men and Women in the Restoration Comedy of Manners* (Durham: Duke University Press, 1947), which easily proves that the transition was from derision to overawed respect. "Overawed respect" describes exactly the sentimental attitude toward parents (A4). Act, scene, and line numbers of Cibber's comedies are those in the edition of Maureen Sullivan (1973); see p. 25 below. Thomas Shadwell, *The Complete Works*, ed. Montague Summers, 5 vols. (London: Fortune, 1927) IV 276.

vrai," which terminates in the nonsense of "The Child is father of the man."[36]
Animals are endowed with human feelings and even inanimate objects are
assumed to be living (folklore motif F990). The non-sentimental attitude
toward animals is expressed in Pope's *Windsor Forest* (1713). A German critic
supposes that Pope betrays sentimentality in his image of a dying pheasant.[37]
But Pope wastes no sympathy on the prey. He is intent to communicate the
intense excitement of flushing a game bird in the field, balanced by the beauty
of the dead bird. There is no pathetic fallacy, no anthropomorphizing, only a
quick sketch from the life and a wry question:

> [the bird] feels the fiery Wound,
> Flutters in Blood, and panting beats the Ground.
> Ah! what avails his glossie varying Dyes,
> His Purple Crest, and scarlet-circled Eyes?
> (113–16)

The true sentimental reaction is described a few years later by Pope's friend,
James Thomson. Thomson's game bird is a cock pigeon, escaped from the
shot that killed the hen:

> again
> The sad idea of his murdered mate,
> Struck from his side by savage fowler's guile,
> Across his fancy comes; and then resounds
> A louder song of sorrow through the grove.
> (*Summer*, 617–21)

Thomson can even invite pity for withered flowers:

> Who can unpitying see the flowery race
> Shed by the morn, their new-flushed bloom resign
> Before the parching beam?
> (*Summer*, 212–14)

But the classical expression of pity for animals (A7) is, of course, Blake's
Auguries of Innocence (c. 1803):

> A Robin Red breast in a Cage
> Puts all Heaven in a Rage.
> (K431)

Jesus, it will be recalled, "overthrew ... the seats of them that sold doves"
(Matthew 21.12).

The non-sentimental attitude toward the lower orders (A6) may be
illustrated by a vote of the House of Commons in April 1711 about "the poor

---

[36] Addison, *The Whig-Examiner* 21 September 1710; Wordsworth, *Ode: Intimations of Immortality*
(1807) Epigraph.
[37] Bernhard Fehr, *Palaestra* 148 (1925): 308.

Palatines." "Poor" meant "destitute," not "pathetic." Drawn by the promise of naturalization and the hope of freedom of worship, more than 10,000 German Protestants from the Rhineland crowded into England in the summer of 1709. In 1711 Parliament repealed the naturalization act and voted that "whosoever advised the bringing over the poor *Palatines* into this Kingdom, was an Enemy to the Queen, and this Kingdom."[38] It was not until 1770 that Richard Cumberland undertook to represent "the victims of ... national, professional or religious prejudices" as "heroes for ... dramas."[39]

The sentimental attitude toward the emotions (A8) follows as a corollary to the foregoing disorders (A2–7). Reason is subordinated to emotion and instinct: "In this [instinct] 'tis God directs, in that [reason] 'tis Man"; "the feelings never can draw us into any mistake."[40] This "moral sense," as it came to be called, was assumed by Adam Smith to be infallible: "What is agreeable to our moral faculties, is ... right."[41] The unsentimental attitude is illustrated in the *Leviathan* (1651): "our naturall Passions ... carry us to Partiality, Pride, Revenge, and the like," in *Pilgrim's Progress* (1678–84): "He that trusts his own heart is a fool," and in Congreve's comedies (1693–1700). But the next generation of English comic dramatists inclines toward the sentimental. Osborn Waterhouse observes that the characters in sentimental comedies "do what is right by spasmodic impulses, for which no sufficient motive can be found."[42]

The sentimental attitude toward vice, sin, crime, and death (A9) follows as a corollary to cosmic optimism (A1). Evil is a fiction, Lord Shaftesbury assures us, and Lord Kames insists that "all evil tends to good."[43] Human vice can be dismissed, as Pope did in *An Essay on Man*, as the small price we pay for free will. And in this best of all possible worlds, this morally self-regulating universe, "'tis surely an undeniable [truth]," Steele tells us,

---

[38] *Journals of the House of Commons* XVI 598. The Rev. Jonathan Swift, D.D., supplied the usual rationalizations for xenophobia: the "*Palatines,*" he said, "understood no Trade or Handicraft; yet rather chose to Beg than Labour; [and] besides infesting our Streets, bred Contagious Diseases" (*The Examiner* 7 June 1711).

[39] Cumberland 1806, 136. Oliver Goldsmith's essay, "An essay on the theatre; or, A comparison between laughing and sentimental comedy" (*The Westminster Magazine* January 1773), the first attack on the subgenre, is strangely aristocratic and prescriptive. "The Beggar who accosts us in the street ... has ... our contempt," Goldsmith said, completely misjudging the humanitarian thrust of his time (Goldsmith 1966, III 211).

[40] Pope, *An Essay on Man* (1733–4) III 98; Hugh Kelly, *The Babler,* 2 vols. (London, 1767) II 184.

[41] Adam Smith, *The Theory of Moral Sentiments* (Edinburgh, 1754) 282; cf. Kames 1779, II 277: "By intuitive perception, without reasoning, we acquire knowledge of right and wrong."

[42] *Leviathan* II 17; John Bunyan, *The Pilgrim's Progress,* ed. James B. Wharey and Roger Sharrock (Oxford: Clarendon, 1960) 145; cf. "Passions are unreasonable and involuntary" (Congreve, *The Complete Works,* ed. Montague Summers, 4 vols. [London: Nonesuch, 1923] II 144); Waterhouse 1907, 281.

[43] Boswell: *The Applause of the Jury 1782–1785,* ed. Irma S. Lustig and Frederick A. Pottle (New York: McGraw-Hill, 1981) 36.

"that Vice is its own Punishment."[44] This is another sentimental attitude that Goldsmith ridicules. "It is my maxim, Sir," the hero of *The Good Natur'd Man* (1768) pontificates, "that crimes generally punish themselves." Shakespeare, who believes in the reality of crime, makes King Lear imagine that he burns in Hell "bound Upon a wheele of fire" (IV vii 46), but "we know that George [Barnwell]," the idle apprentice who murders his master, "is safely in heaven, and Christian tragedy thus takes on some of the characteristics of sentimental comedy."[45]

The sentimental attitude towards money (A10), namely that it does not matter, is a common topic. Phrases such as "Why hang an Estate, marry *Emilia* out of hand!" and "So vile a thing as money must not come between us" ring down through English comedy from James I to George III. Dr. Branfman speculates that the sense of loss resulting from such heroic renunciations lies close to the primal sentimental scene. "Without the basic feeling of personal deprivation," he says, "there is no sentimental sadness." But the emergence in the eighteenth century of a recognizable moneyed class greatly increases opportunities for feelings of personal deprivation. "By Anne's reign it was becoming apparent that money was gaining importance over birth or station in conferring power and influence."[46] Sentimentality about money may be a reaction to this development.

In the sentimental attitudes known as chronological and cultural primitivism (A11), greater values are imputed to the past and the elsewhere than to the here and now.[47] The past is always available, to quote Dr. Branfman again, as "potential material for masochistic fantasies." And John Evelyn learned the standard, unsentimental attitude toward the elsewhere during his grand tour of France and Germany. "There was little more to be seene in the rest of the world," he was told, "but plaine and prodigious Barbarisme."[48] It was Richard Cumberland again who discovered greater value in "that warm sunny region, where naked nature walks without disguise" than in "this cold contriving artificial country" of England.[49]

The validity of this sentimental paradigm can be tested by applying it to works in other languages and other periods. And when this is done some surprising results emerge. "The sentimental comedy of Marivaux," for example, turns out not to be sentimental at all. The characteristic tone of

---

44 Steele 1701, sig. A7r.

45 Goldsmith 1966, V 68; Arthur Friedman, *The Augustan Milieu*, ed. Henry K. Miller *et al.* (Oxford: Clarendon, 1970) 258–9.

46 George Etherege, *The Man of Mode; or, Sr Fopling Flutter* (London, 1676) 15; Cumberland, *The West Indian* (London, 1771) 56; Branfman 1954, 633; James R. Jones, *Country and Court. England 1658–1714* (Cambridge MA: Harvard University Press, 1978) 79.

47 Arthur O. Lovejoy *et al.*, *Primitivism and Related Ideas in Antiquity* (Baltimore: Johns Hopkins Press, 1935) 1–22.

48 Branfman 1954, 634; *The Diary of John Evelyn*, ed. E. S. de Beer, 6 vols. (Oxford: Clarendon, 1955) II 354.

49 *The West Indian* (London, 1771) 60.

marivaudage is distinctly anti-sentimental. There is no sentimentality about the lower orders (A6) in *Le Jeu de l'amour et du hasard* (1730):

> DORANTE. . . . tout valet que je suis, je n'ai jamais eu de grandes liaisons avec les soubrettes, je n'aime pas l'esprit domestique.
> [Although I am a valet, I have never carried on with maids. I don't enjoy the servant mind.]⁵⁰

nor about money (A10) in *Les Fausses confidences* (1737):

> MARTON. . . .c'est de Dorante que vous parlez? C'est pour se garder à moi qu'il refuse d'être riche?
> [Dorante is refusing all this wealth for me?]
> MONSIEUR REMY. Tout juste, et vous êtes trop généreuse pour le souffrir.
> [Exactly; but you're too generous to let him.]
> MARTON (*avec un air de passion*). Vous vous trompez, Monsieur, je l'aime trop moi-même pout l'en empêcher, et je suis enchantée: oh! Dorante, que je vous estime! Je n'aurais pas cru que vous n'aimassiez tant.
> [You're wrong, Monsieur, I love him too much to set him free. This is heavenly. Oh, Dorante, how noble you are! I never thought I was so dear to you.]⁵¹

But Dorante is not noble at all. He undertook in the first scene to win the girl *and* her entire fortune, exactly as Mirabell did in *The Way of the World* (1700), another comedy notoriously unsentimental.

Rousseau's *Emile, ou de l'éducation* (1762) is equally unsentimental about women (A3), parents (A4), children (A5), the lower orders (A6), animals (A7), and money (A10). But *Emile* is invariably and emphatically sentimental about the universe (A1):

Ce qui est est bien [What is, is good] (712, 732),⁵²

about man (A2):

l'homme est naturellement bon [Man, by nature good] (525),

and about crime, evil, and death (A9):

leur propre coeur les en punit [their own heart punishes those crimes] (535) . . . La mal que l'homme fait retombe sur lui [The evil that man does reacts upon himself] (587) . . . la suprême justice . . . employe les maux que vous vous faites à punir les crimes qui les ont attirés. [Justice uses self-inflicted ills to punish the crimes which have deserved them] (591–2) . . . le cri des remords qui punit en secret les crimes cachés [the voice of remorse, the secret punishment of hidden crimes] (597) . . . la peine et le vice sont inséparables [suffering and vice are inseparable].

(815)

If Rousseau never deviates in *Emile* from his sentimental belief that crime is

---

⁵⁰ Marivaux 1968, I 808; Mandel 1968, 150.   ⁵¹ Marivaux 1968, II 382; Mandel 1968, 280.
⁵² The page references in the text are to Jean-Jacques Rousseau, *Oeuvres complètes*, vol. 4, ed. Bernard Gagnebin and Marcel Raymond (Paris: Gallimard, 1969). The translations are those of Rousseau, *Emile*, trans. Barbara Foxley (London: Dent, 1911).

self-punishing (A9), he is ambivalent and even contradictory in his shifting evaluation of reason and the emotions (A8):

Posons pour maxime incontestable [he says in Book II] que les premiers mouvemens de la nature sont toujours droits: il n'y a point de perversité originelle dans le coeur humain.

[Let us lay it down as an incontrovertible rule that the first impulses of nature are always right; there is no original sin in the human heart.]

(322)

But in Book V the first impulses of nature need to be validated by the application of reason:

Il leur importe donc de cultiver une faculté ... que ne laisse point égarer la conscience ... Cette faculté est la raison.

[It is, therefore, important to cultivate a faculty ... which does not permit conscience to go astray ... That faculty is reason.]

(730)

The apparent contradiction, however, is easily resolved on the sentimental side. Rousseau's most deeply held conviction is revealed in his phrase "vile reason" (758) and in his long exposition of "l'instinct moral" (598) in the creed of the Savoyard priest:

Exister pour nous, c'est sentir [To exist is to feel] (600) ... Conscience! ... juge infaillible du bien et du mal [Conscience! ... infallible judge of good and evil] (600) ... On a beau vouloir établir la vertu par la raison seule [Reason alone is not a sufficient foundation for virtue] (602) ... nos prémiers penchans sont légitimes [our first impulses are always good.]

(604)

It is hardly unexpected that a paradigm invented to analyze sentimental comedy of the eighteenth century finds an applicability to Rousseau. But the applicability of the paradigm to the Bible is less to be expected. Here are a few random examples:

Sentimentality about children (A5): "Except ye ... become as little children, ye shall not enter into the kingdom of heaven" (Matthew 18.3).

Sentimentality about the lower orders (A6): "The sleep of a labouring man is sweet, whether he eat little or much: but the abundance of the rich will not suffer him to sleep" (Ecclesiastes 5.12).

Sentimentality about animals (A7): "a man hath no preeminence above a beast" (Ecclesiastes 3.19).

In all of these examples the sentimentality results from inverting the traditional hierarchical relationships between parent/child, master/servant, and man/animal (p. 11 above). And as in the case of Rousseau, the paradigm is equally helpful in determining what the Bible is *not* sentimental about. It is *not* sentimental about the past (A11), for example:

Say not thou, What is the cause that the former days were better than these? for thou
dost not enquire wisely concerning this.

(Ecclesiastes 7.10)

The paradigm functions equally well in detecting the absence of sentimentality. Ashley Thorndike calls *The Provok'd Husband: or, A Journey to London*
(1728) by Vanbrugh and Cibber "the most 'sentimental'" of Cibber's
plays.[53] But the paradigm affords ample evidence that the play is *un*sentimental. There is no sentimentality

About women (A3): "Let Husbands govern ... Wives obey,"[54] says the
madcap Lady Townly, played by the incomparable Ann Oldfield;

About parents (A4): "am not I to take Place of Mama" (89), asks 15-year-old
Jenny Wronghead;

About the lower orders (A6): "Trades-people are the troublesomest Creatures"
(78), complains Lady Townly, and a casual figure at a masquerade is openly
anti-semitic (86);

About the emotions (A8): in the conversion scene Lady Townly renounces the
"Passions" that had led her astray (83);

There is no *sentimental disregard for money* (A10): "I would take her in her
Smock" (57) is spoken by a 16-year-old lout, Richard Wronghead;

Cultural primitivism (A11) is dismissed by Lady Townly as "primitive
antediluvian Notions of Life [that] have not been in any Head these thousand
Years" (50).

Manly, the hero of the play, has "a satyrical Turn" of mind (7) and the
thrust of the satire in the play is directed equally at the extravagant, wasted
lives of London women of quality and at hunting squires who buy themselves
seats in Parliament expecting to recoup their wasted fortunes. The coarse
language of the play – "kiss my ——" and "jig their Tails" (35, 36) – would
please neither Jeremy Collier nor Mrs. Grundy. It is a delightful play, without
a trace of sentimentality.

Robert D. Hume calls Benjamin Hoadly's *The Suspicious Husband* (1747)
"the most popular 'sentimental' comedy in the 1747–76 period."[55] But again
there is not a trace of sentimentality in the play. And again the paradigm
affords positive evidence that the play is *not* sentimental. There is no
sentimentality

About the nature of man (A2): the *phrase* "good nature" recurs frequently in the
play.[56] But it is not a by-word for Pelagianism, as it is in *The Careless Husband*

---

53 Thorndike, 1929, 362.
54 *The Provok'd Husband: or, A Journey to London*, 2nd ed. (London, 1729) 85. Subsequent page
    references are to this edition.
55 Hume 1972, 272.
56 Benjamin Hoadly, *The Suspicious Husband. A Comedy*, 2nd ed. (London, 1747) 6, 14, 60, 68, 71.
    Subsequent page references are to this edition.

(p. 37 below). It is an antonym for "ill-natur'd." "The World" and Mr. Strictland are ill-natured (17, 22, 51), but the eirons are "good-natured";

Sentimental disregard for money (A10) is expressed by Clarinda, played originally by Hannah Pritchard, the leading comedienne of her day. Clarinda is an heiress, "a Lady of such Fortune!" (66). "I don't care what his Fortune is," she says of her lover. But she immediately takes it back and draws a laugh, "No, Psha! Prithee! I don't mean so neither" (70).

The best evidence of the play's *un*sentimentality lies not in the primary elements (A1–11) but in the secondary differentia of sentimental comedy (B1–4). There is one phrase of "tender melancholy Conversation" (B1) in the play: "You will do what you please with me" (73). But its uniqueness emphasizes the fact that the dialogue is decidedly not "tender melancholy." It is even more vulgar than that of *The Provok'd Husband*. "Dissolute small talk" is what Charles Macklin called it. It is full of open references to sex (4–5, 23, 28, 30, 34 &c.), full of sexual innuendo, called "double Tenders" (57) in the play, and full of threats of sexual violence (37, 43, 58). "*Throws down his Hat, and seizes her*" and "*Going to lay hold of her*" are stage directions (37, 43). Sexual innuendo might be assumed to cancel out or nullify sentimental effects in any case. But in a work as complex as *A Sentimental Journey* "double Tenders" and sentimentality happily coexist and even seem to reinforce each other. In *The Suspicious Husband* there are only "double Tenders."

The plot of the play, a version of the Griselda motif (H461), *requires* Mrs. Strictland to suffer a great deal of undeserved distress (B3). She is abused, "suspected," and "ill treated" (38–9, 43, 66). But this is only comic distress and it cannot be imagined that the audience suffered very much. A miraculous conversion (D1881) leaves Mr. Strictland "ready to love and trust" his wife (77). Explicit moralizing (B4) is ridiculed – "Pho! none of your musty Reflexions now!" (29) – and laughed off the stage:

CLARINDA. What? Moralizing, Cousin! Ha! ha! ha!   (61)

Clarinda's cousin is the opportunistic Ranger, "the Hero of the Day," a Georgian Davos whose "damn'd Tricks" (77, 48) insure that every Jack has his Jill. The part was created by David Garrick and it became his greatest comic role. It is not surprising therefore that *The Suspicious Husband* became "the most popular comedy of the Garrick era at Drury Lane."[57] But without the essential stigmata (A1–11) it could not be a sentimental comedy.

Sentimental comedy, at last, may be defined *ad hoc* as comedy on the stage that arouses sentimental reactions (A1–11). This is assumed to be the essential and primary nature of the subgenre. But there may be, as well, secondary characteristics that are its occasional and non-essential differentia:

---

[57] Bevis 1980, 60.

B1 "A sprinkling of tender melancholy Conversation"
B2 Reckless, self-sacrificing virtue
B3 Undeserved distress
B4 Overt moralizing[58]

Goldsmith maintained that a sentimental comedy was as easy to write as a novel. "It is only sufficient," he said, "to ... make a Pathetic Scene or two, with a sprinkling of tender melancholy Conversation (B1) through the whole, and ... all the Ladies will cry, and all the Gentlemen applaud." Goldsmith's phrase, which he could have found in Fielding, perfectly describes the kind of dialogue that characterizes sentimental comedy, or, indeed, sentimental novel or sentimental elegy: "Alas! my heart bleeds for him ... do what you will with me ... I am the offspring of distress and every child of sorrow is my brother."[59]

"The thrill of reckless virtue" (B2), in L. J. Potts's fine phrase,[60] seems to have been lifted straight out of Restoration heroic plays into the comedies of the next age. "So to your welfare I of use may be," Aureng-Zebe tells the empress, "My life or death are equal both to me." These magic gestures recur frequently in eighteenth-century sentimental novels as well as in sentimental comedy. Clarissa Harlowe's cry, "No matter what becomes of me," finds its reprise in Sir John Dorilant's wish to "make her happy whatever becomes of me."[61] But not even Jack Bevil's heroic willingness to marry the girl of his father's choice would make *The Conscious Lovers* a sentimental comedy if it raised none of the sentimental attitudes outlined above (A1–11).

When Goldsmith complains that in *"Sentimental* Comedy ... the Distresses [B3], rather than the Faults of Mankind, make our interest in the piece,"[62] he is wrong on four counts. In the first place, distress is endemic to comedy. There can be no comedy without the pain felt by lovers as long as they are kept apart. This pain can be very acute and very funny, "as Fantastick as the Misery of Lovers," in Steele's phrase.[63] Indeed, "who ever heard the Name of Love mention'd *without* an Idea of Torment?" (16). In the second place, the

---

[58] While B1 seems to be an eighteenth-century innovation, B2–4 are staples of Elizabethan, Jacobean, and Restoration comedy.

[59] Goldsmith 1966, III 213; Fielding, *The Author's Farce*, 3rd ed. (London, 1750) 17 (Bernbaum 1915, 148).

[60] L. J. Potts, *Comedy* (London: Hutchinson, n.d.) 147.

[61] Dryden, *Aureng-Zebe: A Tragedy* (London, 1676) 39 [misnumbered 25]; Richardson, *Clarissa*, 7 vols. (London, 1748) III 253; Whitehead, *The School for Lovers* (London, 1762) 30.

[62] Goldsmith 1966, III 212.

[63] Steele 1701, sig. A7r; cf. "scenes of comic suffering – fear where there is no cause for fear, anxiety where there is no cause for anxiety, embarrassment, desperation, absurd beatings, etc., are in fact among the funniest in comedy; and so we must have comic suffering" (Olson 1968, 51). This line from a *copla, Quien tiene amor tiene pena* (He who loves suffers pain), is very affecting until we recall that it is a whale that speaks; cf. A. J. Greimas and F. Nef, "Essai sur la vie sentimentale des hippopotames," *Grammars and Descriptions: Studies in Text Theory and Text Analysis*, ed. Teun A. van Dijk and János S. Petőfi (Berlin: de Gruyter, 1977) 85–104.

introduction of exemplary characters into sentimental comedies has nothing
to do with the essential nature of the subgenre, but is an accidental effect of the
subgenre being appropriated for reformation-of-manners propaganda.[64]
"The Contemplation of Distresses," Steele believed, "softens the Mind of
Man, and makes the Heart better."[65] In the third place, the perverse pleasure
that we take in the distresses of others – *suave . . . magnum alterius spectare laborem*
– is a commonplace that recurs in one century:

> The broadest mirth unfeeling Folly wears,
> Less pleasing far than Virtue's very tears,

as well as in another:

> . . . the soothing thoughts that spring
> Out of human suffering.[66]

Years before it was called "sentimental," the new comedy was called weeping
comedy. Congreve remarked that "Some Weep, and others Laugh at one and
the same thing."[67] Steele thought that it might be an improvement of comedy
"to introduce a Joy too exquisite for Laughter."[68] Perhaps he was right, but
without laughter there could be no comedy.[69]

In the fourth and final place, Goldsmith's complaint that "the Faults of
Mankind" are underrepresented in sentimental comedy is not supported by
sentimental comedy itself, which is prodigal of fools, including sentimental
fools.

The last secondary characteristic of sentimental comedy, overt moralizing
(B4), is not mentioned by Goldsmith at all. But it is by almost all the other
hostile critics of the new comedy.[70] In fact the first characteristic of the new
drama to be called "sentimental" was the intrusion of direct moral instruction
in the form of maxims or grave sentences, the very thing that the Abbé

---

[64] "How little do they know of the Nature of true Comedy, who believe that its proper Business is
to set us Patterns for Imitation" (Dennis 1943, II 245); "sentimental comedy and exemplary
comedy . . . are not identical" (Loftis 1952, 199); "there is no necessary connection between
sentimentalism and exemplary drama" (Calhoun Winton, in *Quick Springs of Sense. Studies in the
Eighteenth Century*, ed. Larry S. Champion [Athens: University of Georgia Press, 1974] 99).

[65] *The Tatler* 18 October 1709.

[66] Lucretius, *De rerum natura* II 1–2; Pope, *An Essay on Man* IV 319–20; Wordsworth, *Ode:
Intimations of Immortality* 183–4.

[67] *Letters upon Several Occasions: Written by and between Mr. Dryden, Mr. Wycherly, Mr. —, Mr. Congreve,
and Mr. Dennis* (London, 1696) 91.

[68] *The Conscious Lovers. A Comedy* (London, 1723) sig. A5v; cf. "elegy . . . has discovered sweets in
melancholy which we could not find in *mirth*" (William Shenstone, *The Works*, 2 vols., 2nd ed.
[London, 1765] I 18).

[69] Ernest Bernbaum, the first historian of sentimental drama, inadvertently calls Philip Francis's
Eugenia (1752) "the only sentimental comedy . . . [that] entirely lack[s] a comic element"
(Bernbaum 1915, 201). But this is a contradiction in terms. Without a comic element *Eugenia*
cannot be a comedy. It is something else, a melodrama perhaps. Francis called it a tragedy.

[70] William Cooke, *The Elements of Dramatic Criticism* (London, 1775) 141, called sentimental
comedy "a drivling species of morality."

d'Aubignac had warned against.[71] The prologue to William Whitehead, *The Roman Father, A Tragedy* (1750), boasts that *"Moral,* Sentimental *Stroke[s], / Where not the Character but Poet spoke,"* had *not* been intruded. And this is the phrase that is cited as the first use of "sentimental" to describe a *literary* effect. But for Henry Mackenzie, the sentimental novelist, "there are no passages more captivating both to the writer and the reader, than those delicate strokes of sentimental morality."[72]

Aristotle supposed that a tragedy arouses in the audience feelings of pity and fear and purges off these irrational poisons. By analogy Northrop Frye has said that a comedy "seems to raise the corresponding emotions, which are sympathy and ridicule" and to effect, not a purgation, but a communion. The individual members of the audience are drawn together by their common feelings of sympathy for the young lovers and ridicule for anyone who stands in the way of true love.[73] By a further analogy it might be said that sentimental comedy rouses the comic "sympathy and ridicule" *plus* the sentimental reaction (A1–11). Then what happens is described by Steele in the halting verse of his epilogue to *The Lying Lover* (1704):

> ... Laughter's a distorted Passion, born
> Of sudden self Esteem, and sudden Scorn;
> Which, when 'tis o'er, the Men in Pleasure wise,
> Both him that mov'd it, and themselves despise,
> While generous Pity of a painted Woe
> Makes us our selves both more approve, and know.[74]

It is remarkable that Steele describes the effects of a sentimental comedy in almost the same words in which Samuel Johnson describes the effects of alcohol: "Wine makes a man better pleased with himself," Johnson says. And what Johnson goes on to say about the effects of alcohol may apply with equal grace to the effects of sentimental comedy: "To make a man pleased with himself, let me tell you, is doing a very great thing."[75]

---

[71] D'Aubignac argued that maxims or grave sentences are cold and intellectual and obstruct the action of a play that is intended to produce an emotional effect on the audience. The moral instruction in a comedy, he concluded, must operate indirectly "by the *Entermise* of the Actions themselves" (D'Aubignac 1927, 314–15, 318). William Hazlitt repeats this argument in *Lectures on the English Comic Writers* (Hazlitt 1902–06, VIII 156–8).

[72] William Whitehead, *The Roman Father, A Tragedy* (London, 1750), sig. [A]3v; *Oxford English Dictionary*, s.v. **Sentimental**; *The Mirror* 25 April 1780.

[73] Aristotle, *De Poetica*, 1449b; Frye 1957, 177, 164.

[74] *The Lying Lover: Or, The Ladies Friendship* (London,1704) Epilogue, sig. A3v. The first of these couplets paraphrases Hobbes, *Leviathan* (1651) I vi, and the second paraphrases Dryden's preface to *An Evening's Love, or The Mock Astrologer* (1671) (Dryden 1800, I ii 200).

[75] Boswell 1934–50, III 327–8.

Practice

2

Colley Cibber, *Love's Last Shift* (1696)

Out of his necessities as an immigrant's son with no more education than
Shakespeare, and as a young actor trying to support a growing family on 30s. a
week,[1] Colley Cibber wrote his first play. He was having trouble getting good
parts, so he wrote one for himself, Sir Novelty Fashion, a role that is part
stage-history (reaching down from the Marquis de Mascarille in Molière's *Les
Precieuses ridicules* [1659] through Sir Fopling Flutter in Etherege's *The Man of
Mode* [1676]) and part wish-fulfillment. For Sir Novelty Fashion is everything
that Colley Cibber was not. He is the first Restoration rake to be called
"Beau." He is resourceful enough to create fashions, not simply to follow
them, and rich enough to keep a mistress, a coach, and a footman. But even at
twenty-three, Colley Cibber's head was practical as well as stuffed with
shaping fantasies. So he also created a role for his wife and one more for his
brother-in-law, a musician.

Forty years later, all unaware that he was echoing Ariosto and Milton, he
remembered only that he had "resolv'd to leave nothing unattempted that
might shew me in some new Rank of Distinction. Having then no other
Resource, I was at last reduc'd to write a Character for myself." It is not
surprising that what the happily married man wrote is a celebration of
marriage. It was called *Love's Last Shift* and it opened at the Theatre Royal in
January 1696.[2]

The plot of *Love's Last Shift* is generated in the classical fashion by a conflict
between generations, between one alazon, Sir William Wisewoud, and three
pairs of eirons.[3] The first of these, Amanda and Ned Loveless, are the
abandoned wife and the prodigal husband, patient Griselda and Don Juan.
Amanda's trouble is that she is not patient enough. She resents her husband's
infidelities and when he found that he "cou'd not Whore in quiet" (V ii 52),[4]

---

[1] *Apology* 1889, I 194. A good edition of Cibber's *Apology* is a major desideratum. In her biography
of Cibber, Helene Koon points out that several stars of the Drury Lane company, Thomas
Betterton, William Mountfort, and George Powell, had written plays to exhibit their particular
talents (Koon 1986, 25).
[2] *Apology* 1889, I 212.   [3] Frye 1957, 172–5.
[4] The line (and page) numbers of *Love's Last Shift* and *The Careless Husband* are those of *Colley
Cibber: Three Sentimental Comedies*, ed. Maureen Sullivan (New Haven: Yale University Press,
1973), but the text is that of the first edition of each play. By taking as her copy-text *Plays Written*

25

Loveless left her. "The World ... is a Garden," Loveless says, "stockt with all sorts of Fruit," whereas a wife is "no more than ... a half Eaten Pippin, that had lain a Week a Sunning in a Parlor Window" (I i 42–8). So Loveless took off on a seven-year pursuit of shiny new apples and we catch a glimpse of him paying a pope's ransom for the enjoyment of a Venetian exotic (I i 31–4). As the play begins, he returns to London, dirty, broke, and unreformed, still in pursuit of "a Dinner and a brace of Whores" (I i 206). It has been objected that there is nothing in the play "to prepare us for Loveless's Conversion" in Act V.[5] Even if this were true, a playwright cannot be denied his surprises. But in fact it is not true. Every detail of Loveless's conversion is anticipated in two of young Will Worthy's speeches in Act I (I i 415–32). In the opening speech of the play Loveless says, "Sirrah! leave your Preaching." In the last speech of the play Loveless is preaching. What he preaches is subsumed by the theme of the comedy: "Change" is obsessive, but marriage is curative. Or, in other words, "change" is alazonic, but marriage is eironic. Loveless has earned his right to preach by experiencing these disjunctions.[6]

The second pair of lovers, young Will Worthy and Narcissa Wisewoud, daughter of Sir William and an heiress, are the bright, hard juveniles of Restoration comedy. Will is "a beggerly unaccountable sort of Younger Brotherish Rake-hell" (III i 191) whose derelictions include heiress chasing, lawyer bribing, and whoring. He is "The vice ... combined with the hero ... a cheeky, improvident young man who hatches his own schemes and cheats his rich father or uncle into giving him his patrimony along with the girl." "I am as much in Love with Wickedness, as thou canst be," he tells Loveless, "but I am for having it at a Cheaper rate than my Ruine!" (I i 118). Will experiences no conversion before he is rewarded by marriage to his heiress, but his being the "first promoter" (V iii 37) and undertaker of Love's successful Last Shift atones for his derelictions, because in comedy Love is "*Victorious*" "*In Spight of Reason*" (V iv 1, 15).

"The Fair *Narcissa*" (III i 24) conforms exactly to the model of the female eiron in Richard Blackmore's preface to *Prince Arthur. An Heroick Poem*:

by Mr. Cibber (1721) Sullivan bowdlerizes and misrepresents the play that was performed and published twenty-five years before. For the edition of his collected plays in two volumes Cibber undertook a thoroughgoing revision of *Love's Last Shift* to conform to the more refined sensibilities of the Georgian period. He cut out a few phrases like "lye in a naked bed" (I i 501, p. 300) and "her stinking breath" (IV i 25, p. 302). He changed "What the Devil shall we do?" (III ii 197, p. 302) to "What shall we do?", "Maidenhead" (IV i 37, p. 302) to "Maid," "hot Raging Lust" (IV i 108, p. 302) to "the Dotage of undone Desire," and "new Ravish'd" (IV iii 210, p. 302) to "new-blest." He also cut out an entire low-comedy episode (IV i), the importance of which to the structure of the play is set forth below (p. 28).

5 Bateson 1928, 22.

6 The terms "alazon" (impostor) and "eiron" (self-deprecator) for the blocking characters and heroes/heroines in comedy were made current in *Anatomy of Criticism* (Frye 1957, 40, 172); Frye 1957, 174.

this *Accomplish'd Person* [Blackmore says] entertains the Audience with confident Discourses, immodest Repartees, and prophane Raillery. She is throughly instructed in *Intreagues* and *Assignations*, a great *Scoffer* at the prudent Reservedness and Modesty of the best of her Sex, She despises the wise Instructions of her Parents or Guardians, is disobedient to their Authority, and at last, without their *Knowledge* or *Consent*, marries her self to the *Fine Gentlemen* above mentioned.[7]

Being an heiress, Narcissa can afford to be fashionably *difficile* (I i 178–80). She pretends that love is "old stuff" (I i 378), but she is not unwilling that a duel be fought over her because "*Narcissa* wou'd sound so great in an Expiring Lover's Mouth" (II i 243). And she pays for her pretensions by falling in love with a wastrel who thinks that she is "a strange affected piece," but can find "no fault in her 1000 *l.* a year" (I i 523). She is redeemed by her beauty, her wit, and her mischievous "Satyrical Smile" (II i 318).

The third pair of lovers, Tom Worthy and Hillaria, Narcissa's cousin and Sir William Wisewoud's ward, are less interesting. Tom Worthy is a humorless (V iii 82–4) prig whose interpretation of the meaning of *Love's Last Shift* is a fine example of the device of the deliberately inadequate interpretation. Amanda's "Example," he intones, "shou'd perswade all constant Wives ne'er to Repine at unrewarded Virtue" (V iii 35–6). But if Amanda had *not* repined, her virtue would have remained unrewarded.

Hillaria is almost indistinguishable from her cousin Narcissa. She is vain, high-spirited, and cynical (I i 236, 292, 318). In her "Mad humour" (III i 11) she thinks it foolish to be agreeable to her lover (II i 151). But she is redeemed by confessing her folly (II i 191) and also, of course, by her "Wit and Beauty" (I i 235, 270, 276). Her beauty was self-evident, supplied by the playwright's young wife, but her wit has to be taken on faith, for she has few witty lines.

Cibber's observance of poetic justice in the play is a hilarious parody of the virtue-rewarded motif. As in many Restoration comedies, "the price of Women" (V iii 104) is plainly marked. Hillaria is worth about £750 a year in her own right (V i 78). Narcissa has about £1250 a year (I i 162; V 37–8). Amanda has an income of £2000 a year (I i 322; V ii 211). In awarding his "several Prizes in the Lottery of Human life" (V iii 244), Cibber exercises impeccable economic justice: the least rich girl gets the richest man, Tom Worthy; the richer girl gets young Will Worthy and £5000; the richest girl gets Loveless, whose estate is heavily mortgaged.

Arrayed against these young lovers is the one alazon, Sir William Wisewoud, a humor character in Shadwell's definition:

> A Humor is the Byas of the Mind,
> By which with violence 'tis one way inclin'd:
> It makes our Actions lean on one side still,
> And in all Changes that way bends the Will.[8]

---

[7] Richard Blackmore, *Prince Arthur. An Heroick Poem* (London, 1695) sig. A2r.
[8] Thomas Shadwell, *The Humorists* (London, 1671) Epilogue.

Sir William represents an interesting switch on the traditional *senex iratus* figure; he is *senex stoicus*. "Old Philosophy" (III i 229) "fancies himself a great Master of his passion, which he only is in trivial matters" (*Dramatis Personae*). Even before he says "'tis impossible to make me angry" (IV i 52–3, p. 278) we know that he is going to blow. His temper is tested three times in the play and these tests supply a skeleton for the structure of the plot. He is tested in III i by Sir Novelty Fashion's declaration that he is to marry "the Fair *Narcissa*," in IV i by two bullies provoking him to a duel, and finally in V iii by the discovery that he has been cheated by the Worthy brothers and a crooked lawyer. Structurally, therefore, these three tests constitute the backbone of the plot and the suspense generated in the first two insures that the third will culminate in a big comic bang.

Besides helping to polarize the comic tone by repeating his obsession, Sir William also functions importantly to obstruct the course of true love.[9] His avarice would marry off the richer girl, Narcissa, to the richest man, Tom Worthy, in manifest violation of Cibber's version of poetic justice. His blocking role is dramatized when he places his daughter's hand in that – of the wrong man (V i 36) and urges his niece and ward to give her hand – to the wrong man (V i 72). Thus the "Comical old Gentleman" of III i 149 becomes a vicious old gentleman whose plaintive cry, "Ay, but the 5000 *l.*, Sir!" (V iii 200) recalls Harpagon's "O ma cher cassette."[10] But unlike Harpagon, Sir William grows ashamed of his avarice in time to be reconciled to the eironic world at the play's end.[11]

The great role in *Love's Last Shift*, however, and the one that Colley Cibber wrote for himself, is none of these, but that of Sir Novelty Fashion, a clown, a fool, a scapegoat sacrificed to our laughter (II i 211). Like all young actors, Colley Cibber wanted to be a tragedy hero and play opposite Anne Brace-girdle. But he had enough sense to recognize that neither his voice nor his "meagre Person" qualified him. "What was grave and serious did not ... become me," he said.[12] So he became a great comedian, like Pinky (plate 1).

The character invented by Molière is developed in Cibber's imagination into "a true Original" (II i 45). He is another humor character like Sir William Wisewoud, "an Egregious Fop" (III i 148), whose obsession is fashion. And like Sir William he functions, though less importantly, as a blocking character, by his gallantries with Hillaria and Narcissa. Sir Novelty's "business is Love" (II i 236), as he says. But all his love is for himself (II i 312; III i 144–5).

The language of *Love's Last Shift* juxtaposes the hero with the alazons and fools of the play. Like Sir William Wisewoud, Loveless is "Insensible" (III i 137; III ii 74). Don Juan, in Colley Cibber's conceit, turns out to be, not a free spirit, but an alazon living in ritual bondage to an obsession, "Fashionable

---

[9] Frye 1957, 168, 172.   [10] Molière, *L'Avare* (1668) V iii.   [11] Frye 1957, 165.
[12] *Apology* 1889, I 182–3.

Plate 1   William Penkethman created the role of Snap, Loveless's servant, in *Love's Last Shift*.
His mobile face made him a great success as a clown.

Fornication" (III ii 106). Loveless enunciates the principle in his first speech:
"They that will hunt pleasure ... must never give over in a fair Chase" (I i
5–6). The "Chase" turns out to be an irrational compulsion. Like Sir Novelty
Fashion, Loveless affects "Variety" and "change" in love (I i 43; IV iii 160–1;
III i 109–11; III ii 60–1). But Sir Novelty's "Understanding goes naked"
(III i 147) and even Mistress Flareit regrets her affair with him, not on moral,
but on intellectual grounds: it was stupid, a "forfeiture of [her] Sense and
Understanding" (IV i 52). By association, therefore, "Variety" and "change"
become irrational, the product of "deluded Fancy" (I i 425–6). In these terms,
Loveless's conversion becomes a disenchanting. He is unspelled. "Reason ...
breaks forth" (V ii 230) and Loveless is cured of the compulsive "Chase." The
equation of reason and marriage, the recurring image of marriage as a remedy
(I i 146; II i 390; V i 14), and the case history of Loveless, all combine to
enforce "a favourable Opinion of Poor Marriage" (II i 350).

"Lewd for above four Acts" (Epilogue, 16) the play certainly is. While not
sustainedly pornographic, it reverts frequently to the sexual act (I i 501,
p. 300; IV iii 213–15; V iii 126). Even the trees in St. James's Park are
"lovingly ... joyned" (III ii 2). The tone of all but the last two scenes is
worldly and cynical. One determining device that Cibber could have learned
from George Etherege is the potentially sentimental phrase uttered in an
ironic voice. What Dorimant *says* is, "I have always my arms open to receive
the distressed."[13] What Dorimant *means* is, "I am always ready to seduce
young girls who have run away from home." In Love's Last Shift the "Unhand
me, you villain" kind of melodramatic injunction, concluding with tears (IV i
86), is spoken, not by an innocent to a villain, but by one villain to another,
both acting disingenuous parts. Sentimental disregard for money – "Hang an
estate! true Love's beyond all Riches!" (V i 77) – is articulated by Sir William
Wisewoud who regards nothing but money.

So it becomes necessary to define the sentimentality of the play very
carefully. It is mainly the last two scenes, dismissed as "out of fashion stuff"
(Epilogue, 15), that account for its inclusion here. The "stuff" that was out of
fashion in 1696 became "so much in fashion" that by 1773 Goldsmith felt
threatened by it.[14] Like his creature, Sir Novelty, Colley Cibber proved to be
resourceful enough to create fashions (II i 269). Even more symptomatic,
however, are the sentimental details and motifs scattered throughout the play.
The most important of these is the heterodox assumption that human nature
is essentially good (A2). The good nature of Amanda, Hillaria, and Tom
Worthy is made explicit (I i 83; V iii 209; I i 142). Sir Novelty pretends to good

13 Etherege, *The Man of Mode* (1676) V ii 121.
14 Goldsmith 1966, III 210. Estimates of the number of sentimental comedies produced in the
    eighteenth century have been made, but the estimates lack credibility because the criteria for
    inclusion are not defined (Sherbo 1957, 161; *The London Stage*, part 4, I clxii–clxix; Hume 1972
    257).

nature (IV i 61). And even Loveless's vice is understood to be not real but assumed, "an Affectation of being Fashionably Vicious" (I i 417–18).[15]

There is "a sprinkling of tender melancholy Conversation" (B1):

ELDER WORTHY. I am your Slave, dispose of me as you please.

(II i 196)

AMANDA. Forgive this innocent attempt of a despairing passion, and I shall die in quiet ...
          Falls on the Ground.
LOVELESS. Ha! she faints! Look up fair Creature! Behold a Heart that bleeds for your distress.

(V ii 150–6)

There is heroic virtue rewarded (B2):

HILLARIA. Why d'ye persist in such a hopeless Grief?
AMANDA. Because 'tis hopeless.

(I i 309–10)

Amanda's persistence in this hopeless grief turns, of course, into "a Triumph of rewarded Constancy" (III i 78). And there is overt moralizing (B4): "goodness gives you ... Power" (II i 199); "sure there are Charms in *Vertue*" (V ii 4–5).

Loveless's conversion looks like it might be an example of what has been called the "subversive alteration of character" that "regularly" concludes sentimental comedies.[16] But in fact "a conversion ... is the ordinary way which our poets use to end [their plays]," as Dryden said in 1668. "The poet is to be sure," Dryden cautioned, that "he convinces the audience that the motive is strong enough."[17]

Love's Last Shift easily meets this requirement. Loveless's conversion gains some credibility because it follows the pattern of religious conversion reiterated in countless spiritual autobiographies.[18] His "motive," furthermore, may have been reinforced by the fear that he has had sexual intercourse

---

[15] Although human nature is assumed to be essentially good, virtue, inconsistently, is assumed to require that "Conscience and ... Reason" be deployed to overcome nature (V ii 121).

[16] Stanley T. Williams, *Sewanee Review* 33 (October 1925): 408.

[17] Dryden 1800, I ii 80–1. "The manipulation of plot does not always involve metamorphosis of character, but there is no violation of comic decorum when it does. Unlikely conversions ... are inseparable from comedy" (Frye 1957, 170). Kenneth Burke, making a further distinction, calls it "violating repetitive form in the interests of syllogistic progression" (*Counter-Statement* [New York: Harcourt, Brace, 1931] 164).

[18] Loveless's comic conversion follows very closely the stages of religious conversion made known through the extensive literature of spiritual autobiography: 1. provocation to repentance (V ii 86); 2. reflection or consideration, a "coming to oneself" (V ii 112); 3. conviction or godly sorrow, remorseful self-accusation (V ii 141–3, 173–4); conversion proper, when God intervenes to relieve and reclaim the sufferer (V ii 193–4) (George A. Starr, *Defoe and Spiritual Autobiography*, Princeton: Princeton University Press, 1965) 106. The God in this case is Love.

with his dead wife's ghost.[19] And finally, on the new assumption that Loveless is essentially good, his "Conversion" amounts only to the displacement of "an Affectation of being Fashionably Vicious" (I i 417–18) or an unspelling. And while this magic is taking place (V ii 88–191), Loveless acts very much like a male Sleeping Beauty waking out of his seven-year delusion. The main plot of *Love's Last Shift* is a recapitulation of folklore motif D1978.4: "Hero wakened from magic sleep by wife who has purchased place in his bed from false bride."

  Love's Last Shift was a success both critically and at the box office. In "every way" it exceeded Colley Cibber's expectations.[20] Charles Sackville, Earl of Dorset, the patron of Dryden and Wycherley and representative (Lord Chamberlain) of the theatre at court, called it "the best First Play that any Author in his Memory had produc'd; and that for a young Fellow to shew himself such an Actor and such a Writer in one Day, was something extraordinary."[21] Congreve, who had praised Cibber's acting in *The Double Dealer* (1694), grew jealous of Cibber's success as a playwright and found – "justly," Cibber said – that *Love's Last Shift* "had only in it a great many things that were *like* Wit, that in reality were *not* Wit."[22] But Cibber is being too modest, or perhaps ironical, for there are "in reality" a great many things in *Love's Last Shift* that *are* Wit and even some that recall Congreve's wit. "I'll hang my self, and swear you Murder'd me" (IV iv 22–3), for example, is a delightful Irish bull. This exchange:

> YOUNG WORTHY. 'Tis business of Moment, Madam, and may be done in a Moment.
> NARCISSA. ... my business is not so soon done as you imagine.
>
> (I i 468–71)

exhibits the same kind of word play as "I hope I may be offended, without any offence to you, Sir" from *The Old Bachelour* (III i 293), in which Cibber played Fondlewife in May 1695, eight months before the opening of *Love's Last Shift*. And whereas everyone knows that night is the time for love, not everyone knows that "what made *Daphne* run away from *Apollo*, [was] that he wore so much Day-light about his Ears" (III ii 34–5).

  The length of the original run of *Love's Last Shift* is not known, but it is said to have been "uncommon."[23] The play was immediately added to the repertoire of the Theatre Royal and performed "over two hundred times" during the next seventy-seven years. Quarto editions of the play appeared in 1696 and 1702. In 1720 it was included in *Plays Written by Mr. Cibber* and

---

[19] If this is the "Thought" that shocks Loveless's soul (V ii 157), the operative folklore motif is the taboo against sexual intercourse with unearthly beings in general (C112) and with a ghost in particular (E474). Almost no one in the audience in 1696 would have doubted the existence of revenants.

[20] Dedication to Richard Norton of Southwick, Esq., sig. A3v.   [21] *Apology* 1889, I 214.

[22] *Apology* 1889, I 220.   [23] Davies 1783–4, III 412.

editions in the classical Lintot duodecimo format were published in 1730, 1733, 1735, 1747, and 1752. Pirated editions were printed in Dublin and The Hague. Samuel Foote recalled that when the play was included in *Le Théâtre anglois* it was entitled *La dernière Chemise de l'amour*.[24]

It may never be known for sure whether the first night audience did in fact shed "honest tears" during the reconciliation scene between Loveless and Amanda, but even the theatrical legend is instructive. Nor shall we ever know exactly what the anonymous critic meant when he said "that Play was the Philosopher's Stone . . . it did wonders."[25]

---

[24] Bryan R. S. Fone, *Restoration and Eighteenth Century Theatre Research* 7 (May 1968), 34; *The Comic Theatre*, ed. Samuel Foote *et al.*, 5 vols. (London, 1762) I sig. a6r.

[25] Davies 1783–4, III 412; *A Comparison between the Two Stages* (1702), ed. Staring B. Wells (Princeton: Princeton University Press, 1942) 16. Hostile, moralizing criticism of *Love's Last Shift* in the twentieth century is summarized in Koon 1986, 196–7.

3

Colley Cibber, *The Careless Husband* (1704)

"Now, whatever Contempt Philosophers may have for a fine Perriwig," there can be no doubt that the full-bottomed wig he wore in *Love's Last Shift* helped Colley Cibber to another successful comedy.[1] Into the green room at Drury Lane in January 1696 strolled a young rake, heir to an encumbered estate at Cowley, in Gloucestershire, who had recently left Balliol College without a degree to study law in the Middle Temple. But like many students at the Inns of Court, Henry Brett's researches were undertaken in the streets, taverns, coffeehouses, and theatres of London. He surprised Colley Cibber by offering to buy Sir Novelty's wig and a bargain was struck "that Night over a Bottle." That bottle was succeeded by many more during the next months and the drinkers became fast friends and eventually co-managers of the Drury Lane theatre.[2]

But long before that, sometime in 1700, this dashing rake married a "Handsome, Wild, Well-jointured Widow," Anne Mason, divorced wife of Charles Gerard, second Earl of Macclesfield, and late mistress to Richard Savage, fourth Earl Rivers. To Lord Rivers the Countess of Macclesfield had borne two children, of whom the poet Richard Savage later claimed to be one. By the terms of divorce granted by the House of Lords in April 1698, her huge estate was returned to the control of Lady Anne.

She was "a Lady who had enough in her Power to disencumber [Henry Brett] of the World and make him every way easy for Life."[3] In Colley Cibber's mind his friend's new wife became Lady Easy. But Henry Brett's "frequent Successes" with women were not terminated by marriage. They were simply extended into new territory. "Mrs. Brett came into a room one day in her own house, and found [her husband] and her maid fast asleep ... She tied a white handkerchief round her husband's neck, which was sufficient proof that she had discovered his intrigue; but she never at any time took notice of it to him." It was in this way that Sir Novelty Fashion's full-bottomed wig provided Colley Cibber with a hero, a heroine, and a

---

[1] *Apology* 1889, II 36. "This remarkable Periwig usually made its entrance upon the stage in a sedan, brought in by two chairmen, with infinite approbation of the audience" (Pope, *The Dunciad* (B) [1742] I 167n).

[2] *Apology* 1889, II 37, 56.   [3] *Apology* 1889, II 39.

discovery scene for the new comedy that he began to write in the summer of 1702. As he wrote it, "he submitted every scene . . . to Mrs. Brett's revisal and correction."[4]

Help came from other quarters as well. First from "Red John" Campbell, who succeeded as second Duke of Argyll in September 1703. Already at twenty-two he was a very handsome colonel of horse guards with a weakness for the stage and for stage actresses. "If the Dialogue of the following Scenes flows with more easie[!] Turn of Thought and Spirit," Cibber wrote in dedicating the play to the duke, "I owe most of it to . . . your Grace's manner of Conversing."[5]

Help also came from Ann Oldfield, a twenty-year-old actress for whom, after a false start, Cibber wrote the best female part in the play, Lady Betty Modish. "Whatever favourable Reception this Comedy has met with from the Publick," Cibber wrote nearly forty years later, "it would be unjust in me not to place a large Share of it to the Account of Mrs. *Oldfield*; not only from the uncommon Excellence of her Action [acting], but even from her personal manner of Conversing."[6] Not yet a successful actress, Ann Oldfield was already the mistress of a successful man, Arthur Mainwaring, of Ightfield, Shropshire, a poet, musician, Member of Parliament, Whig propagandist, and confidant of Sarah, Duchess of Marlborough. "The Summer [1704] before the Appearance of the *Careless Husband* on the Stage, Mr. *Maynwaring* and Mrs. *Oldfield* spent the Recess of a whole long Vacation at *Windsor* . . . where they lodged in the Castle, at the House of Mr. *John Sewell*, Treasurer and Chapter-Clerk to the Dean and College."[7]

In summary, therefore, Colley Cibber was helped to his main plot by the marital mishaps of Mrs. Brett.[8] Ann Oldfield supplied the female lead for the subplot, and probably some of the Windsor atmosphere. The Duke of Argyll may have supplied phrases for genteel, upper-class dialogue. "Mr. *Cibber*'s Cotemporaries would not allow him to have been the Author of [*The Careless Husband*]; some attributing it to the D. of *Argyle*, to whom it was dedicated, some to Mr. *Defoe*, some to Mr. *Manwaring*, &c."[9] But there is no doubt now

---

[4] Boswell 1934–50, I 174n.

[5] Colley Cibber, *The Careless Husband. A Comedy* (London, 1705) sig. A2r. This kind of flattery provides no evidence of Argyll's wit. Congreve likewise attributes the wit in *The Way of the World* (1700) to Charles Montagu's "Conversation." But Cibber's gratitude for Argyll's "Favourable Influence in the Bounties that were rais'd me for the Third and Sixth Day" indicates that his patron's generosity was real.

[6] *Apology* 1889, I 309. Again Cibber is being too modest; cf. p.32 above.

[7] [William Oldys?], *Memoirs of Mrs. Anne Oldfield* (London, 1741) 12.

[8] Despite an impeccable *historical* provenance the main plot of *The Careless Husband* also reenacts folklore motifs J1112.1: "Wife reforms wayward husband" and K1271.3: "Amorous intrigue exposed and faithless husband humiliated."

[9] David Erskine Baker, *The Companion to the Play-House*, 2 vols. unpag. (London, 1764) I s.v. *The Careless Husband;* cf. *A Series of Letters between Mrs. Elizabeth Carter and Miss Catherine Talbot*, ed. Montagu Pennington, 4 vols. (London, 1809) I 191: "was ever so original an author as Mr. Cibber?"

that Colley Cibber wrote the play and wrote it all. Ann Oldfield played her
part so well that it seemed to contemporaries that she *was* Lady Betty Modish:
"it was not the Part of Lady *Betty Modish*, represented by Mrs. *Oldfield*; but it
was the real Mrs. *Oldfield* who appeared in the Character of Lady *Betty
Modish*."[10] But this is only the illusion of stagecraft. It was the part of Lady
Betty, written by Colley Cibber, that was played so well by Ann Oldfield that
she made her reputation by it.

All the action of the play that Cibber wrote takes place during one long, idle
Sunday at Windsor Castle (plate 2) and it conveys a wonderful sense of the life
there while the court was in residence: the chocolate house just outside Henry
VIII's gatehouse, promenades on the terrace, tennis, serenades, hunting in
Windsor Forest, paying visits, and even a glimpse of the queen returning from
vespers in St. George's chapel. The grossness of Sir Charles Easy's whoredom
with his wife's servant, and even of his so-called "*Honourable* Affair" (V i 53)
with Lady Graveairs, become more apparent when played out against the
background of this venerable, almost sacred enclave.

The characters in *The Careless Husband* are peers. Morelove and Foppington
are barons. Sir Charles Easy is presumably a baronet. Lady Betty Modish is
"your Great Lady" (II ii 209), the daughter of a peer. All of them have
fortunes.[11] These are not the persons below the level of our world that
Aristotle said comedy should imitate. But Cibber's departure from Aristotelian decorum is deliberate and acknowledged. Even these characters of
"Birth, and Education," he says, are not without comic flaws "that call for
Satyr's Rage" (Prologue, 20, 3). Their folly is pride, the weakness, not of
clowns, but of heroes. And not of real heroes, of course, but of mock heroes
who squabble over a snuff box (III i 254) very much in the manner of *The Rape
of the Lock* (1712). "How little do our Passions make us" (IV i 179), says Lady
Easy, Cibber's heroine.

"But what shall we do with our-selves 'til Dinner" (I i 407), asks Lord
Morelove, and immediately we know where we are: in the midst of a leisure
class fighting off ennui with sex and games. It is, of course, the society of
Restoration comedy, like *The Way of the World* (1700) which opens to comic
hero and comic villain playing cards before noon in a chocolate house. But
into this familiar world Cibber introduces some strange elements. Goldsmith
discovered that if the characters in sentimental comedy have "Faults or
Foibles, the Spectator is taught ... to applaud them, in consideration of the
goodness of their hearts."[12] However flawed and compromised his characters

---

[10] [William Oldys?], *Memoirs of Mrs. Anne Oldfield* (London, 1741) 3.
[11] I i 69, 400; II i 84; II ii 25, 148; V vi 159.
[12] Goldsmith 1966, III 212.

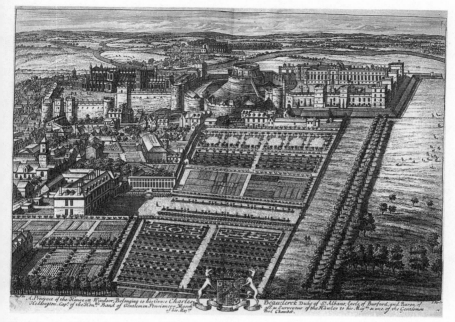

Plate 2   In this bird's-eye view of Windsor Castle, the terraces are on the right, St. George's Chapel is at upper left, and Charles II's enclosed tennis court is at center left. Engraving by Johannes Kip after a drawing by Leonard Knyff.

may appear – and he goes as far as the genre will permit him[13] – Cibber makes it perfectly clear that beneath the surface beats a heart of gold.

Lady Betty Modish is "a strange giddy Creature" (II i 111) with an apparent streak of sadism in her, but we are told very early that her "Heart don't want good Nature" (II i 155) and this, of course, is confirmed in the dénouement (V vii 230). Sir Charles Easy is "A vile, licentious Man" (I i 2) who manages to sound sometimes like W. C. Fields:

My Dear, your Understanding startles me.

(V vi 75)

and sometimes like an advertising flack:

Thou Easy Sweetness.

(V vi 174)

But in the end we learn that he is only "Carelessly Good Natur'd" (V vi 63).

---

[13] Some of the excitement in *The Careless Husband* may be generated by Colley Cibber's scorn for the characters he has created. These representatives of the lesser nobility are not so attractive as the middle-class characters in *Love's Last Shift*. My guess is that Cibber unconsciously disliked them and that a little of this dislike leaks out in the prologue where he calls them "slaves to a vile Tainted Mind" (sig. A3r).

Besides this one primary characteristic of sentimental comedy, the Pelagian heresy (A2), *The Careless Husband* exhibits all of the secondary characteristics:
A *"sprinkling of tender melancholy Conversation"* (B1):

from the soft Heat of his distilling Thoughts the Tears have fall'n.   (IV i 130–1)

Receive me then Intire at last, and take what yet no Woman ever Truly Had, my Conquer'd Heart.
(V vi 112–13)

Heroic virtue (rewarded) (B2): Lady Easy's "Exalted Virtue" (V vii 314), her "Heart-breaking Patience" (V v 28), is rewarded, as she says herself, "more than I had Merited" (V vi 152), with "something more than Happiness," with "Double Life, and Madness of Abounding Joy" (V vi 118). Lord Morelove's "vast Merit" (III i 487), which also is patience, is similarly rewarded. "O let my Soul, thus Bending to your Power," he tells this now penitent coquette, "adore this soft Descending Goodness" (V vii 175–6).

Undeserved distress (B3): At the beginning of the play Lady Easy is a neglected wife who has been left to "cry [her] self sick in some dark Closet" (I i 218). Lord Morelove is a rejected suitor "whose whole Life's but one continued Torment" (IV i 97–8).

Overt moralizing (B4):

there's a Pleasure ev'n in the Melancholy of a Quiet Conscience.
(V vi 12)

Another remarkable thing about the play is the absence of "City Husbands" and "old fumbling Keepers," who provide obstacles to the realization of the lovers' happiness in earlier Restoration comedy. There are no angry old men on the stage at all; no ancestral voices crying, No! There is nothing to prevent the lovers from falling into each others' arms but their own states of mind, their own follies, their silly belief that "Free Love" is preferable to marriage. The obstacles are completely internalized.

The plot of *The Careless Husband* cannot be generated in the classical manner by a conflict between generations because there is only one generation. All these characters of "Birth and Education" and fortune are also young – "only children of a larger growth." What Cibber does, therefore, is to conceal the essential good nature of some of the eirons in order to let them function, temporarily, as alazons. Lord Foppington and Lady Betty, Sir Charles and Lady Graveairs, are all "Slaves," as Cibber says in the prologue, to some "vile" obsession. They set the comic tone by repeating their obsessions: self love, coquettish "Power," the sexual "Chace," and generate the comic plot by providing obstacles to the course of true love.[14]

The good nature of some of the characters must also be concealed so they

14 Frye 1957, 168, 172.

can ill-naturedly provide distress for the obviously good-natured characters. And this pain, in the sentimental paradox, is pleasure. *Suffering* pain is "much superior" to inflicting it. "How low are Vicious Minds, that Offer Injuries," Lady Easy is made to exclaim, "How much superior Innocence that Bears 'em?" (V vi 11–12). And in the end Lady Easy is made "Happy ev'n to a Pain of Joy" (V vii 4).

When the obstacle-making, distress-providing characters have served their dramatic purposes, their disguises can be stripped off and their essential good nature revealed. Sir Charles calls this process "Conversion" (V vii 279) and it is not unlike baptism. The comic hero is indeed "regenerate and born anew." In the sacrament of baptism this cannot happen "by nature," whereas in a comedy it can. The "Conversion" is an undisguising, a dismantling, an unmasking, revealing the essential good nature that has always been there. Only when the lovers' faults have been confessed and renounced and the disguises stripped off, are the lovers free to enjoy each other, and the play free to end.

But sentimental details do not predominate. *The Careless Husband* is essentially a Restoration comedy of manners – praised by Alexander Pope – with some of the symptoms of sentimentality. It is a Restoration comedy in the process of becoming sentimental, *sentimentalisante*.

The language of the play can be remarkably "Restoration":

LORD FOPPINGTON. Why that for my Part, I had rather have a Plain Slice of my Wife's Woman [personal maid], than my Guts full of e'er an Ortolan Dutchess in Christendom.

(II ii 168)

There is not as much of this as there is in *Love's Last Shift*, but there is still enough to generate a cynical, dissipated tone during all but the last scenes of the play. "What good has your Virtue done you" (I i 192), Sir Charles asks his wife in the first scene of the play. The recurrent imagery reinforces this cynicism. Lady Betty Modish and Lord Foppington are agreed that a fine lady is a commodity, a "Dish" (II i 107; II ii 174; III i 355, p. 310). What is heard in the play is "the laugh of Noisy Fops, Coquettes, and Coxcombs, Dissolutely Gay" (V vii 92–3), and even fashionable baby-talk (V vii 235). Cibber satirizes polite society in the age of Queen Anne by letting it speak in its own voice. "This comedy," it is said, "contains, perhaps, the most elegant dialogue, and the most perfect knowledge of the manners of persons in real high life, extant in any dramatic piece."[15]

With an instinctive feel for comedy, Cibber sensed that "nothing is more ridiculous than the Fall of Pride" (II i 149) and with an equally sensitive

[15] Baker 1812, II 83.

responsiveness to the reforming tendency of the times,[16] he plotted "the Fall of Pride" as a kind of masque reenacting on the stage the moral reformation that everyone in London was talking about. Plot and subplot in this masque are mirror images of each other. Lady Easy is another patient Griselda, the very model of the neglected and uncomplaining wife. She loves her husband, but Sir Charles is preoccupied by a mistress and a passing *tendresse* for Lady Easy's maid. In the subplot Lord Morelove is a male Griselda, who has been "us'd like a Dog for Four or Five Years together" (II i 71). He loves Lady Betty Modish, but she is engaged in infamous dalliance with the Baron of Foppington. Lord Foppington's relationship with *his* neglected wife (II ii 106–8) provides a parallel with, and perspective upon, the main plot.

Sir Charles's pride is self-indulgence, which he calls "Carelessness," and which enables him to blame his wife for his own marital shortcomings (III i 42). Lady Betty Modish's pride is love of power, that "Pontifical" power over men afforded by her "Estate and Beauty" (II i 131), which she knows will terminate when she marries. It is Lady Betty who verbalizes the eironic norms, "Free Love, Disorder, Liberty and Pleasure," (III i 536), which "are seldom defined or formulated."[17] The irony is that while she articulates "Liberty" she enacts coquetry to which she is in ritual bondage. The theme of *The Careless Husband*, like that of *Love's Last Shift* is a paradox: "Free Love" is bondage; "Freedom, Order and Tranquility" (III i 175) exist only in marriage.

Perhaps the most interesting feature of the play is Cibber's handling of the traditional Griselda motif (H461). He undertakes to investigate the reasons *why* Griselda is patient, *why* the wife endures rejection, a question that Boccaccio, for example, ignores. This is the problem with which the play begins:

> LADY EASY. Was ever Woman's spirit, by an injurious Husband, broke like mine
>   A vile, licentious Man! must he bring Home his Follies too? Wrong me with my
>   very Servant! O! how Tedious a Relief is Patience! and yet in my Condition 'ti
>   the only Remedy.
>
>   (I i 1

Cibber suggests two reasons why Lady Easy accepts this situation: partly she is afraid to reproach her husband, and partly she is too proud. The latter, and more interesting insinuation, is made first about Lady Foppington, an off-stage replica of Lady Easy. Lady Betty observes that Lady Foppington endures her husband's infidelities because she is too proud to complain: "her Pride indeed makes her carry it off without taking any Notice of it" (II i 117)

---

[16] In the dedication Cibber sets up, very impudently, as a competitor of Jeremy Collier. In *Defence of the Short View of the Profaneness and Immorality of the English Stage* (London, 1699) i–ii Collier had declared that *Love's Last Shift* was "scandalously Smutty and Profane." The language of *The Careless Husband* is notably less gamy.

[17] Frye 1957, 169.

And Sir Charles, as we have seen, is of the same opinion: "Virtues in a Wife are Good for nothing but to make her Proud" (II ii 154). But Lady Betty and Sir Charles are themselves proud characters in need of a chastening conversion, so their testimony may be suspect. And the evidence of the other characters is not unequivocal. Lord Morelove exclaims that Lady Easy is "A Woman truly Good in her Nature" (III i 35), but Lady Easy herself believes that "The Fault's in me" (V v 16). Yet when Sir Charles's conversion has been accomplished and Lady Easy can relax a bit, she – who has never deluded herself – admits that "it's a Joy to think it over: A secret Pride, to tell my Heart my Conduct has been Just" (V vi 9).

The lesson seems clear: on the surface *The Careless Husband* enacts a fable of masculine pride-in-irresponsibility and feminine pride-in-power. The surprising development is that the victim of masculine irresponsibility, the rejected wife, remains patient at least partly out of pride. It is an interesting paradox: Lady Easy enjoys "giving Ease" and Lady Betty Modish delights to cause "Pain" – from the same motive of pride (V vii 250). Not even the most virtuous of these characters is without guilt.

The Careless Husband was even a greater success than *Love's Last Shift*. It was played "with very great Applause" sixteen times in its first season, revived in October 1705 and again nearly every season to the end of the century.[18] Congreve, further embittered, perhaps, by the unsuccess of *The Way of the World* in March 1700, was again hostile, but even his sneer testifies to the play's success: it is "a play ... which the ridiculous town for the most part likes," he said, "but there are some that know better."[19] Horace Walpole helps to explain Congreve's hostility: "The delicate and almost insensible touches of The Careless Husband are the reverse of Congreve's ungovernable wit," he said.[20]

In 1706 the play was cited for "Swearing and Blasphemy ... undermining Religion ... [and] undermining Virtue."[21] But *The Careless Husband* survived, and survived to become a standard of excellence in the eighteenth century. An anonymous review of *The School for Lovers* in *The British Magazine*, February 1762, found that "the delicacy of sentiment, purity of language, and elegance of character, which shine through this piece, must raise it ... far above the level of the generality of our comedies, (the Careless Husband excepted)." A review of *False Delicacy* in *The London Magazine*, January 1768, pronounced that there had been "no piece since the Careless Husband, in which the dialogue so happily imitates the conversation of people of fashion." Horace Walpole said simply that "The Careless Husband and Vanbrugh are standards."[22]

---

[18] Giles Jacob, *The Poetical Register: Or, The Lives and Characters of the English Dramatick Poets* (London, 1719) 39; *The London Stage*, part 2, I 82–95.

[19] George Monck Berkeley, *Literary Relics* (London, 1789) 342.   [20] Walpole 1797, II 317.

[21] Arthur Bedford, *The Evil and Danger of Stage-Plays* (London, 1706) 29, 100, 113.

[22] Walpole 1797, II 322. Edmund Burke was aware "with how much Success the excellent Writers of this Age have imitated *Cibber*" (*The Reformer* 31 March 1748).

By the middle of the century, however, the discovery scene was found to be "vicious and indelicate."[23] But at the same time literary ladies were finding "Colley Cibber a much more moral and entertaining writer" than Terence.[24] And in the next century another actor-playwright declared that the dialogue of *The Careless Husband* is "so very natural, that its force will admit of no augmentation, even from the delivery of the best actors." The characters "talk, they think, they act, they love, and hate, like people of rank this very day," Elizabeth Inchbald asserted, "Change but their dinner hour from four to seven, and blot out the line, where a lady says, 'she is going to church,' and every article, in the whole composition, will be perfectly modern."[25] Today there is no problem of distinguishing "between what's Meant for Contempt, and what for Example" (V iii 69). "After all," said an anonymous critic of Jeremy Collier, "my Lord *Foppington* was never design'd to teach People to speak or act like him."[26] What the play celebrates are "those real Comfortable Advantages in Marriage, that our Old Aunts, and Grand-mothers wou'd persuade us of" (V i 65).

---

[23] Wilkes 1759, 39–40. The copy of *The Foundling* submitted to the Lord Chamberlain for license in 1748 included these lines: "I know a certain Lady of Quality in this very Street, that wou'd blush to Death at the Handkerchief Scene in the Careless Husband, – when to my Knowledge a certain motherly Gentlewoman ... has reliev'd her twice within these three Years from the Burden of her Indiscretions with John the Butler" (Huntington MS L68, p. 74). These lines are *not* included in the published text of the play.

[24] *Bluestocking Letters*, ed. R. Brimley Johnson (London: John Lane, 1926) 223.

[25] Inchbald 1808, IX 55–6.

[26] *A Letter to A. H. Esq; Concerning the Stage* (London, 1698) 11.

4

Sir Richard Steele, *The Conscious Lovers* (1722)

"A greater Concourse of People was never known to be assembled" in London than on the opening night of *The Conscious Lovers* on Saturday 7 November 1722.[1] It would be nice to be able to report that the crowd in Drury Lane proved the popularity of sentimental comedy. But such, alas, is not the case. What the crowd proved was the effectiveness of advance publicity.

The Conscious Lovers had a longer period of gestation than an elephant. It is virtually certain that the play of which Steele said in June 1710, "only the Out-Lines [are] drawn,"[2] is the same play that opened on 7 November 1722, more than twelve years later. At first it was called *The Fine Gentleman*, then *Sir John Edgar*, then *The Unfashionable Lovers*, and finally, only a few days before the curtain went up, *The Conscious Lovers*.[3] The word "conscious," in Steele's usage, retains something of its original meaning, *con scius*, "sharing a secret together," and something of the latest fashionable meaning, "self-conscious."[4] Jack Bevil and Indiana Danvers are "conscious" in both senses. And both senses are reinforced by dominant images in the play, the image of reciprocal peeking (*con scius*) and the image of being stared at (making one self-conscious) (I i 255; II ii 24–5; II iii 182; III i 157–60, 211, 294, 422–4; V i 25).[5] Phillis, Lucinda Sealand's maid, summarizes all this in a gnomic sentence of blinding nonsense: "not to see, when one may," she says, "is hardly possible; not to see when one can't, is very easy" (III i 161).

Steele plugged his new play shamelessly in *The Theatre*, the last in the long line of his periodical essays, which he wrote in the first months of 1720.[6] Then, in October 1722, while the play was in rehearsal, the following advertisement was placed in the newspapers: "Sir Richard Steele's excellent new Comedy,

---

[1] *The Daily Journal* 8 November 1722 (quoted in *The London Stage*, part 2, II 694).

[2] *The Tatler* 8 June 1710. The provenance and composition of *The Conscious Lovers* are described in Loftis 1952, 183–93 and in *The Plays of Richard Steele*, ed. Shirley S. Kenny (Oxford: Clarendon, 1971) 275–9.

[3] Victor 1761–71 II 99; Steele, *The Theatre* 5 April 1720; note 7 below.

[4] Steele, *The Spectator* 5 March 1711: "she knows she is handsome, but she knows she is good. Conscious Beauty adorn'd with conscious Virtue" (*OED*).

[5] *The Conscious Lovers* is quoted in the definitive edition of Shirley S. Kenny, which takes as copy text the first edition (1723).

[6] Steele, *The Theatre* 9 January, 5 March, 5 April 1720.

called *The Unfashionable Lovers*, will be acted on the sixth of next month. It is thought that this Play is the best modern Play that has been produced."[7]

Since advance publicity was not yet common enough to be totally discounted by critics, the old critic John Dennis was outraged by these "scandalous Artifices" and proceeded to write a footless attack on a play that he had neither seen nor read.[8] Dennis's pamphlet, rushed into print on 2 November 1722 to warn people away, can only have drawn greater numbers to the Theatre Royal on 7 November.

Sir Richard Steele himself was an attractive character. He was another witty Anglo-Irishman, like Congreve and Swift. But unlike Congreve and Swift, he was short, fat, and good-natured (plate 3). He believed in alchemy and other get-rich-quick schemes that always failed. "He was a man of undissembled, and extensive benevolence; a friend to the friendless, and as far as his circumstances would permit, the father of every orphan,"[9] several of whom he begat himself. In November 1722 he was at the top of his career. He had just been reinstated in the management of the Drury Lane company (May 1721) after a long legal battle. He had just been reelected to Parliament (March 1722) for the third time.[10] His new comedy had been touted and discussed for a dozen years. When Steele read it to his three co-patentees in the Theatre Royal, Barton Booth and Robert Wilkes "dozed over the perusal." "Too moral and serious," they declared. But Cibber took it in hand and made "many additions."[11] While the play was in rehearsal he acted as stage director, "instructing the Actors, and altering the Disposition of the Scenes."[12] At last it was ready for the stage.

[7] *The Epistolary Correspondence of Sir Richard Steele*, ed. John Nichols, 2 vols. (London, 1809) II 621n.

[8] *A Defence of Sir Fopling Flutter, A Comedy Written by Sir George Etheridge. In which Defence is shewn, That Sir Fopling, that merry Knight, was rightly compos'd by the Knight his Father, to answer the Ends of Comedy; and that he has been barbarously and scurrilously attack'd by the Knight his Brother, in the 65th Spectator. By which it appears, That the latter Knight knows nothing of the Nature of Comedy* (London, 1722).

[9] Cibber 1753, IV 121.

[10] Steele was a Whig Member of Parliament for Stockbridge, Hants (August 1713 to 18 March 1714), Boroughbridge, Yorks. (1715 to 1722), and Wendover, Bucks. (1722 to 1727) (Romney Sedgwick, *The History of Parliament 1715–1745*, 2 vols. [New York: Oxford University Press, 1970] II 442).

[11] Cibber 1753, IV 120; cf. Wilkes 1759, 43. Theophilus, who at the age of eighteen played Daniel in the original cast, implies that his father wrote the parts of Tom and Phillis. But this is most unlikely, for Tom is the slave Davus in Steele's source (Terence's *Andria*) and Steele adapted the part to "fit the Genio's" of his friend, Colley Cibber (*The Tatler* 8 June 1710). The germ of Tom and Phillis is in *The Guardian* 20 June 1713 (Kenny 1971, 413). What Cibber added may have been the two scenes of broad farce (III i 339–426 and all of V i) which have no necessary relationship to the plot or subplot but which definitively polarize the comic tone of the play. Nor is there any evidence that Cibber rewrote the play in the summer of 1722 at Twickenham (Koon 1986, 104). In the preface to the printed play Steele records that Cibber convinced him, with difficulty, to substitute a masquerade for "*Terence*'s celebrated Funeral" in the *Andria*.

[12] *The Conscious Lovers. A Comedy* (London, 1723) sig. A6v.

Mr STEELE.

I. Thornhill pinxit. G. Vertue sculpsit.

Plate 3   Richard Steele (before he was knighted in April 1715), an engraving by George Vertue after a portrait by Sir James Thornhill.

For the stage itself, two new painted scenes were ready. In that of Charing Cross for Act V, scene ii, "You [could] see as far as from Whitehall to Temple Bar, and the shops and all: Then, there is the very sentry-box, the old soldier, my Lord's chair, and the trees, just as though they were all alive."[13] For the entire cast, including Barton Booth as Jack Bevil, the incomparable Ann Oldfield as Indiana, Colley Cibber as Tom, new costumes had been made. So it would have required very little curiosity indeed to have "ventur'd to squeeze into the Crowd that went to see it the first Night."[14]

Of the play that they saw, the plot was borrowed from the first comedy of Terence, the *Andria* (166 BC). It goes like this: an agreeable and privileged young man has for three weeks (II ii 88) been keeping a mysterious and attractive young woman in lodgings near Charing Cross. His father wants him to marry the daughter of a rich businessman. Our hero, of course, wants to marry the mysterious stranger, but to stall for time he agrees to marry the woman of his father's choice. Fortunately the rich businessman grows suspicious and breaks off the match. But then, in the recognition scene, Act V, scene iii, the mysterious stranger turns out to be the elder daughter of the rich businessman, so our hero can marry her, and his friend can marry the younger daughter, whom he has wanted all along.

This well-worn and improbable fiction, which teeters constantly on the edge of farce, was, Steele said, "writ for the sake of the Scene of the Fourth Act, wherein Mr. *Bevill* evades the Quarrel with his Friend."[15] But the evidence of the play itself shows that "the whole was writ for the sake of" the recognition scene. The build-up for this scene begins in the first lines of the play – when a mysterious "Lady in the *Indian* Mantle" (I i 68) is said to have been seen at a masquerade last week with Jack Bevil – and continues into the last act. The mystery of this woman's identity is not long allowed to be forgotten. She is "the Lady at the Masquerade ... this secret Lady ... this Woman they talk of ... your *Indian* Princess ... this strange Lady ... this *Incognita* ... This unknown Lady ... this unknown Lady that Mr. *Bevil* is so great with" (I i 96–7; I ii 223; III i 150; IV i 149; IV ii 76–7, 93; V i 108). The suspense created by this repetition, together with that created by the repeated clues to the solution of the mystery (I i 89; I ii 164; II ii 93; IV ii 68), effects a powerful release when Indiana's identity is revealed (V iii 176):

> MR. SEALAND. O my Child! my Child!
> INDIANA. All-Gracious Heaven! is it Possible! do I embrace my Father!
> MR. SEALAND. And do I hold thee! These Passions are too strong for Utterance. Rise, rise, my Child, and give my Tears their Way.

---

[13] Aitken 1889, II 285.
[14] *The Freeholders Journal* 14 November 1722 (quoted in Loftis 1952, 195).
[15] *The Conscious Lovers. A Comedy* sig. A5v.

Even Steele's worst enemy agreed that this scene is very moving[16] and there can be no doubt that it, rather than the declined duel in Act IV, scene i, is the reason for *The Conscious Lovers* to exist. In *The Winter's Tale* Shakespeare declined a similar opportunity and removed offstage the recognition scene between Leontes and Perdita (V ii).

The contrast here with *Love's Last Shift* is also instructive. Colley Cibber builds up suspense in a very similar fashion.[17] Cibber's big bang brings laughs, while Steele's evokes a sentimental response, "Why didn't my father treat *me* that way?" It is the response, not the recognition scene, that makes comedies sentimental. A recognition scene by itself cannot generate sentimentality. "The *cognitio* in comedy, in which the characters find out who their relatives are … is one of the features of comedy that has never changed much."[18] The recognition scene in *The Conscious Lovers*, however, reaches back, through Terence, to the beginnings of New Comedy in the fourth century BC. And behind New Comedy lie the folklore motifs that generate the sentimental response: abandoned children, tests of patience, search for the lost father, recognition by tokens,[19] and reversals of fortune.

What is being tested in Indiana, besides her patience, is whether she is "worthy" (V iii 197) of Jack Bevil, whether she is an "Object worthy his Acceptance" (V iii 220). Is she really only "a handsome Beggar" (II ii 81), an "Object of Desire" (V iii 123), or is she a fairy princess in disguise? Steele develops his plot, in the approved fashion of the soap opera, by the principle of "Aggravation of the Distress" (V iii 4), or "Get the heroine behind the eight-ball and keep her there" (B3). So Indiana suffers the loss of her father while still an infant (IV ii 68). She survives the ordeal by water while only a child (I ii 173). She passes her chastity test in the dangerous terrain of Toulon (I ii 197). And in London she is subject to her final trial, the test of her belief in Jack Bevil.

Jack Bevil is indeed hard to believe in. He refuses to seduce the orphan he has rescued from a fate worse than death in Toulon and brought back to London, even though he keeps her in expensive lodgings (V iii 24) and pays her a big allowance (II ii 17), and even though the girl herself is under the spell of "a languishing unreserv'd Passion" for him (V iii 2). Although he "doats on her to death" (I ii 227) and intends to marry her, he refuses even to speak of love (I ii 230; V iii 109) until he can secure his father's consent (I ii 135; IV ii 139–40). And most ingloriously of all, he risks shame and dishonor

---

[16] Dennis 1943, II 267. Dennis goes on to insist that Steele should have made it "more surprizing." But this would have been impossible without removing the suspense on which the effect of the scene depends.

[17] See p. 28 above. [18] Frye 1957, 170.

[19] Steele had joked about recognition by tokens in his last comedy, *The Tender Husband; Or, The Accomplish'd Fools. A Comedy* (London, 1705) 18: "Many an Infant has been placed in a Cottage with Obscure Parents, till by chance some Ancient Servant of the Family has known it by its Marks."

by refusing to fight when challenged to a duel (B2). So it is not surprising that the rich businessman, Sealand, cannot believe that Jack Bevil's relations with the mysterious stranger are innocent (IV ii 27). Even Jack's father has doubts (IV ii 118).

To try to make Jack Bevil credible, Steele invented a character, Isabella Danvers, with no counterpart in the *Andria*, whose main function is to disbelieve in Jack Bevil. Presumably what Steele hoped was that by making a sour old maid proclaim that "Mr. *Bevil* ... is a Man, and therefore a Hypocrite" (II ii 54), he could convince the audience to believe otherwise. He tries further to insulate his hero against incredulity by making the mysterious stranger herself proclaim that "the Fools that laugh at Mr. *Bevil*, will but make themselves more ridiculous" (II ii 82). But in spite of all Steele's rhetoric, this fool, at any rate, cannot help laughing at Jack Bevil, all dressed up (V iii 100) for his wedding to the girl of his father's choice and putting on "an Easy Look with an Aking Heart" (I i 192; I ii 5), a perfect instance of the funny-sadness of sentimental comedy.

The trouble, of course, is that the character of Jack Bevil suffers from having to embody Steele's idea that "A Man that is Temperate, Generous, Valiant, Chaste, Faithful and Honest, may, at the same time, have Wit, Humour, Mirth, good Breeding, and Gallantry."[20]

The truth can be concealed no longer. Sir Richard Steele was also a reformer and, even worse, a disciple of Jeremy Collier and Sir Richard Blackmore. His first published work was *The Christian Hero: An Argument Proving that no Principles But Those of Religion Are Sufficient to make a Great Man* (1701) and his second play, *The Lying Lover* (1703), was written to prove that "a Comedy ... might be no Improper Entertainment in a Christian Common-wealth."[21] But Steele the Reformer and Steele the Entertainer were the same man. Jeremy Collier wanted to close the theatres and Sir Richard Blackmore urged playwrights to "take up some honest, lawful Calling."[22] But Steele loved the theatre. "One of my greatest Delights," he said, is "to sit unobserved and unknown in the Gallery, and entertain myself ... with what is personated on the Stage."[23] And unlike most reformers, Steele understood something about human nature. In the spring, he said, "a Woman is prompted by a kind of Instinct to throw her self on a Bed of Flowers."[24] Like everyone in the eighteenth century, what Steele wanted was censorship of the stage: "nothing ... but what is agreeable to the Manners, Laws, Religion and

---

[20] Steele, *The Spectator* 28 April 1711.

[21] Steele, *The Lying Lover: Or, The Ladies Friendship. A Comedy* (London, 1704) sig. a1r; cf. *Diary of Mary Countess Cowper* (n.p., 1864) 46–7: "It were to be wished our Stage was chaster; and I cannot but hope, now [15 February 1715] it is under Mr. *Steele's* Direction, that it will mend."

[22] Richard Blackmore, *Prince Arthur. An Heroick Poem* (London, 1695) sig. a1r.

[23] Steele, *The Tatler* 8 June 1710. The two hours of a theatrical performance, Steele goes on to say, is "a Duration of Bliss not at all to be slighted by so short-lived a Creature as Man."

[24] Steele, *The Spectator* 29 April 1712.

Policy of the . . . Nation."[25] Steele wanted to harness the propaganda power of the stage to the cause of virtue, so that "the whole Soul is insensibly betrayed into Morality, by bribing the Fancy with beautiful and agreeable Images." This is certainly no innovation. Congreve wanted to do the same thing in *The Double Dealer* (1694). "I design'd the Moral first," Congreve said, "and to that Moral I invented the Fable."[26] Steele's mistake was in believing that "the Theatre has much the same Effect on the Manners of the Age, as the Bank [of England] on the Credit of the Nation."[27] It is true that a central bank controls the money supply of a nation. But it is not true that the stage controls manners. The truth must be that an uncensored stage reflects, rather than controls, the manners of the age. The English dramatists of the eighteenth century did not invent the behavior that is represented in sentimental comedies. It is, as Horace Walpole said, "the effect of observation."[28] But in any case, we can't get mad at Steele because he thought "Virtue worth contending for."

Indiana's belief in Jack Bevil's virtue is forged in the other big scene in the play, Act II, scene iii, in which Jack Bevil comes to pay his usual morning call on the mysterious stranger. It is a passage of high gallantry, full of extravagant compliment, well-bred conversation, and a command performance of a violin sonata. But Indiana is determined to "know the worst" (II iii 7) about her anomalous situation, to know whether Jack Bevil's "Care" of her can really proceed from "no private Interest in the Action" (II iii 151). So it is also a passage of high comedy, with Indiana pressing for an answer and Jack Bevil artfully and good-humoredly evading her questions. In the end, when he is gone, Indiana is forced to conclude that "he is wholly disinterested, in what he does for me . . . and has neither Good or Bad Designs upon me" (II iii 172). Indiana's disappointment that Jack Bevil is not even a serpent who lies in wait for doves, as her aunt insists, is one of the touches that make her irresistible. Because so many critics today find Indiana listless and dispirited, it is important to imagine how witty and spirited Ann Oldfield must have seemed to the original audience.

So in the end we only come to believe in the possibility of disinterested virtue because Indiana does. In the agony of her confrontation with the father of the girl whom she thinks Jack Bevil will marry that very night, her faith remains unshaken. She, alone in the play, is able to believe in Jack Bevil:

---

[25] See note 21 above.

[26] Steele, *The Tatler* 24 November 1709; Congreve, *The Double-Dealer, A Comedy* (London, 1694) sig. A3r.

[27] Steele, *The Tatler* 7 May 1709. Blackmore makes the same mistake: "The *universal* Corruption of Manners . . . that infects the Kingdom, seems to have been in a great Measure deriv'd from the Stage" (*Prince Arthur. An Heroick Poem* [London, 1695]) sig. A2v. To argue that the Restoration stage corrupted English manners is like arguing that *The Raj Quartet* brought down the British Empire.

[28] Walpole 1797, II 320.

"From his mere Delight in Virtue," she tells this rude, cynical businessman, "I have been his Care" (V iii 111–12).

Thus Indiana passes the final test of belief in Jack Bevil and becomes "the Reward of all his Virtues" (V iii 193) because *she* can believe in the possibility of disinterested virtue. The joke, of course, is that Jack Bevil is not disinterested at all. He is in love, that most "interested" and "conscious" of human situations. But in order for Indiana to become acceptable to Jack Bevil's father, she must be rich. So in the final transformation, the "handsome Beggar" (II ii 81) becomes, not an old-fashioned fairy princess, but the daughter of a new-fangled merchant king who "trades to all parts of the World" (V i 12). The plot of *The Conscious Lovers* looks as though it is going to be an example of folklore motif L162 (Lowly heroine marries prince), but it turns out in the end to be L213 (Poor girl chosen rather than the rich. Treasure follows).

The second pair of lovers in the play are only sketched in. Charles Myrtle is a young man-about-town – "so Gay, so Open, so Vacant" (II i 6) – with a great talent for mimicry. His suit for the hand of Lucinda Sealand was once encouraged by her parents (V iii 266–7) but now he is suffering violent attacks of the lover's disease, jealousy. In the throes of one of these attacks he challenges his friend Jack Bevil to a duel. Otherwise he provides much of the low comedy in the play by impersonating successively Serjeant Bramble, a learned barrister who interrupts (III i) and Sir Geoffry Cimberton of Cimberton Hall (V i 99, 124), a lecherous old baronet who is "half blind, half lame, half deaf, [and] half dumb" (IV iii 46).

Lucinda herself is sole heiress to the vast estate of the rich businessman, Sealand. She is also very young: the time-table of the play (V iii 26; I ii 168) would hardly allow her to be more than thirteen. She is still very much under the influence of her mother: "My Mother says, it's indecent for me to let my Thoughts stray about the Person of my Husband ... Mamma says ... My Mother says I must not converse with my Servants" (III i 155, 165, 200). And she is still somewhat vague about sex: "Who is to have this Body of mine," she says, "is nothing to me" (III i 154–5). Her "Body" is important in the play because it has been "expos'd, and offer'd to some aukward Booby ... in every County of *Great Britain*" (III i 174–6). Her cousin, Sir Geoffry Cimberton's nephew, inspects it as if he were buying a brood mare. When she objects to this scrutiny, her mother overrules her: "Oh, Child, hear him, he talks finely, he's a Scholar, he knows what you have" (III i 283–4). And Charles Myrtle, impersonating lecherous old Sir Geoffry, is able to appraise it lovingly (V i). Besides her fortune and her youth, she has "a great many [other] needless and superfluous good Qualities" (I ii 74; cf. Cibber, *The Careless Husband*, I i 192, quoted above, p. 39).

The third pair of lovers are servants, Tom (Jack Bevil's valet "or

Gentleman, as they call it"[29]) and Phillis (Lucinda Sealand's maid). They are funny because they impersonate the great rakes and coquettes of Restoration comedy. Phillis pretends to be fashionably *difficile* and willing to have her lover suffer "a little longer," but she is really "a pert merry Hussy" with an eye firmly fixed on the main chance (III i 58, 136, 113–14). Tom, her lover, pretends to be "as false and as base, as the best Gentleman of them all" (I i 265), but he too is looking forward to escape to "one Acre, with *Phillis*" (III i 78). It is Tom who articulates the archetypal distress of the lover: it is "miserable to be in Love," he says, "and under the Command of others than those we love" (III i 63).

The "others," of course, are the alazons in the play and there are four of these: Sir John Bevil, presumably a baronet; Sealand, who is in foreign trade; Mrs. Sealand, who has married beneath herself and is determined "to return our Blood again into the *Cimberton*'s" (V i 104) by marrying her daughter to old Sir Geoffry Cimberton's nephew, an insufferable coxcomb. Collectively the alazons function in the classical manner (1) to put obstacles in the lovers' way, and (2) by "the extravagance of their Humours" (V i 38) to polarize the comic tone. The same thing, of course, happens in Steele's source, the *Andria*, and presumably in the two lost comedies of Menander that Terence put together in *his* comedy. What is new in *The Conscious Lovers* is the way Steele develops this classical conflict. He does it, summarizing now, (1) by building up the suspense around Indiana for the big emotional bang in the recognition scene, (2) by subjecting two of his heroines to a series of harrowing tests, and (3) by authenticating the virtue of his hero.

The first of these developments has already been shown to be *not* sentimental but the second and third may seem to be sentimental because they encourage such responses as pitying the poor little orphan, or pitying the poor little rich girl, or admiring "A Man that is Temperate, Generous, Valiant, Chaste, Faithful and Honest." But all comedy is concerned with the distresses of lovers (p. 20 above). It is indeed "miserable to be in Love, and under the Command of others than those we love." And the tests of Indiana and Lucinda are completely within the comic (as opposed to the sentimental) tradition.

But not all eirons are "Temperate, Generous, Valiant, Chaste, Faithful and Honest." In the famous passage from Aristotle's *Rhetoric* that Dennis quotes:

Young Men ... have strong Appetites, and are ready to undertake any thing, in order to satisfy them; and of all those Appetites which have a Relation to the Body, they are most powerfully sway'd by Venereal [i.e. sexual] ones, in which they are very changeable, and are quickly cloy'd. For their Desires are rather acute than lasting; like

---

[29] Steele, *The Theatre* 9 January 1720.

the Hunger and Thirst of the Sick. They are prone to Anger, and easily provok'd;
vehement in their Anger, and ready to obey the Dictates of it.[30]

Jack Bevil is clearly none of this. He is a Christian hero. But he is a comic
version of the Christian hero and in order to qualify as a comic hero he must
have some weakness. His comic *hamartía*, of course, is his absurd "Religious
Vow" (II i 123) not to marry without his father's consent.

Sixty years ago Ashley Thorndike affirmed that "*The Conscious Lovers* is
sentimental comedy par excellence" and his judgment is commonly accepted
today.[31] But no one yet has been able to say exactly what *The Conscious Lovers* is
sentimental *about*. Now it is possible to say. *The Conscious Lovers* is primarily
sentimental about parents (A4).

The traditional attitude toward parents in comedy is extremely unsentimental. Parents exist in comedy to be circumvented, ridiculed, and defeated.
But Jack Bevil's "Religious Vow" not to marry without his father's consent
puts an alazon in control of the action of the comedy, which is clearly one of
the "new and desp'rate Rules" (Prologue, 16) by which Steele fashioned *The
Conscious Lovers*. Although Jack Bevil has an independent fortune, "He is as
dependant and resign'd to [his father's] Will, as if he had not a Farthing" (I i
39–40). Twice he affirms, "I never will Marry without my Father's Consent"
(I ii 135; IV ii 140) and thrice he acknowledges his "Obligation to the best of
Fathers" (I ii 233; II i 14; IV i 165). The fantasies induced by these details, so
different from the cruelties of the real world, enable any parent to experience
the authentic sentimental response: this is the way children *should* behave, "*I
am merely observing, passively . . . how I should have been treated.*" The cruelties of the
real world were borne in upon Steele one night at the theatre. When an old
woman collapsed and was carried out in agony, the audience laughed and
applauded. Something of Steele's sympathy for this old woman and for the
father he could barely remember may be incorporated in Jack Bevil's
exaggerated reverence for Sir John (A4).[32]

Secondarily, *The Conscious Lovers* expresses sentimental attitudes

Toward Woman (A3): Indiana is "one of the Ornaments of the whole
Creation" (II iii 118–19), a phrase that Goldsmith parodies in *She Stoops to*

[30] Aristotle, *Rhetoric* II xii, quoted in Dennis 1943, II 246–7.
[31] Thorndike 1929, 343; cf. Maximillian E. Novak, "The sentimentality of *The Conscious Lovers*
revisited and reasserted," *Modern Language Studies* 9 (1979): 48–59. Complaints about Jack
Bevil's sentimental regard for his father – "the filial Obedience of young *Bevil* is carried a great
deal too far" (Dennis 1943, II 263); "the character of *Bevil* is strained beyond all reason" (*The
Gentleman's Magazine* September 1762, but "Written at the time of exhibition") – measure the
difference between *The Conscious Lovers* and the unsentimental comedy with which playgoers
were familiar.
[32] Branfman 1954, 626; *The Spectator* 6 October 1712.

Conquer (1773) where the hero calls "a modest woman ... in all her finery," "the most tremendous object of the whole creation."[33]

Toward the lower orders (A6): Servants, including musicians, are not inferiors, but "Friends" (I i 19, 138, 239) to whom "something more" than wages is owed (II iii 94).

Toward money (A10): Jack Bevil plays the dutiful son by telling his father only what he knows his father wants to hear: "For, Sir," he says, "a Woman that is espous'd for a Fortune, is yet a better Bargain, if she dies; for then a Man still enjoys what he did marry, the Money" (I ii 66). But this is completely ironical. The woman whom Jack Bevil's father wants him to marry "for a Fortune," is "no Bargain" (V iii 257) at all for Jack Bevil, who wants to marry a penniless orphan. The device of uttering a cynical phrase in a sentimental voice exactly reverses a detail in *Love's Last Shift*[34] and illustrates the marked difference of tone between the two plays. Charles Myrtle reflects young Bevil's true feelings when he says of Lucinda, "No Abatement of Fortune shall lessen her Value to me" (V iii 267). And Lucinda's reply is an endearing specimen of sentimental paradox: "I love you more," she says, "*because* I bring you less" (V iii 274, italics added).

Two of the secondary characteristics of sentimental comedy, reckless virtue (B2) and undeserved distress (B3), have already been discussed (pp. 51–2 above). But the other two are also present:

A *"sprinkling of tender melancholy Conversation"* (B1): Phrases like "more than Life," "worse than Death," and "bleeding Heart" run through the play like refrains (I ii 146; II i 109; IV i 147; II ii 78; IV i 180; II ii 21), but the show piece of sentimental dialogue occurs in the recognition scene:

INDIANA. All my Comfort must be to expostulate in Madness, to relieve with Frenzy my Despair, and shrieking to demand of Fate, why – why was I born to such Variety of Sorrows?

(V iii 131)

Overt moralizing (B4): "A good Sentence," Steele said in *The Spectator*, 29 October 1711, "describes an inward Sentiment of the Soul," and a good one in *The Conscious Lovers* is this: "the best Condition of Human Life is but a gentler Misery" (II i 127).

After all this, it is hardly necessary to add that *The Conscious Lovers* was a "prodigious success" on the stage. It drew tears as well as laughter on the opening night and a generation later it was said that it "never fails to draw tears."[35] It ran for eighteen nights, a remarkably long run for the period, and

---

[33] Goldsmith 1966, V 130. There is no trace of Pelagian heresy (A2) in the play. "The Infirmity of Human Nature" (IV i 153) is everywhere assumed and virtue is explicitly stated to be an achievement, or "Escape from our selves" (IV i 206), not a natural endowment.
[34] See p. 30 above.   [35] Cibber 1753, IV 119, 115.

was revived every year for the next seventy-five years.[36] At the box-office it earned £2536 3*s*. 6*d*., more money than any play previously performed by the Drury Lane company. Even George I was moved to present Steele with an honorarium of £500. There were amateur productions as well. In April 1728 it was "acted by the young Ladies educated at Mrs. Defenne's French Boarding-School," at Wandsworth in Surrey.[37]

The play was equally successful in print. Three editions were required in 1722–3 and forty-five more in the next seventy-seven years, including translations into French, Italian, and German.[38] In the press the play was attacked and defended with equal spirit.[39] But its defenders show clearly the marks of the new sensibility. "There are Sentiments so generous in many parts of the *Conscious Lovers*," Aaron Hill said, "that the nobly-sighted ... could never look for its Errors."[40] And at the end of the century Elizabeth Inchbald could look back and find that it was *The Conscious Lovers* that had taught an audience "to think and to feel, as well as to laugh and applaud, at the representation of a comedy."[41]

[36] *The London Stage*, parts 2–5 passim.
[37] Aitken 1889, II 314; *The London Stage*, part 2, II 968.
[38] Kenny 1971, 288, 290.   [39] Aitken 1889, II 280–6; Loftis 1952, 205–12.
[40] Victor 1761–71, II 172.
[41] Inchbald 1808, XII [3]5.

5

Edward Moore, *The Foundling* (1748)

"Gentle *Neddy More*," as he once designated himself, was neither a foundling nor an orphan. Born in Abingdon, Berkshire, in March 1712, he was the son and grandson of dissenting ministers. But his father died when he was ten and he was raised by a schoolmaster uncle and apprenticed to a London linen-draper. His first job was in Dublin, where he was factor to a London merchant. There he met an Irishman, in partnership with whom he set up a linen-draper's shop in Cheapside, London. Edward Moore would have taken very seriously Mr. Sealand's admonition to Sir John Bevil in *The Conscious Lovers*: "we Merchants are a Species of Gentry, that have grown into the World this last Century, and are . . . almost as useful as you landed Folks, that have always thought your selves so much above us" (IV ii 50–3). But unfortunately the business failed and there is no successful merchant in *The Foundling*. Both the alazon figures, Sir Roger Belmont and Sir Charles Raymond, are baronets, "landed Folks."

Even before he failed in the linen trade, Moore had begun publishing anonymous verse in *The Gentleman's Magazine*.[1] And now, like John Gay in the same circumstances a generation earlier, he turned from trade to fable. His next published work, however, was a libretto for Dr. William Boyce's *Solomon; a Serenata, taken from the Canticles*, performed in 1742 and published the next year.[2]

In June 1743 Thomas Cooke wrote in his diary: "I read sixteen Fables in manuscript, wrote by Mr. *Edward Moore*. The ninth, 'The Farmer, the Spaniel, and the Cat,' is a very pretty Fable . . . The sixteenth and last Fable, called, 'The Female Seducers,' is a charming, elegant piece. – These two Fables are far superior to the rest."[3] Of the sixteen fables that Cooke read only the first thirteen are Moore's. The last three are by another Irishman whom Moore may have met in Dublin, Henry Brooke, already established in London as a successful playwright.

---

[1] Caskey 1927, 8.
[2] *Grove* 1980 III 138, 143. Moore's libretto is reprinted in Moore 1756, 203–15. Some of Moore's songs from *Solomon* were revived and performed every season from 1789–90 to 1799–1800 (*The London Stage*, part 5, II–III, Index s.v. Boyce, William).
[3] *The Gentleman's Magazine* December 1791.

In 1745–7 Moore wrote librettos for Thomas Augustine Arne and for Georg Friedrich Handel. For Arne, whose success had already been sealed by a command performance of his masque, *Alfred*, in August 1740 at Cliveden House, Moore wrote the delightful lyrics to the dialogue, *Colin and Phoebe*, which played the entire season of 1744–5 at Vauxhall Gardens and was tacked on to most performances at Drury Lane that season, no matter how inappropriate.[4] For Handel Moore wrote the stirring lyrics to the patriotic song *For the Gentlemen-Volunteers of the City of London*, "Stand round my brave boys, with heart and with voice," sung at Drury Lane on 14 November 1745 when the army of Charles Stuart, the Young Pretender, was marching on London.[5] It must have been about this time that Moore met David Garrick: "my best Services to . . . all Friends," Garrick writes to Francis Hayman, the painter, "particularly Mr. Moore, his Song is rattled in my Ears all Day & most part of the Night."[6]

Fables for the Female Sex with seventeen engravings after Francis Hayman was published anonymously in May 1744 and immediately established Moore's reputation. At least eighteen editions in English (including one published in Philadelphia), one in French (translated by a Dutchman, as Jacob Grimm complained), and one in German, appeared in the eighteenth century. For his next work, however, Moore turned to the stage. Arne's sister, Susanna Cibber (separated from Colley Cibber's disastrous son, Theophilus) was at the height of her remarkable career as concert singer and tragic actress. At eighteen she created the role of Galatea in a pirated production of Handel's opera, *Acis and Galatea*, in London in May 1732. In April 1742 in Dublin she sang songs that Handel composed for her mezzo-soprano voice in the world première of the *Messiah*. Then, as if this was not enough, she became Garrick's leading lady in the Drury Lane company in 1744. A production of *The Beggar's Opera* at Drury Lane on 12 December 1747, in which she was cast as Polly Peachum with Kitty Clive as Lucy Locket, "created a furore: Mrs. Clive considered Polly her speciality, not to be usurped by a younger rival." But the younger rival usurped the role four more times that season and three times in the next before Polly was restored to Mrs. Clive when Mrs. Cibber was too ill to play the part. It was Susanna Cibber who persuaded her brother to re-set Addison's opera libretto, *Rosamond* (1707), which launched Thomas Arne's career as a composer when it was performed at Lincoln's Inn Fields in March 1733. So it may have been Susanna Cibber who persuaded Edward Moore to write *The Foundling*, which launched his career as a dramatist when it was performed at Drury Lane in February 1748 with Susanna Cibber in the title role. It was for her remarkable mezzo-soprano voice that Moore wrote Fidelia's song, "for a Shape, and a Bloom, and an Air, and a Mein," in Act III

[4] Caskey 1927, 29; *The London Stage*, part 3, II 1182–1236.
[5] The text was published in *The London Magazine* November 1745 and in Moore 1756, 187–8.
[6] Garrick 1963, I 54.

scene i, which was set to music by Thomas Arne, the house composer for Drury Lane.[7]

Critics in the twentieth century emphasize the *historical* importance of *The Foundling*: "The only new sentimental comedy of this period [1732–50] which achieves a fair measure of permanent success," "the culmination of the sentimental comedies of the early eighteenth century," "a play ... of the utmost importance ... the connecting link between the sentimentalism of the early and the sentimentalism of the late eighteenth century. It aids in bridging the gap from the times of Cibber and of Steele to those of Cumberland and of Mrs. Inchbald."[8]

Although he wrote it in prose, Moore called his play "my first Attempt in Dramatic Poetry," perhaps in the generic sense of creative literature or perhaps inadvertently.[9] But in either case Moore's mind was full of poetry when he wrote *The Foundling*. The play is not the libretto for a musical comedy, but it could easily be adapted to recitativo and song.[10] Moore's mind was also full of fable when he wrote *The Foundling* (9, 24, 52). On the title-page he identified himself as "*Author* of *Fables for the Female Sex.*"

Without minimizing the historical importance of the play it may be possible here to convey something of its *intrinsic* value. In the first minutes of the play the story of the foundling, known only as Fidelia, is shrouded in "Mystery and Hieroglyphic" (5), like Indiana in *The Conscious Lovers* (1722) (p. 46 above). Finally in Act V scene iv the hero, Charles Belmont, begins to talk: "The Story will amaze you!" he says, "At twelve Years old – " (58), but here he is interrupted by the entrance of the villain and the audience is held in suspense another few minutes until the telling can be resumed, now by the heroine: "Hear but my Story," Fidelia says, "He bought me, Gentlemen – for the worst of Purposes" (60). That last phrase raises considerable unconscious irony; it applies unambiguously to the villain but also uncomfortably close to the hero as well. The play is acutely constructed.

Moore's friend, Henry Brooke, who had contributed three of the *Fables for the Female Sex*, now contributed a prologue presumably describing Moore's intentions:

> He rather aims to draw the melting Sigh,
> Or steal the pitying Tear from Beauty's Eye;
> To touch the Strings, that humanize our Kind.
>   (sig. A4r)

---

[7] Caskey 1927, 20, 169–70; *Grove* 1980, IV 388; *The London Stage*, part 4, I 19–120; *ABDA*, III 275–6; *Grove* 1980, I 605, 609.

[8] Bernbaum 1915, 179; Frederick T. Wood, *Neophilologus* 18 (1933): 284; Allardyce Nicoll, *A History of Early Eighteenth Century Drama 1700–1750* (Cambridge: Cambridge University Press, 1925), 206–7.

[9] *The Foundling. A Comedy* (London, 1748) iv; hereafter cited by page number only.

[10] There is verse or snatches of song on 13, 16, 22, 29–30, 34, 36, 42, and 66. Further opportunities for song were found in later productions of the play (*The London Stage*, part 4, II 1130, III 128–9).

The first critics of the play were divided on this point, but there can be no doubt now that Moore based his play on *The Conscious Lovers*. Besides "the principal drift of the plot,"[11] concluding in an emotional discovery scene, there are a sufficient number of verbal parallels to make it clear that Moore had *The Conscious Lovers* in mind when he was writing *The Foundling*:

The Conscious Lovers (1722)	*The Foundling* (1748)
they are made for one another, as much as Adam and Eve were (V iii 6)	so compleat a Couple – ... the first Pair in Paradise (23)
Why, can't you fire our House (IV iii 25)	set the House in such a Flame (28)
What have I to do, but sigh, and weep (V iii 126)	To retire and weep, must now be my only Indulgence (38)
plunder'd in my Cradle! ... an Infant Captive! (V iii 136)	from my Cradle, the very Child of Misfortune (38)
he ... was dragging her by Violence to Prison (I ii 200)	he had Recourse to Violence (60)

When Faddle says to Charles Belmont, "Suppose I ... make Interest to be Commode to him, hah!" (46), we know *exactly* what he means because Mr. Sealand had supposed that Rachel was "one of those Commode Ladies, who lend out Beauty, for Hire" (V iii 45).

There are other influences as well of course:

The Careless Husband (1704)	*The Foundling* (1748)
Ha! ha! ... [she] makes as ridiculous a Figure, as a beaten General marching out of a Garrison (V iii 38)	Ha! ha! ha! – How like a beaten General do'st thou look now! (13)

Some readers see in Act IV scene i of *The Foundling* a faint reflection of the proviso scene in Act IV of *The Way of the World*.[12]

Although the plot and even some of the phrasing of *The Foundling* derive from *The Conscious Lovers*, the characters are quite independent of *The Conscious Lovers*. "Between the idea / And the reality / Between the motion / And the act / Falls the Shadow" of *Pamela, or Virtue Rewarded* (1740). David Garrick could not understand why a man who wanted to seduce a woman would

---

[11] Horace Walpole, Charles Dibdin, Arthur Murphy, and David Erskine Baker noticed the resemblance to *The Conscious Lovers*. Francis Gentleman found "no striking similitude" (Walpole 1937–83, XIX 464–5; Dibdin 1800, V 178; Murphy 1801, I 148; Baker 1812, II 248; Gentleman 1770, II 218).

[12] Nienhuis 1974, 88, 111.

install her in his father's house in St. James's parish. He expressed his bewilderment in the epilogue he wrote for his new friend's play (to be spoken by Susanna Cibber but *not* in the character of Fidelia):

> ... the Rake's an Ass.
> Had I like Belmont, heard a Damsel's Cries,
> I wou'd have pink'd her Keeper, seiz'd the Prize,
> Whipt in a Coach, not valu'd Tears a Fardin',
> But drove away like Smoke – to Covent Garden,

a more convenient parish for seduction. But with *Pamela* in his mind – and he refers to it twice (4, 25) – Moore may have had a purpose in bringing Fidelia to the "haunted House" (28) in St. James's parish. By locking up Fidelia in the same house with her would-be seducer, Moore may have hoped to reproduce those scenes of great sexual excitement and great comedy in *Pamela*: the agon in the summer-house ("he kissed me two or three times, with frightful Eagerness"), the agon in milady's dressing-room ("He by Force kissed my Neck and Lips ... He then put his Hand in my Bosom"), the closet trick ("out rushed my Master, in a rich Silk and Silver Morning Gown").[13]

Viewed at a sufficient distance the plots of *Pamela, or Virtue Rewarded* and *The Foundling. A Comedy* are identical:

Lower-class woman avoids seduction by gentleman rake (T320 Escape from undesired lover);

Lower-class woman effects conversion of gentleman rake (D1881 Magical transformation);

Marriage follows (Q87 Reward for preservation of chastity; L162 Lowly heroine marries prince).

Besides a common infrastructure the two works share a number of themes and motifs of which these are a representative sample:

Gentleman rake falls in love with lower-class woman whom he had intended to seduce (*Pamela* I 55; *The Foundling* 57);

Lower-class woman writes verse (*Pamela* I 116; *The Foundling* 29);

Lower-class woman deplores custom which licenses fashionable vices (*Pamela* I 181; *The Foundling* 66);

Gentleman rake deplores marriage (*Pamela* I 292; *The Foundling* 4, 52).[14]

---

[13] Samuel Richardson, *Pamela, or Virtue Rewarded*, 4 vols. (Oxford: Blackwell, 1929) I 19, 31, 79; cited hereafter by volume and page number.

[14] The parallels should not obscure the essential differences between the two works. The problem of *mésalliance*, for example, is easily solved in *The Foundling* by the discovery that the "ugly Gipsy" (24), as Faddle calls her, is really the daughter of Sir Charles Raymond. In *Pamela* the problem is solved by attributing egalitarian and evangelical notions to Pamela: "we were all on a foot originally," she says, "and ... Surely these proud people never think what a short Stage Life is; and that ... a Time is coming, when they shall be obliged to submit to be on a Level with us" (II 22). But this bold solution creates another *mésalliance*: the mind of a libidinous and sycophantic middle-aged tradesman is grafted onto the body of a fifteen-year-old servant-girl from the country.

The unities of time and place are strictly observed in *The Foundling*. All the action of the play takes place in the town house of Sir Roger Belmont in St. James's parish during the daylight hours of one day. Most of the residents in the house go out and come back during the day. The women go to the rehearsal of a new opera in the morning and some of the men go to White's Chocolate House and the King's Arms tavern in the afternoon (6, 40). No less than four letters are delivered to the house during the same day. If *The Foundling* does not project as powerful a sense of place as *The Conscious Lovers* or *The School for Lovers* (pp. 46, 71), the reason may be that the important action of the play is interior: "Situation of the Mind!" Rosetta exclaims, "Very geographical!" (22). All the action on the stage takes place in three rooms of Sir Roger's house in London.[15]

In this constricted space two love affairs are struggling to survive. Three months ago the only son and heir to the title and estates of Sir Roger Belmont and a "riotous young Dog" (55), while invigilating the streets at midnight, was alarmed by a woman's cries. He broke open doors, wounded the woman's ravisher, and carried her off in his arms. Without thinking much about it (28, 41–2) young Belmont carried off his prize, the fair Fidelia, to his father's house. There he extorted a promise from her to pose as the sister of a recently deceased college friend, whose deathbed request was that young Belmont act as her guardian. This flimsy story convinces no one but Charles's sister, Rosetta, who is charmed with her new friend and housemate. Unknown to everyone, including herself, Fidelia is the long-lost daughter of Sir Charles Raymond, a pardoned Jacobite and temporary guest in Sir Roger's house. Although Charles is intent only to make Fidelia a whore, and tells her so (52), Fidelia has managed to survive intact in the "haunted House" for three months. It is hard to reconcile this fact with Horace Walpole's remark that "the Bevil of the new piece is in more hurry." Today an audience might suspect some kind of hormonal imbalance or dietary deficiency.[16]

The second love affair struggling to survive in the "haunted House" is that of Colonel Raymond, who has been brought up in the Belmont household, and Rosetta Belmont, Charles's sister, a hard-shell coquette (plate 4). This "mighty Colonel" has "laid violent Siege" to Rosetta for a whole year (7, 8) without a sign of a white flag. Like Lady Betty Modish in *The Careless Husband*, Rosetta is in love with power.[17] She has been called one of "the liveliest characters in the play" and as played by Peg Woffington, whose liaison with Garrick was "productive of some scandal,"[18] there can be no doubt that this is

---

[15] The scene design requires a minimum of three sets, "*An Apartment in Sir Roger Belmont's House*" (1), "*Another Apartment*" (6), and "*Another Apartment*" (40). The first two are reception rooms, open to guests like William Faddle, while the third is "*Fidelia's Chamber*" (40) which Faddle invades as an eavesdropper (41).

[16] Walpole 1937–83, XIX 464–5.   [17] *The Careless Husband* II i 25–132; *The Foundling* 2, 7.

[18] Caskey 1927, 48; *DNB* VII 897.

THE FOUNDLING.

Stothard ad viv. del   Scot Sculp

Plate 4   In a 1786 revival of *The Foundling* at Covent Garden, the comic leads, Young Belmont
and his sister Rosetta, were played by the great Joseph Holman at the beginning of his career and
an otherwise unknown actress named Ann Warren. Holman's later career took him to New York,
Philadelphia, and Charleston.

true. Her character is ticked off at Faddle's toasting club: "a Wit ... a Scold
... a little freckled ... Damnationly padded ... And painted like a Dutch
Doll" (25). The wit begins in the first act. Fidelia cannot understand why
Rosetta rejects the Colonel's proposal of marriage "or how it should ever enter
her Thoughts, that the Rigour of a Mistress can endear the Submission of a
Wife." Rosetta has a quick answer (heavily breathed) to this silly question.
"As certain, my Dear, as the Repentance of a Sinner out-weighs in Opinion
the Life of a Saint" (8).[19] The proof of her power is that she has reduced a
brave soldier to a self-confessed baby in leading-strings (13). She admits the
advances of William Faddle only to tease the Colonel. And she teases him
"into Madness" on the dubious premise that this will "sweeten Kindness"
(29) after marriage. "All I know is, that I'm a Woman" (43), she replies to the
Colonel's entreaties, and since the Colonel has already confessed, "I am but a
Man" (13), the audience is assured that this marriage will soon be consum-
mated. "Now Pox catch me," Faddle exclaims, "if Nature ever form'd so
compleat a Couple – since the first Pair in Paradise" (23).

The remarkable symmetry in the character relations of *The Foundling* can be
represented diagrammatically:

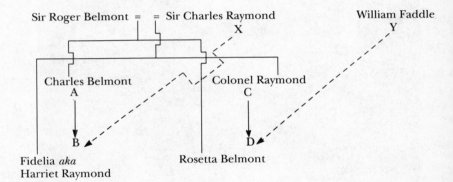

While the arrows of desire AB and CD are pure and flaming, XB is notional (it
exists only in the minds of Faddle and Young Belmont) and YD is pretended
(by Rosetta to make Colonel Raymond jealous). Faddle and Young Belmont
suspect that Sir Charles has "a liquorish Look-out for *Fidelia*" (6). If *The
Foundling* were a Jacobean rather than a Georgian comedy, the suggestion of
incest in XB would not be ignored.

Although their "Hearts took Fire at first Sight" (28), the objectives of

---

[19] Another difference between *Pamela* and *The Foundling* is illustrated by this cynical (but true)
observation of Rosetta, contrasted with Pamela's pious recollection of Luke 15.7: "*There is more
Joy in Heaven over one Sinner that repenteth, than over Ninety-nine just Persons that need no Repentance*" (II
96).

Fidelia and young Belmont remain quite different. Charles's objective is "a little simple Fornication" (28), but "between the Jealousy of Sir *Charles*, the Gravity of the Colonel, the Curiosity of a Sister, and the awkward Care of a Father" (28) this has proved impossible. As the play begins, Charles's plot is to defame Fidelia so that Rosetta will demand her removal from the house and Fidelia's "Ruin" (41) can be accomplished in private lodgings. Charles Belmont is repeatedly characterized as a rake of the worst kind, "a Town-Rake" (55), "a licentious young Fellow" (15) devoted to "nothing but [his] own Pleasures" (4). "What a Rogue am I," he boasts, "throw but coy Beauty in my Way, and all the Vices, by Turns, take Possession of me" (39). But no raking is dramatized in the play and no raking is narrated until Act V scene v when Fidelia recounts her rescue from the villain, George Villiard; "By Violence, and at Midnight [Charles] stole her" (59). And even this rakery was accidental rather than deliberately undertaken: "He was accidentally passing by," Fidelia admits (60). There is no low debauchery at Pontack's or deep play at White's, as in *The Rake's Progress*, plates III and VI.

One of the first critics of the play observes that "the Matter is lost in the Beauty of the Expression."[20] If the audience does not *see* Belmont raking, it *hears* him articulating all the fashionable rakish clichés: coquettes are easy to seduce because a coquette is herself a rake in petticoats (20), which recalls Pope's equally callow assumption that "ev'ry Woman is at heart a rake" (*Epistle II. To a Lady*, 216); "Preniac may serve one's Turn [in a seduction] ... when Champain is not to be had" (26); rakish vices are "authoris'd by Custom" (20, 66); "Marriage ... is the Trick of Priests, to make Men miserable, and Women insolent" (52). When Colonel Raymond urges him to marry Fidelia, Charles explodes:

And hang myself in her Garters next Morning, to give her Virtues the Reward of Widowhood! Faith, I must read *Pamela* twice over first.

(4)

Charles is a strangely introspective, unHogarthian kind of rake. He is even something of a poet (16). The same hostile critic suggests that Charles *needs* to seduce Fidelia "to find out an Excuse for his Baseness."[21] His baseness in the play is limited to causing Faddle to write a letter traducing Fidelia as a woman of the town (32) and then refusing to tell Rosetta the truth about Fidelia (37, 56). The truth about young Belmont is that he is deeply self-deceived. "I am a Fellow of Principle" (40), he tells himself, even while allowing his sister to believe that Fidelia is false. His conversion is an act of undeceiving himself.

Fidelia's objectives are more complex. She is hopelessly in love with her deliverer (9, 62), and she is no coquette. She is not one of those charmed birds that drop "plum into [Charles Belmont's] Arms" (20). Fidelia is aware, in

[20] *A Criticism* 1748, 14.   [21] *A Criticism* 1748, 13.

another unconscious irony, that Belmont "pursues me to my Ruin" (41), but she is also aware that keeping men at distance "is not always what we wish" (7). Charles thinks she has "Wit ... Beauty ... Pride ... and Desire ... In short, she has every Thing" (4). Played by Susanna Cibber her beauty, pride, and desire would be evident in her appearance, but her lines provide few opportunities for wit. On one occasion she teases Rosetta by telling the Colonel of Rosetta's love for him. "Do you call this Wit?" (10), Rosetta asks. The answer to this rhetorical question must be, No.

As a "Counterfeit" (37) in the Belmont household Fidelia is forced to weigh the alternatives of wife and mistress. But she knows that marriage to Charles would disgrace the Belmont family and she will not consent to become his mistress. As "the new Face" (25) in St. James's parish she is the object of scrutiny at the King's Arms. Another of Faddle's friends unwittingly discloses the secret of Fidelia's character. What about exhibiting her in a freak show, Billy Cruel asks, "keeping her in a Show-glass, by Way of – Gentlemen and Ladies, walk in, and see the Curiosity of Curiosities – the perfect Pamela in High Life!" (25). As "the perfect Pamela in High Life" Fidelia never wastes an opportunity for high-minded moralizing:

ROSETTA. Power, Power! my Dear, sleeping or waking, is a charming Thing!
FIDELIA. Now, in my Opinion, a Woman has no Business with Power.[22]

(7)

ROSETTA. *Fidelia*, you must oblige me with your Company to Rehearsal ...
FIDELIA. I am no Friend to public Places; but I'll attend you, Madam.

(12–13)

Like Pamela, Fidelia tells a sad, sad story: "a poor wretched Out-cast of Fortune ... a helpless Stranger" (33). It is literally "a Tale ... that will exceed Belief" (63), as the first reviewers quickly pointed out. When her widowed father left England to serve the Young Pretender, he entrusted his son to Sir Roger Belmont and his three-year-old daughter to the child's governess with funds for her support. After nine years the governess sold the child to one George Villiard. Villiard, for purposes that are easily imagined, gave Fidelia, as she is now called, "the best of Educations" for six years (58). At the very moment that Villiard chooses to execute his vile purposes, Fidelia is carried off to the "haunted House" by Charles Belmont. Or, in Charles Belmont's version of the story, she was "foster'd by a Hag, sold for a Whore, sentenc'd to a Rape, and rescu'd by a Rogue" (5).

Young Belmont's foppish friend, William Faddle, "a Fellow, form'd only to make one laugh" (9), is pure clown, and a very funny one. His vocabulary is funny, compounded of words like "tremulated" (23) and "Cumbustibles"

---

[22] "Power ... sleeping" (unless disqualified as an Irish bull) may constitute wit. Critics who find no comedy in Fidelia's role (Nienhuis 1974, 83–7) overlook the fact that repeated goody-goody moralizing, like Pamela's, can be as funny as any other compulsion (Frye 1957, 168–9).

(25). His mimicry of other characters in the play is funny (25, 46, 47).[23] And his single-minded pursuit of self-interest is funny. Even his "Twitches of Compunction" (39) are faked – to extort more money from Belmont. Essential to his clownish character is his love of mischief for its own sake (19, 38). So, like Volpone, he cannot resist taunting his victim, Sir Charles Raymond, "For a little Sport" (46). And like Volpone he over-reaches himself and has to betray his friend to save his skin (48).

H. G., one of the first reviewers of *The Foundling*, claimed that Sir Charles "has no distinguishing characteristic" at all.[24] But this is not quite true. He is actually a romantic figure – suffering exile for his loyalty to the House of Stuart, pardoned and restored to his estate by George II only three months ago (8, 64) – and potentially a sentimental figure (9, 42). His tears in the discovery scene (63–4) are highly infectious. Sir Roger Belmont, on the other hand, has only one distinguishing characteristic, his insistence upon "a little Money" (6, 14) in a marriage contract.

The handling of the obstacles in the affair of Belmont and Fidelia is highly original in that they change. Initially it is Belmont himself who puts "a few Mountains" (4) in his own way, first by insisting that Fidelia "be ravish'd by her own Consent" (5) and second by his mistake in bringing her to his father's house (28). Then, after his conversion begins in the scene with Sir Charles (IV v), he sets up another mountain. By this time he is ashamed of his designs on Fidelia. But his pride prevents him from proposing marriage to "the Outcast of a Beggar" (4, 54). In the second stage of his conversion he overcomes his pride and proposes marriage (57–8).[25] But this time it is Fidelia's pride that provides the block: "I have been the innocent Disturber of your Family – but never will consent to load it with Disgrace" (58). Yet she objects not when Belmont asks Sir Roger's consent to marry her. Sir Roger is predictably adamant: "What, without a Shilling? . . . no marrying!" (62). The plot cannot

[23] The character of Faddle very nearly caused a riot on opening night. The violence "so terrified our Heroine," Sophia Western, that she returned early to Lady Bellaston's, encountered Tom Jones, and fainted (*The History of Tom Jones, a Foundling* (1749), XIII xi). Apparently the first-night audience thought that the part of Faddle "copied too closely" a certain Mr. Russell, presently languishing in debtors' prison (Garrick 1963, II 627; Murphy 1801, I 147; Baker 1812, II 248; Fitzgerald 1868, I 222.) As a result Moore says he shortened the part of Faddle "in almost every Scene, where it was not immediately connected with the *Fable*" but ventured to publish the play "in its original Dress" (v). In 1756 he published the play "As it is Acted at the Theatre Royal in Drury-Lane" (Moore 1756, sig. 2F1r). If the quarto text of 1748 represents Moore's manuscript (of which the Larpent manuscript is a fair copy) and if Moore 1756 represents the acting version, the differences are very slight indeed: Moore changed "Toad" to "Angel" (23), omitted one phrase, "and Darkness seal my Eye-lids" (24), and 53 lines of Faddle's account of his toasting club's appreciation of Fidelia and Rosetta (24–6).
[24] *The Gentleman's Magazine* March 1748.
[25] Henry Fielding thought that Belmont's "Redemption from evil, by the conscious Shame which results from having a base Action set before him in its true and genuine Deformity, shews great Knowledge of Human Nature in the Author" (*The Jacobite's Journal* 19 March 1748, quoted in Caskey 1927, 45).

be resolved without the discovery scene in which Fidelia is revealed to be the daughter of "an elderly Gentleman, of Title and Fortune" (51). Rosetta's reservations about early marriage are swept away in the general ebullience and the comedy ends, as comedies so often do, in anticipation of a double wedding.

By this time it should be apparent that *The Foundling* is not a sentimental comedy at all. The only trace of a sentimental attitude in the five acts of the play is Colonel Raymond's ill-considered suggestion that Rosetta's entire fortune be given to Fidelia (62). Otherwise *The Foundling* is blankly un-sentimental. There is not a shadow of cosmic optimisim or Pelagian heresy. Men and women in the play are cast in the common mold. Charles is a self-confessed rake and Rosetta is not "a Bit better than a Woman" (43). Parents are ignored and servants are blockheads (55). Richardson's Mr. Booby can marry Pamela because he has sentimental ideas about serving-maids (A6), but Charles cannot marry Fidelia until she stands revealed as "a Lady of Birth and Fortune" (14). Animals, emotions, and evil are not in the script. And except for Colonel Raymond's single lapse everyone in the play is agreed that money is important; "the Certainty of a little Money" (6, 14) is Sir Roger's only requisite for happy marriage and Sir Charles agrees that Sir Roger's "Determination is just" (62). Colonel Raymond's requisites are more various, but "a Competency" is one of them and Rosetta quietly insists that "the Competency shall be divided between us" (44–5). Neither cultural nor chronological primitivism figures in the text.

Despite the absence of the essential stigmata, all the differentia of senti-mental comedy are present in *The Foundling*. The text is rich in "tender melancholy Conversation" (B1): "I am not what I seem" (33), "I have a Heart, that feels for your Distresses, and beats to relieve 'em" (42). Fidelia yearns to immolate herself (B2): "I can forego Happiness" (58), she says, "I will obey him in this, whatever happens" (41). Both Fidelia's distresses (32, 58) and Colonel Raymond's distresses (22) are undeserved (B3). The text is equally rich in sentimental "Strokes" (B4): "'Tis a fickle World, and nothing in it is lasting, but Misfortune" (42); "Ignorance is the Mother of Love, as well as Devotion" (43). Despite the absence of the sentimental stigmata, the play presents us with an outstanding sentimental paradox: "When I us'd you worst," young Belmont confesses, "I lov'd you most" (57). Despite the sentimental embroidery (B1–4), *The Foundling* is not a sentimental comedy, because (except for Colonel Raymond's lapse) it embodies none of the sentimental essentials (A1–11). This point has already been made (p. 19 above), but *The Foundling* has been included here to illustrate it.

Since Steele put together *The Conscious Lovers* by sentimentalizing Terence's *Andria*, it might be supposed that by desentimentalizing *The Conscious Lovers* Moore might have restored to *The Foundling* some qualities of the *Andria*. But such does not seem to be the case. The *Andria* is resolutely unsentimental. Even a detail like this,

SIMO. sed nunc ea me exquirere
iniqui patria est . . .
dum tempus ad eam rem tulit, sivi, animum ut expleret suom

(186–8)

[I am not an unreasonable parent, and . . . as long as circumstances permitted I left
him free to do as he liked],

that might arouse a sentimental response today: "I am only observing,
passively, how I should like to have been treated" (A4), is not really
sentimental. What is really communicated in these lines is the almost
unlimited power of a Roman father. *Patriae potestas* was the peg upon which
Steele hung his sentimentalizing of the *Andria*. Moore takes down the peg. But
there is no evidence that he was aware of the *Andria* while doing so.

None of the first-generation critics of *The Foundling* called it a sentimental
comedy or even mentioned sentimentality in writing about it. In 1768,
however, Garrick recommended the play to Marie Jeanne Riccoboni as
"something in your Larmoyante way" that she might wish to include in her
Nouveau Théâtre Anglois (1769). Charles Dibdin called the play "one of the first
attempts at what was called sentimental comedy, which the French under the
term *drame* have classed as superior in a moral sense to either tragedy or
comedy." Up to this moment Dibdin's ridiculous claim has gone un-
challenged.[26]

The 1747–8 season was Garrick's first as co-patentee (with James Lacy) of
the Drury Lane theatre and *The Foundling* was the only new mainpiece
presented at Drury Lane that season. To produce the first play of an unknown
playwright involved considerable risk for the patentees, but they spared no
expense to make it a success. Lacy provided new sets and costumes and
Garrick from the fifty-three actors and actresses in the Drury Lane company
chose seven of the most talented for the cast and wrote the incredulous
epilogue himself.[27]

Sir Charles Raymond was played by Spranger Barry, the rising young
tragedian who was in his second season with the company. The great tragic
actress and principal singer, Susanna Cibber, for whom Moore wrote
Fidelia's song (29), played opposite Garrick in the title role. Casting himself
as Young Belmont enabled Garrick to capitalize on his success as Ranger in
The Suspicious Husband, a role that he had created and played for twelve
performances during the previous season and that became his most successful
comic role. Ranger is a more Hogarthian "Town-Rake" (55) than Young
Belmont. Nor is it quite accurate to say that Garrick "played" Ranger.
Hoadly "wrote the Character for my own . . . when I was young," Garrick
acknowledged. So in playing Ranger and Young Belmont Garrick was really
playing Young Garrick. Certain to have drawn a laugh on the opening night

[26] Garrick 1963, II 626–7; Dibdin 1800, V 176.   [27] *The London Stage*, part 4, I 30.

was Faddle's allusion to Garrick's size – "Not so big neither" (40). In his *Ode to Garrick* (1749) Moore calls him "a shrimp."[28]

Faddle would also have drawn an appreciative laugh when he addresses Rosetta as "you slim Toad you" (24), for Rosetta was played by Peg Woffington whose incomparable figure enabled her to play breeches parts. Her most popular role, in which Hogarth painted her, was that of Sir Harry Wildair in Farquhar's *The Constant Couple*. But Woffington had also played Lady Betty Modish in her first season at Drury Lane in 1741 and this was the role she resumed in Rosetta. Casting the great comic actor and playwright, Charles Macklin, as Faddle was particularly brilliant. The character of Faddle appears to have been based on a historic Mr. Russell, "admired for his agreeable manner of imitating the opera singers" and Macklin had begun his career in Dublin as a mimic. Faddle was also a fop and Macklin had played Lord Foppington in *The Careless Husband* during *his* first season at Drury Lane in 1733–4. Sir Roger Belmont was played by Richard Yates, a favorite Shakespearean clown and creator of the role of Mrs. Jewkes in Henry Giffard's adaptation of *Pamela* (1741). An audience of 1748 would be ready to laugh at the first lines that Yates spoke.[29]

The sober Colonel Raymond was played by William Havard who excelled in such sober parts as Horatio in *Hamlet* and the Friar in *Romeo and Juliet*. He had created the role of Bellamy in *The Suspicious Husband* in February 1747 and played Elder Worthy in *Love's Last Shift* in November 1747. The villain, Villiard, was played by Luke Sparks, another young actor, in his third season with the company. He was primarily a Shakespearean actor, playing Iago and Cassius, but also First Spirit in *Comus* and Mr. Sealand in *The Conscious Lovers*. The celebrated Mrs. Pritchard, who had just rejoined the Drury Lane company, spoke the Prologue.

The effect of this brilliant casting is described by Percy Fitzgerald:

> Mrs. Cibber had another opening for her enchanting melody in *Polly* . . . Barry showed all his handsome grace in *Sir Charles*; Macklin, as *Faddle*, found a part that suited his oddities and convulsed the audience . . . Mrs. Cibber was all softness and music; and Woffington, in *Rosetta*, all pertness and prettiness; but Garrick, who had taken *Young Belmont*, a sort of walking gentleman, by his extraordinary spirit and versatility turned it into a leading character.[30]

Even Horace Walpole, who liked *The Conscious Lovers* better than *The Foundling*, agreed that the new play was "extremely well acted." Colley Cibber said he "had not seen so good a play these fifteen years," i.e. since his retirement in 1733.[31]

---

[28] Garrick 1963, II 626; Moore 1756, 26.
[29] Baker 1812, II 248; *The London Stage*, part 3, I 389.
[30] Fitzgerald 1868, I 221–2.
[31] Walpole 1937–83, XIX 465; Joseph Spence, *Anecdotes of Books and Men*, ed. James M. Osborn, 2 vols. (Oxford: Clarendon, 1966) I 357.

Many in the audience would have sensed some of the tensions that obtained between the players on the stage. In the autumn of 1742 Garrick and Peg Woffington moved into Macklin's house on Bow Street, Covent Garden. But this arrangement "was soon broken up." In 1743 another quarrel between Macklin and Garrick precipitated a pamphlet war. Mrs. Woffington would have needed no reason to be jealous of Mrs. Cibber, Garrick's new leading lady.[32]

The Foundling provides a good example of E. M. Forster's important observation about actors. "Is it not extraordinary," Forster asks, "that plays on the stage are often better than they are in the study, and that the introduction of a bunch of rather ambitious and nervous men and women should add anything to our understanding of Shakespeare and Chekov?" "Mr. *Garrick's* peculiar qualifications, and happy use of them," reported an eyewitness of the original production, "added amazing spirit to the piece; giving young Belmont much more consequence than can well be imagined."[33]

It is not surprising that *The Foundling* more than repaid Garrick's investment. It played fifteen performances in its first season and earned £2500 for the company. It was revived in fourteen subsequent seasons and played a total of forty-three performances in the eighteenth century. And the collaboration between Garrick and Moore continued to flourish. In the spring of 1749 Garrick became engaged to marry Eva Maria Veigel, a dancer at the Haymarket theatre who called herself Violette. To honor their engagement Moore wrote his *Ode to Garrick* with its playful evocation of Violette sitting in a side box at Drury Lane and flirting with her future husband:

> No, no; the left-hand box, in blue;
> There! don't you see her? – *See her! Who?*
> Nay, hang me if I tell.
> There's GARRICK in the music-box!
> Watch but his eyes; see there! – *O, pox!*
> *Your servant,* MA'MOISELLE![34]

---

[32] Fitzgerald 1868, I 131; *ABDA*, VI 11–12.

[33] E. M. Forster, *Aspects of the Novel* (New York: Harcourt Brace, 1927) 67; Gentleman 1770, II 220.

[34] Moore 1756, 24.

6

William Whitehead, *The School for Lovers* (1762)

When the poet-laureate, Colley Cibber, died on 12 December 1757, the laureateship, worth £100 a year, "And that too tax'd, and but ill paid,"[1] was offered to Thomas Gray. The post was already a joke in 1730 when Cibber had succeeded Laurence Eusden, "a Parson, much be-mus'd in Beer," and Gray, predictably, refused it.[2] The offer to Gray had been communicated through his admirer, the Reverend William Mason, whom Gray called Scroddles. Neither Mason's letter nor Gray's reply has survived, but a few days later, on 19 December 1757, Gray wrote again to Mason:

for my part I would rather be Serjeant-Trumpeter, or Pin-Maker to the Palace. Nevertheless I interest myself a little in the History of [the laureateship], & rather wish somebody may accept it, that will retrieve the credit of the thing.[3]

There had even been rumors that the post would be offered to Mason,[4] but on the very day that Gray was writing, it was bestowed upon William Whitehead, who did indeed retrieve the credit of the thing. Scroddles survived to become Gray's literary executor and the biographer of both Gray and Whitehead.

In December 1757 Whitehead was a forty-two-year-old bachelor, sometime Fellow of Clare Hall, Cambridge, now resident in London with his patrons, the "superannuated" Earl and Countess of Jersey, in their house on Berkeley Square. He was already well known as the writer of "an agreeable variety of miscellaneous verse" and two successful tragedies in which Garrick had played leading roles.[5] So his appointment as poet-laureate seems to have surprised or angered no one.

Besides annual visits to Middleton Park, Lord Jersey's seat in Oxfordshire,

---

[1] "A Pathetic Apology for all Laureates, Past, Present, and to Come" (Whitehead 1774–88, III 96).

[2] Broadus 1921, 134; Alexander Pope, *An Epistle to Arbuthnot* (1734) 15.

[3] *Correspondence of Thomas Gray*, ed. Paget Toynbee and Leonard Whibley, 3 vols. (Oxford: Clarendon, 1935) II 544.

[4] *Lloyd's Evening Post* 14 December 1757, cited in Broadus 1921, 136.

[5] *DNB* XXI 107; Austin Dobson, *Old Kensington Palace and Other Papers* (London: Oxford University Press, 1926) 141. "He could write heroics like Pope's, blank-verse like Thomson's, anapaests like Prior's, elegies like Gray's. He had considerable humour, and a convenient gift of epigram" (*ibid.*, 171).

Whitehead was a frequent visitor at Nuneham, Lord Harcourt's estate nearby. Austin Dobson imagines that *The School for Lovers* was a product of "that placid, sauntering, summer-day life in the gardens of Middleton Park or Nuneham."[6] And Whitehead points out in the prologue that there are no scene shifts in *The School for Lovers*: "In one poor garden's solitary grove, / Like the primaeval pair, his lovers rove."[7]

On 17 December 1761 Garrick reported to George Colman that *The School for Lovers* had "been once read, & has a great deal of Merit."[8] The play must have gone into rehearsal soon after, for it opened on 10 February 1762 at Drury Lane with David Garrick in the leading role of Sir John Dorilant.

The scene revealed to the audience on the opening night is a familiar one. It is "the lover's corner" (III i 11) in the garden of an English country house "with an Arbour, Garden Chairs, &c." Other features of the garden are mentioned as the play progresses: "the close walk by the house" (IV i 272) and the "old fashioned cradle work [that] makes the hedges so thick, there is no seeing through them" (IV i 288–9). In this propitious soil, the audience is asked to imagine, two love affairs are flourishing. The lord of the manor, Sir John Dorilant, a bachelor in his 30s and full of "rapture" (II i 180), has fallen in love with his ward, Caelia Beverley, a green girl of seventeen who has suddenly "grown a woman, you see, and . . . has her allurements" (II i 126–7). But there are impediments to the happy resolution of this affair beyond the difference of ages. Sir John's "delicacy" (II i 17) prevents him from declaring his love until he knows that Caelia's feelings for him are more than filial. And although her feelings for Sir John are more than filial (IV i 12), Caelia is inhibited by unnamed and perhaps unnameable "delicacies" (I i 318) on her part as well.

To the happy resolution of the second love affair of the garden, that between "the accomplished Mr. Modely" (I i 163–4) and Araminta Dorilant, Sir John's younger sister, there seem to be no impediments at all. Two weeks before the time of the play, Mr. Modely has come up from London with his friend Mr. Belmour, to be married to Araminta as soon as the lawyers can write out the settlements (II i 224). So the *status quo ante* looks like this:

Mr. Modely	Sir John Dorilant
$\updownarrow$	$\updownarrow$
Araminta Dorilant	Caelia Beverley

But "the insinuating Mr. Modely" (V i 230–1) proves to be the serpent in this rural Eden. He is infatuated with Caelia and flatters her until, like Eve, "She does not know what she does" (I i 82). His friend Belmour complicates matters further by falling in love with Araminta. And to complicate matters still further, Caelia's mother, the widowed Lady Beverley, is discovered to be

---

[6] *Ibid.*, 162, 172.
[7] See pp. 129–30 below. The play is quoted by act, scene, and line number of the text in the appendix below.
[8] Garrick 1963, I 349.

in love with Sir John. As the play opens, therefore, the innocent relationships of two weeks ago have assumed the diabolical form of triangles (T92.1):

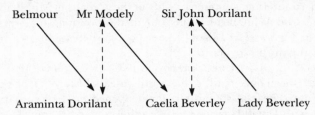

The obstacles to the course of true love are partly psychological, the "delicacy" of Sir John and Caelia, and partly conventional, the fickleness of Mr. Modely and the mother–daughter rivalry of Caelia and Lady Beverley (T92.6). But the real elegance of the design, and a refinement of what Colley Cibber did in *The Careless Husband*, is that it allows an eiron, the Machiavellian Mr. Modely, to function temporarily as a blocking alazon for both affairs:

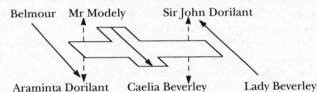

Belmour and Lady Beverley are clearly peripheral in the design, and they are paired off together at the end (V i 270–2).

By interposing himself in exactly this way, Modely makes it impossible for Sir John to object to Modely's conduct. Objecting would make Sir John appear to be mercenary, i.e., afraid to lose Caelia's "great fortune" (I i 36), and would, Sir John thinks, cause "real pain" to Araminta and Caelia, both of whom he now supposes to be in love with Modely (IV i 21–4). But then, in quick succession, Caelia and Araminta reject Modely (IV i 147, 231). Now the insinuating Mr. Modely finds himself exactly in Sir John's dilemma: if he begs Araminta's forgiveness, it "will only look like a mean artificial method of patching up" his disappointment over losing Caelia (IV i 260). Mr. Modely recognizes that he has overreached himself and breaks down into abject penitence.

With both of the heroes *hors de combat*, the plot is resolved by the unblocking actions of the heroines. Caelia very *in*delicately tells Sir John for the third time that she loves him:

> CAELIA. ... O Sir ... Shield me from the world, shield me from the worst of misfortunes, your own unkind suspicions.
>
> ARAMINTA. What fooling is here? Help me, Mr. Belmour. There, take her hand. And now let it go if you can.
>
> SIR JOHN (*grasping her hand*). O Caelia. May I believe Modely? Is your heart mine?

CAELIA. It is, and ever shall be.
SIR JOHN (*turning to* CAELIA). Transporting extacy!

(V i 184–93)

Since Araminta has never been troubled by unnamed delicacies (II i 91–5), it is much easier for her, after a little diversion testing Mr. Modely's penitence and love, to accept him back in her good graces:

> ARAMINTA. To shew how willing I am to conceal everything, now I have had my little female revenge, as my brother has promised us the fiddles this evening, Mr. Modely, as usual, shall be my partner in the dance.

(V i 261–3)

Sir John Dorilant is "quite a different creature" (I i 103, 156) from the London "wits" (V i 53), Modely and Belmour. He is a "rustic moralist" but not of the country churchyard, an honorable gentleman, who under all conditions insists upon doing what is right and proper (IV i 3–4). He is a man whom we should be proud to know. Yet without his comic weaknesses, he might be tedious, like his prototype, Sir Charles Grandison. There were times, indeed, when his sister hated him, but the times were only cancelled dances (II i 52). His old-fashioned, garden-variety virtues are reflected in the love of an old family servant (IV i 47, V i 100) and are contrasted with the newfangled amorality of Mr. Modely (IV i 133–7).

Sir John's weakness, his comic *hamartía*, is an excess of honor (V i 44–56), a refusal to exercise the sultanic "power" (IV i 101) bequeathed to him in the will of Caelia's father: "Sir John, you know, by her father's will, may marry her if he pleases, and she forfeits her estate if she marries any one else" (I i 94). In tacit condemnation of arranged marriages Sir John refuses to take Caelia's "lifeless form" without her "heart" (III i 114–15), a refusal that is called "delicacy" (V i 82) in the play. It is this "delicacy" that makes Sir John a comic hero. He makes one comical mistake after another until he is finally saved from himself by Caelia's bold action (V i 183).

Beyond this, almost all that is required of Caelia is that she be sufficiently "handsome" (III i 8) to validate Sir John's passion. Her mother would like to think that Caelia is still "a hoydening girl" (I i 139), but nothing could be further from the truth. Caelia has never been to London, her education has been ludicrous (I i 270), and her social life limited to "a horse-race, or a rural visit" (I i 115–16). But by "early reading" she has made herself "like a sentimental lady in a comedy" (I i 120–1), someone like Susanna Cibber, who had preempted the role of Indiana.

Her "youth and inexperience" (III i 233–4; IV i 83, 144; V i 161) are contrasted with her mother's "prudence and experience" (IV i 63). It is her inexperience that constitutes Caelia's comic weakness. She is a green girl who succumbs easily to Modely's flattery and then has to pay for her foolishness by the grossly *in*delicate action (T55 Girl as wooer) of proposing to Sir John, just as her worldly mother would do (II i 206). It seems to take Caelia's rejection of sensibility to overcome the excessive sensibility of Sir John. Or perhaps it is her rustic "simplicity" (I i 117), her ignorance of the fact that such things simply are not done, that determines her decisive action: a green girl growing to a green thought.

Caelia's gay deceiver, Mr. Modely, is "a man of the town" (I i 110) whose ruling passion is the "affectation of success among the ladies" (V i 6). To achieve his conquests he is willing to "go as near being a rogue as possible" (II i 311) and he has already gone as far as duels with rivals (I i 151). But he is, of course, a lovable rogue with "a certain ... *Gayete de Coeur*" (III i 30).

Although he has pursued Araminta Dorilant for years (II i 281), his Don Juan role (K1315.8) requires success with Caelia, whom he saw for the first time only two weeks ago. Like his predecessors, Will Worthy in *Love's Last Shift* and Mirabell in *The Way of the World*, he wants the girl *and* her money (I i 89). And he comes very close to getting both (IV i 136). But he is *démasqué* by a green girl (IV i 138) and defeated by his "nobler self" (V i 40). After Modely suffers all the stages of guilt and self-reproach, he emerges "a man of honour" (IV i 264) – and a somewhat sententious man of honor like Sir John Dorilant[9] – and then he is eligible to be joined in marriage with Sir John's sister, whose "gayety of ... temper" (IV i 228) matches his own.

Araminta, who hates walking and loves dancing (II i 27, 52–3), is obviously ready for London. But before she goes, she has an important part to play in mediating between the sentimentalists, Sir John and Caelia, and the Machiavellians, Mr. Modely and Lady Beverley. Araminta has no false delicacy. She is ready to marry a man who she knows may not love her because she is very much in love with him (II i 93). With Sir John and Caelia she talks "in plain terms" (II i 67). With her lover and Lady Beverley she can be savagely sarcastic (I i 19; III i 260). And she is not above a little harmless dissembling to punish her erring lover (IV i 188; V i 26).

Lady Beverley is an attractive young widow with "an excellent jointure" (I i 141). She is also a "character" (I i 122), a three-dimensional reflection of Lady Wishfort:

LADY BEVERLEY. He! he! I am so angry with him at present, that I really believe I should refuse him.
MODELY. Your ladyship must not be too cruel.
LADY BEVERLEY. Why, I confess it is not in my nature ...

(III i 97–100)

Like her cousin Modely, Lady Beverley is an eiron who functions momentarily as a blocking alazon. Lady Beverley's imposture is that she is Lady Decency, that she "would not be guilty of an indecorum," even with Sir John (V i 107). So she functions in the play in a dual role: to provide "a thousand obstacles" (I i 309) to the course of true love, and to polarize the comic tone by repeating her obsession, "Decency and decorum require it" (IV i 157).

---

[9] As soon as he is converted, Modely begins to sound like Sir John (IV i 109–10, 261–2) and to utter "sentimental *Strokes*": "How virtuous does a real passion make one" (IV i 286).

Sexual rivalry between mother and daughter (T92.6), which is glanced at in *The Conscious Lovers*, is fully developed in *The School for Lovers*. Lady Beverley encourages Modely's pursuit of Caelia in order to "get this girl out of the way" (III i 289) so she can pursue Sir John herself. But her machinations are soon exposed and savagely rejected (III i 203, 243, 290). She is saved only by the tendency of comedy to include everyone in the final society. So in the closing scene she is paired up in the dancing with Mr. Belmour, "the only disconsolate swain who wants a partner" (V i 272). And the play ends with "one dance in the garden" for three pairs of lovers, with the butler and ladies' maids called in to help out the figure (V i 267–74).

Sentimental attitudes in *The School for Lovers* can be summarized very briefly. There is no trace of cosmic optimism (A1). Whitehead's garden is too prosaic even to imply transcendence. But there are glimpses of Pelagian heresy (A2). The "goodness of [Caelia's] heart" (IV i 83–4) is matched by the "honest, honest heart" (IV i 143) of Sir John, which "if it errs, it errs from too much love" (V i 285), an endearing example of sentimental paradox. Contemporary readers were able to see that not even Modely's "foibles ... have ... arisen from any badness of heart."[10]

Woman is strangely magnified (A3):

> by Nature ... designed.
> Her last best work, to perfect humankind.
> No spot, no blemish the fair frame deforms,
> No avarice taints, no naughty passion warms.
>
> (Epilogue)

Servants sound like doting parents (A6): "Heavens bless his good soul!" old Jonathan exclaims about his employer, "I love to see him merry" (V i 104). Emotions in general are assumed to be more reliable than reason or knowledge (A8): "a lover's eye [is] incapable of erring" (II i 201), whereas "knowledge, without ... the feelings of humanity ... [is] contemptible" (V i 47–50).

It is the penitent Mr. Modely who utters words that come closest to expressing the theme of the play: "Cherish the tender feelings, and be happy" (V i 71), he tells Sir John. Modely's folly as well as Sir John's is said to be self-punishing (A9) in this morally self-regulating microcosm (V i 235–6, 283). For money, of course, there is the greatest contempt (A10): "Fortune! I despise it ... Fortune! Dirt" (II i 171–2), exclaims the landowner whose negotiations to purchase an adjoining estate are interrupted by the emotional crises of the play. The garden in the springtime where these crises are so happily resolved is itself a version of primitivism (A11), a green elsewhere manifestly superior to the "malicious" here (V i 162).

---

[10] David E. Baker, *Biographia Dramatica, or, A Companion to the Playhouse ... Continued from 1764 to 1782* [by Isaac Reed], 2 vols. (London, 1782) II 328–9.

All of the accidents of sentimental comedy are likewise represented:

A *"sprinkling of tender melancholy Conversation"* (B1): "Unhand me ... you have used me cruelly" (IV i 235–6) ... "Honour, Mr. Modely! 'tis a sacred word. You ought to shudder when you pronounce it" (V i 44–5).

Heroic virtue (B2): "SIR JOHN DORILANT. No, I ... [will] make her happy whatever becomes of me" (II i 197–8).

Undeserved distress (B3): "I know my honourable intentions will give her great uneasiness," says Sir John of Caelia (IV i 28), and it is indeed a refinement of plotting to make Caelia distressed and "twice rejected" by her too honorable lover (V i 156–7).[11]

Overt moralizing (B4): "How virtuous does a real passion make one!" (IV i 286–7) ... "The mind which suffers injustice, is half guilty of it itself" (V i 91–2).

While some of these details are more incidental than salient, the number of them is impressive. And even more impressive is the fact that none of the lines of the play quoted above to illustrate its sentimentality have any counterpart in Fontenelle's *Le Testament*, of which *The School for Lovers* is an adaptation. It is literally true, therefore, that what Whitehead did, consciously or unconsciously, was to sentimentalize his source. This helps to explain why *The School for Lovers* was called "the model of the sentimental branch of the modern Comedy."[12] And more particularly, it may help to explain why Hugh Kelly took *The School for Lovers* as his model for *False Delicacy*.

In its plot *The School for Lovers* is a version of the January and May motif (J445.2 Foolish marriage of old man and young girl), of which the comic diversions of Zeus among various accommodating mortals (T111.1) provide mythological analogues. The immediate antecedents and analogues of *The School for Lovers*, however, are utterly secular:

Barthelemi-Christophe Fagan, *La Pupille* (5 June 1734; published 1734)

Bernard le Bovier de Fontenelle, *Le Testament* (written 1731?; not acted; published 1751)

David Garrick, *The Guardian* (3 February 1759; published 1759)

Whitehead, *The School for Lovers* (10 February 1762; published February 1762)

---

11 Fontenelle's Caelia suffers much less. Since she never offers herself to Sir John, she is spared the pain of rejection. She suffers feelings of guilt for wavering in her love for Sir John, but these are overcome by Sir John's offer of marriage (V v–vi), whereas Whitehead's Caelia is made to endure a third offer of herself to Sir John (V i 183).

12 *The School for Lovers* (London, 1793) sig. B1r. In a German study *The School for Lovers* is said to be the model for five later comedies (August Bitter, *William Whitehead – Poeta Laureatus* [Halle: Niemeyer, 1933] 93).

La Pupille is pure comedy of manners. It exhibits none of the sentimental attitudes dilucidated in the present work. The guardian character is a *philosophe*, a
middle-aged rationalist, struggling to retain his footing as he is knocked over
by waves of love by and for a very young girl. In Garrick's adaptation, *The
Guardian*, it became one of the most popular afterpieces on the London stage.

Garrick follows his source very closely, only moving the scene to London,
anglicizing the names, and farcing the dialogue with fashionable phrases, of
which these examples will be sufficient to reveal the intent: "he has too much
delicacy to interpret looks to his advantage . . . 'Tis delicate in you to be upon
the reserve . . . nothing but a little natural delicate sensibility . . . the most
delicate and tender of her sex."[13]

But in spite of these phrases (for none of which is there the slightest suggestion in *La Pupille*), *The Guardian* remains a comedy of manners. "The Similitude
between the Guardian and the School for Lovers" that Garrick imagined,
simply does not exist, beyond the fact that both are versions of the same folklore motif (J445.2), the January and May story.[14]

Whitehead's play owes nothing to *The Guardian*. It is an adaptation of *Le
Testament*, a closet drama that Fontenelle wrote to demonstrate the existence of
a genre between tragedy and comedy, from which buffoonery is eliminated
and "le pitoyable" and "le tendre" are joined to the comic staples of "le ridicule" and "le plaisant."[15] The result, which Fontenelle called "Comédie qui
fait pleurer," or "Comédie mixte," is exemplified in *Le Testament*.[16] Although
it is not a comedy of manners, neither is *Le Testament* a sentimental comedy in
the sense in which this term is used in the present work. It remained for
Whitehead to graft sentimental shoots upon this flourishing stock.

The style of *The School for Lovers* has long been admired. The "purity of the
dialogue" that William Mason noted reinforces the simplicity of the characters of Caelia (I i 117) and Sir John.[17] "I must speak plain," Sir John says
(II i 164), not only because honesty demands it, but also because "rhetorick"
in the play is associated with the Machiavellians, Lady Beverley and Mr.
Modely (II i 8). Out of the most ordinary, unornamented, unmetaphorical
language arranged in the most ordinary, unbalanced, unperiodic sentences,
Whitehead fashions a dialogue of remarkable "purity and grace."[18] He
simplifies his style even further by banishing the frequent topical allusions

---

13 *The Dramatic Works of David Garrick*, 3 vols. (London, 1798) II 168, 171, 174, 176.

14 Garrick 1963, I 358.

15 *Oeuvres de Monsieur de Fontenelle*, 8 vols. (Paris, 1742–51) VII xxv, xxxi–xxxiii.

16 *Ibid.*, VII xiii, xxxi. Mason says that Fontenelle's ideas are "explained, and controverted" by
Richard Hurd (Whitehead 1774–88, III 103). But in fact Hurd's commentary determines
nothing, as he says himself (Richard Hurd, "Of M. de Fontenelle's Notion of Comedy," *Q.
Horatii Flacci Ars Poetica, Epistola ad Pisones: With an English Commentary and Notes*, 2nd ed., 2 vols.
[London, 1753] I 273).

17 Whitehead 1774–88, III 103.

18 Bernbaum 1915, 212. Further evidence of the quality of the diction may be found in the fact
that only two or three words in the play require glosses today, while more than three dozen
words in *The Conscious Lovers* (1722) need glossing.

characteristic of comedy of manners. In this way he achieves a sense of timelessness that is appropriate to the timelessness of the folklore motifs that the play reenacts.

Garrick provided an all-star cast led by Kitty Clive, Whitehead's favorite actress for whom he wrote the part of Lady Beverley. "Gentleman" John Palmer played Modely. But seventeen-year-old Caelia Beverley was played by Susanna Cibber, who was now nearly fifty. And Garrick himself found the role of Sir John Dorilant most uncongenial. On 19 February 1762, during the second week of the opening run, he wrote to his brother: "I . . . don't appear in the Play till the beginning of the 2d [act] when Sir John Dorilant (that's the Name) makes his Entrance – and a fine, polite, Sentimental, *Windling* Son of a Bitch it is." In spite of his hostility to sentimental comedy – he called it "Humbug" in this same letter – Garrick knew what was wanted in 1762. He worked off his resentment (1) by adding an afterpiece to three performances of *The School for Lovers*, viz. George Colman's *Polly Honeycombe* (1760), a satire on sentimental novels, and (2) by writing *The Farmer's Return from London*, a farce in which Farmer John witnesses a performance of *The School for Lovers* in London and returns home to tell about it in his native Staffordshire dialect:

> The Greaat ones dislik'd it – they heate to be taught:
> The Cratticks too grumbled – I'll tell you for whoy,
> They wanted to laugh – and were ready to croy.

In fact the critics grumbled not. They praised *The School for Lovers* for its "delicacy of sentiment, purity of language, and elegance of character." But as soon as the opening run of *The School for Lovers* was over, Garrick assumed the title role of *The Farmer's Return from London* and played fourteen performances, one more than *The School for Lovers*. When the latter was revived in March 1765, Mrs. Cibber was replaced by a much younger actress, Hannah Mary Palmer, the strikingly beautiful daughter of Hannah Pritchard; and Charles Holland, Garrick's popular young understudy, played Sir John Dorilant. The play was revived every year from 1765 to 1770, three times in 1775–6, and twice in 1794–5.[19]

The School for Lovers may have been more popular in print than it was on the stage. Four editions (in quarto) were required between 1762 and 1770. The text was pirated in Dublin (1762), translated into German (1771), and included in Whitehead's collected *Plays and Poems* in two volumes (1774). A less hostile critic than Garrick called it "a perfect comedy." "Mr. Whitehead's fable is conducted with skill," Arthur Murphy acknowledged, "but after all, it is a sentimental comedy."[20]

[19] Garrick 1963, I 354; *The London Stage*, part 4, II 916–21, 1103; Garrick, *The Farmer's Return from London. An Interlude* (London, 1762) 12; *The British Magazine* February 1762; *ABDA*, XI 158–61.
[20] *NCBEL*, II 861; Whitehead 1774–88, III 104; Murphy 1801, I 366.

7

Hugh Kelly, *False Delicacy* (1768)

The early career of Hugh Kelly reads like a Defoe novel. The son of a Dublin tavern keeper, he stayed in school long enough to learn reading, writing, and Latin grammar. But rather than hang on as an idle 'prentice to a Dublin stay-maker, he ran away to sea and learned further that Fitzpatrick's in the Hoogstraat at The Hague is also "a very good house." Then he was put ashore or jumped ship at Bristol and walked to London with his wardrobe in a sheet of brown paper and "about a shilling" in his pocket.[1]

He arrived in the spring of 1760 and almost immediately found work writing – both for the London periodicals and for a solicitor in Chancery Lane.[2] But when he came to write his first novel, Kelly took as his model, not *The Fortunes and Misfortunes of the Famous Moll Flanders* (1722), but Richardson's *Clarissa* (1748). In March 1767 Kelly published *Memoirs of a Magdalen: Or, The History of Louisa Mildmay*, an epistolary novel in two volumes. Since a Magdalen was a penitent prostitute,[3] the work was almost assured of success.

The genre of the work, however, is somewhat less assured. Kelly may have supposed that he was writing a "Comic Romance."[4] And it would be difficult indeed to call a work that ends with a long-separated husband and wife lovingly reunited, and with a double wedding in a fashionable church on Hanover Square, anything but a comedy (II 141–2, 152). But it is "comedy without humor" or melodrama, "which achieves its happy ending with a self-righteous tone that most comedy avoids."[5] The tone is also relentlessly "tragical" and the theme of the action is "the complicated wretchedness"

---

[1] O'Leary 1965, 12, 13; [Hugh Kelly], *Memoirs of a Magdalen: Or, The History of Louisa Mildmay*, 2 vols. (Dublin, 1767) II 40–1 (cited hereafter by volume and page number). Father O'Leary's *Contributions*, the first serious study of the subject, is indispensable.

[2] O'Leary 1965, 16, 27–30.

[3] Johannes H. Harder, *Observations on Some Tendencies of Sentiment and Ethics Chiefly in Minor Poetry and Essay in the Eighteenth Century* (Amsterdam: Portielje, 1933) 260–2; William A. Speck, *British Journal for Eighteenth-Century Studies* 3 (1980): 127–39.

[4] *The Court Magazine* September 1761. Since Kelly contributed a feature, "The Green-Room," and a verse elegy, "Tho' torn from all my tortur'd Soul holds dear" (signed H. K.) to this first number of *The Court Magazine*, it can be assumed that he saw the article defining "Comic Romance" even if he did not write it.

[5] Frye 1957, 40, 167.

and "general ... ruin" caused by "the madness of one guilty moment" between lovers two days before the day set for the wedding (I 117; II 18, 22).

The attitude toward sentimentality in the novel is equally ambiguous. It is full of sentimental attitudes: "The heart of the meanest peasant may be as sentimentally elegant as a prince's" (A6) (II 135–6). But the word "sentimental" is frequently pejorative, sometimes synonymous with "hypocritical" (I 119; II 64).

When Kelly sat down in the winter of 1766–7 to write his first play, he drew on *Memoirs of a Magdalen* for a few incidental details, but he turned elsewhere for his model. In November 1766, on the strength of the notoriety he had achieved by publishing *Thespis: Or, A Critical Examination into the Merits of all the Principal Performers belonging to the Drury-Lane Theatre*, an uninhibited lampoon in the manner of *The Rosciad*, Kelly wrote to David Garrick, the manager of the Drury Lane theatre, to inquire whether, if he should "attempt a theatrical piece," there was "any tolerable hope of getting it exhibited ... next season." Garrick's reply to this bold inquiry from a total stranger has not survived, but it must have been encouraging, for in April 1767 Garrick was writing from Lichfield to his brother in London, "Have you seen *Kelly* yet? – do you know anything of his play?"[6] The play, tentatively entitled *Fortune with Eyes*, was ready for Garrick's perusal in June 1767.[7]

Garrick was delighted with it. "There are thoughts in it worthy of an angel," he told Thomas Cooke. But he also recommended "some slight alterations" and asked to see them before the play was transcribed. In September 1767 Garrick received the revised copy and set about casting the play.[8]

Since nearly every member of the Drury Lane company had been outraged by *Thespis*, this was not an easy task. Garrick did not even dare to approach the aging Kitty Clive or the excitable John Moody. But the cross-eyed Mrs. Ann Dancer, whom Kelly had stigmatized as a "moon-eyed idiot," was won over to play the merry widow, Mrs. Harley, and other stars of the company finally agreed to take parts.[9] Frances Abington, a recent recruit from the Dublin stage and a rising comedienne, took the role of Lady Betty Lambton, and the notoriously indelicate Sophia Baddeley played "delicate" Hortensia Marchmont. The comedian Thomas King was typecast in the role of Cecil. Charles Holland, who had succeeded to the role of Sir John Dorilant in *The School for Lovers*, played Colonel Rivers, and Jack Palmer, at 30s. a week, played "wild" (85) Sir Harry Newburg.

To replace a serious one that Kelly had written, Garrick himself wrote a comic prologue, teasing Kelly, as "a madman, and a stranger," for having

---

6 Garrick 1831, I 278 [letter misdated 1767 (O'Leary 1965, 57)]; Garrick 1963, II 562.
7 Garrick 1831, I 264.
8 Thomas Cooke, "Hugh Kelly," *The European Magazine* December 1793 (quoted in O'Leary 1965, 60); Garrick 1831, I 268.
9 Davies 1780, II 135; Taylor 1832, I 97–8 (quoted in O'Leary 1965, 71).

written a moral play, "a *Sermon* ... preach'd in *Acts*" (A3r). New costumes were provided for all and Kelly's first "theatrical piece," renamed *False Delicacy*, was finally exhibited with much fanfare on Saturday 23 January 1768 at the Theatre Royal.

What the audience was asked to assume on that occasion was simply that three boys want three girls. The three girls are conveniently domiciled in one large house with a garden belonging to the Rivers family in the fashionable suburb of Richmond. These suburban Thames maidens and their suitors are:

Lord Winworth	Charles Sidney	Sir Harry Newburg
↕	↕	↕
Lady Betty Lambton	Hortensia Marchmont	Theodora Rivers

The handsome and affluent Earl of Winworth[10] has for three years (32) been publicly courting an attractive young widow, Lady Betty Lambton, *née* Rivers. Lord Winworth's cousin, Charles Sidney, a penniless younger brother (47), has been secretly courting Hortensia Marchmont, orphan daughter of a clergyman (9), totally dependent upon Lady Betty. Sir Harry Newburg, a fashionable rake with a good estate (8, 15), has asked for the hand of Theodora Rivers, only child and heiress of Colonel Rivers, Lady Betty's older brother.

The first obstacles to the course of true love are provided by two of the ladies themselves. Although Lady Betty loves Lord Winworth, she rejects his suit for a number of reasons. Partly it is a little residual coquetry: she can't help enjoying Lord Winworth's "anxiety" (32). And partly it is a reaction against an unhappy first marriage (17). But mostly it is false delicacy, a feeling that "a woman of real delicacy shou'd never admit a second impression on her heart" (17). Hortensia Marchmont also loves Charles Sidney. Her sole reason for not telling him so is an example not only of false delicacy but of sentimental paradox: I love him too much, she explains, to allow him to marry "a poor orphan" (47).

It is Colonel Rivers, the very model of a modern heavy father figure, who provides the second obstacle to the course of true love. He responds predictably to the possibility of his daugher marrying a fashionable and affluent rake by contracting a marriage for her with a sober and penniless younger brother of family (24, 47). Then, in the opening scene of the play, Lord Winworth inadvertently provides the third obstacle when he redirects his affections to Hortensia Marchmont (L213 Poor girl chosen rather than the rich) and expects Lady Betty herself to promote his suit (T51 Wooing by emissary). These, therefore, are the complications that must be resolved in three hours one morning "a few days" (3) before Charles Sidney and Theodora Rivers are to be married:

[10] Hugh Kelly, *False Delicacy: A Comedy* (London, 1768) 55; cited hereafter by page number.

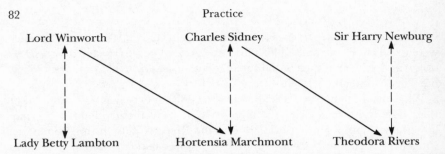

Lord Winworth   Charles Sidney   Sir Harry Newburg

Lady Betty Lambton   Hortensia Marchmont   Theodora Rivers

From this it is clear that Kelly's model is *The School for Lovers*. The double
triangle design of the two plays is in fact identical, even though the outline is
filled in with very different, even contradictory, material. In *False Delicacy* as
in *The School for Lovers* the obstacles to the course of true love are partly
psychological, the false delicacy of Lady Betty Lambton and Hortensia
Marchmont, and partly conventional, the heavy father figure of Colonel
Rivers. In *False Delicacy* as in *The School for Lovers* the eirons, Lord Winworth
and Charles Sidney, function momentarily as blocking alazons for all three
affairs:

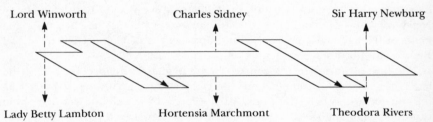

Lord Winworth   Charles Sidney   Sir Harry Newburg

Lady Betty Lambton   Hortensia Marchmont   Theodora Rivers

By switching his affections to Hortensia, Lord Winworth becomes an obstacle
to the realization not only of his own happiness but also that of Lady Betty,
Charles Sidney, and Hortensia. By contracting to marry Theodora, Charles
Sidney becomes an obstacle to the realization not only of his own happiness
but also that of Hortensia, Sir Harry Newburg, and Theodora.

Even more poignant is the fact that the development of the plot allows the
orphan to be persecuted by her benefactress and the benefactress to be driven
to desperation (59) by the unwitting orphan. The first occurs when Lady
Betty urges Hortensia to marry Lord Winworth (50) and the second occurs
when Hortensia agrees to marry Lord Winworth out of "the greatness of [her]
affection" for Lady Betty (82).

The plot also moves forward by a series of cliff-hangers. Lord Winworth
asks Lady Betty to woo Hortensia for him "at the very monent" when Lady
Betty is at last ready to accept him herself (32). Theodora is contracted to
marry Charles Sidney "in the moment" when she has found the man she loves
(73). Lord Winworth learns that Lady Betty loves him at "the moment" when
he must give her up to marry Hortensia (79).

This pitting of cousin against cousin, lover against beloved, patroness
against protégée, and these cliff-hangers create dramatic irony in the plot.

And these larger ironies are reinforced by verbal ironies throughout the play:

LORD WINWORTH [*to Charles Sidney*] ... a few days must make you one of the happiest young men in England.

Exit

SIDNEY (*looking after him*) ... Little does he know.

(3)

LORD WINWORTH. I knew I should please you by it [courting Hortensia].
LADY BETTY. You can't imagine how you have pleas'd me!

(30–1)

LADY BETTY. Has she then betrayed my weakness [her love for Lord Winworth]?
LORD WINWORTH. Madam, I hope you won't think your generous intentions [courting Hortensia] in my favour a weakness.

(78)

These complications are unwound as neatly as they are wound up. The first discovery is made by Charles Sidney. He has learned somehow that Theodora is in love with Sir Harry (72), so he honorably breaks his engagement to her. This enables Colonel Rivers to give his daughter to Sir Harry without losing face (83).

The second discovery is precipitated by Emmy Harley, Lady Betty's confidante. Emmy functions in the play as an unblocking eiron, "entrusted with hatching the schemes which bring about the hero's victory."[11] But she is an eiron with "buffoon affiliations," a merry widow with something of the bustle and leer of a Lady Wishfort (see p. 74 above). Like Lady Betty, she is a young widow, but in every other respect she is Lady Betty's opposite. Since she has already been twice married, she has no false delicacy about second marriages, and she contributes greatly to the comic tone by repeating her obsession – for men (7, 9, 18, 55, 75). And finally, Emmy Harley is a part-time plain-dealer figure, "an outspoken advocate of a ... moral norm which has the sympathy of the audience."[12] This is the role she plays in Act II scene i and in Act IV scene i, where she represents the norm of common sense against the false delicacy of Lady Betty. But she is only a part-time plain dealer, for Kelly undermines her authority, perhaps because he was not certain himself what moral norms would have the sympathy of the audience:

MRS. HARLEY. Well, the devil take this delicacy; I don't know anything it does besides making people miserable: And yet some how, foolish as it is, one can't help liking it.[13]

(20)

So the second discovery of the play is precipitated by Emmy Harley telling Lord Winworth that Lady Betty has a secret to tell him "that must intirely

[11] Frye 1957, 173.   [12] Frye, 1957, 176.
[13] The same kind of ambivalence – probably derived from the same uncertainty in Goldsmith's mind – recurs in *The Good Natur'd Man* (1768): "SIR WILLIAM HONEYWOOD. There are some faults [universal benevolence] so nearly allied to excellence, that we can scarce weed out the vice without eradicating the virtue" (Goldsmith 1966, V 20).

break off the intended marriage with Miss Marchmont" (76). Then she arranges for Lord Winworth and Lady Betty to be alone together and so sets up a confrontation of considerable psychological interest. Lord Winworth's reference to "the secret ... that must entirely break off my marriage with Miss Marchmont" (78) acts on Lady Betty like a thematic apperception test. Consciously she knows no secret. But the secret at the top of her unconscious mind (20) is her love for Winworth and it comes spilling out unbidden:

> LADY BETTY ... since she [Emmy Harley] has told you of the only circumstance which I ever wish'd to be conceal'd, I cannot deny my partiality for your Lordship.
>
>   (78)

This leaves Lord Winworth's just-concluded engagement to Hortensia the one remaining obstacle. It is removed by Mr. Cecil violating the secret of Hortensia's love for Charles Sidney (83).

And now Emmy Harley, "Walking up and down consequentially" as the stage direction in the Larpent manuscript requires, can proclaim that the play enacts "the triumph of good sense over delicacy" (87). But even if this were amended to "the triumph of good sense over *false* delicacy," it would not do justice to the complexity of the play. It ignores the instances of true delicacy that triumph over self-regarding sense.

False delicacy, of course, is very funny. True delicacy, never mentioned in the play, is left to make its points subliminally. False delicacy is associated in the play with stupidity. The intelligence of eirons is seldom an issue in comedies, but in *False Delicacy* it is. False delicacy is represented in the play as a *failure* of sense or "common understanding" (87). In order to dramatize this theme, the sentimental characters must be made to seem stupid. And they do seem stupid.

A few examples will illustrate these "delicate absurdities" (55). In the first scene of the play Lord Winworth, rejected by Lady Betty, fears that Hortensia Marchmont might "think herself insulted by the offer of a rejected heart"[14] (2–3). This is a refinement that ranks with Lady Bracknell's fear that "To miss any more [trains] might expose us to comment on the platform."[15] Hortensia's failure to see that Lady Betty loves Lord Winworth ignores all the obvious signals. "I commend your resolution [not to accept Lord Winworth] *extremely*," Lady Betty says, "So far from being sorry that you have refus'd my Lord – I am pleas'd – *infinitely* pleas'd" (52, emphasis added). Hortensia interprets this to mean, "She's greatly disappointed at my refusal" (52). She misinterprets delight as "manifest proof" of disappointment (53). Hortensia

---

14 The difficulty of interpreting an ironical work in the past is illustrated by this detail. What seems today such an incontrovertible example of false delicacy was interpreted quite oppositely in 1768: "*to save Miss* Marchmont *the pain of a supposed disrespect which might appear in the ... addresses of a lover, whom another had rejected ... surely was true* delicacy" ([John Hawkesworth(?)], *The Gentleman's Magazine* February 1768). Is Hawkesworth(?) being ironical?

15 Oscar Wilde, *The Importance of Being Earnest* (London, 1899), 139–40.

is blinded by an excessive desire to please: "I will not regard my own wishes," she tells herself (53). Theodora is blinded by an "excess of filial affection" (38) and her lover has repeatedly to remind her "what is due to [her] self" (38, 68). She allows her father to believe that she is willing to marry Charles Sidney (73) when she really loves Sir Harry Newburg and the full extent of her muddlement is revealed when she refuses to allow Sir Harry to tell her father that she loves him when Sir Harry is asking her father for her hand (36).

But these examples are only one side of the ledger. If false delicacy is folly and non-sense, true delicacy must at least conform to common sense. Theodora's refusal to elope with Sir Harry is one example of true delicacy that is explicitly called "sense" (68). But the refusal of a penniless orphan to marry "an Earl with a fine person, and a great estate" (55) is an example of true delicacy surpassing self-regarding sense. Charles Sidney's breaking off his engagement when he learns that Theodora is in love with Sir Harry is another example of true delicacy surpassing self-regarding sense, for Sidney is penniless and Theodora will inherit "one of the best fortunes, in England" (73). "There is something shocking," he says, "in a union with a woman whose affections we know to be alienated" (74). Hortensia Marchmont expresses the same sentiment in similar words when Mr. Cecil asks her to marry him: "How utterly improper it would be for me," she replies, "to give a lifeless hand" to one man while another "is entirely master of my affections" (46). If false delicacy falls short of sense on one side, true delicacy goes beyond it on the other.

Although repeatedly called a sentimental comedy,[16] the play is probably best understood as a satire on the false delicacy of *The School for Lovers* (pp. 71, 73 above). Bernbaum in fact comes very close to saying this: "Kelly wished to show that [delicate sensibility in *The School for Lovers*] had absurd as well as amiable aspects." And Arthur Sherbo suspects that some speeches in *False Delicacy* parody *The School for Lovers*.[17] But it is not necessary to guess Kelly's intentions. The identical design of the two plays makes it easy to keep *The School for Lovers* in mind while reading *False Delicacy*. And Kelly makes it easier by repeated similarities of phrasing, of which the following are a sample:

The School for Lovers (1762)   *False Delicacy* (1768)

The lifeless form   a lifeless hand
                 (III i 115)   (46)

---

[16] *The Whitehall Evening-Post* 4 February 1768; Davies 1780, II 134; *PMLA* 28 (1913): xxvi; *The London Stage*, part 4, III 1267. Ricardo Quintana's observation that *False Delicacy* glorifies sentimentality and laughs at it "in alternate scenes" seems mistaken (Ricardo Quintana, *University of Toronto Quarterly* 34 [1965]: 165, quoted in Donohue 1970, 114). The characters in the play glory in their false delicacy but Kelly never does anything but laugh at it.

[17] Bernbaum 1915, 225; Sherbo 1957, 133; cf. Claude J. Rawson, *Journal of English and Germanic Philology* 61 (1962): 11–13.

too much love	too much affection
(V i 285	(47)
cruel generosity!	cruelly kind
(IV i 159–60)	(61)
not . . . for the universe	The universe wou'd'nt bribe me
(I i 310–11; II i 218)	(68)
let me resume my nobler self	restored me to myself
(V i 40)	(71)
a sentimental lady	Lady Sentimental
(I i 121)	(75)
idle bustle	ridiculous bustle about delicacy and stuff
(IV i 202–3)	(76)

The difference between the two plays is that *The School for Lovers* exhibits most of the essentials of sentimental comedy while *False Delicacy* exhibits none. Whitehead adds sentimental attitudes to his source; Kelly subtracts them. Cosmic optimism, children, animals, emotions (other than delicacy, if delicacy is an emotion), evil, cultural and chronological primitivism are simply not in the script of *False Delicacy*. It is the "faults" (7, 71) and follies (17, 25, 41, 49, 54, 85) rather than the inherent goodness of human nature (A2) that are at issue. It is "the depravity" (8) rather than the superiority of women (A3) that is mentioned in the text; women are indeed credited with "more sense" than generally allowed them, but they are also said to have "more vanity" (35). "Excess of filial affection" (A4) is deplored (38). Colonel Rivers's savage tirade against his daughter for want of filial affection is not only baseless but "ridiculously besotted" (74), as he himself confesses later. The lower orders are incidentally "unaccountable" (13) and servants are either "excellent" (56) or "impudent" and "insensible" (37, 67), just as they are in fact. It occurs to none of these rich aristocrats that money is unimportant (A10); in the finale the only penniless characters in the play are endowed with fortunes "guinea for guinea" (86).

The dialogue, however, is rich in "tender melancholy Conversation" (B1): "Do what you will with me . . . You interest me strangely in your story . . . I was born to nothing but misfortune . . . This parting is a kind of death . . . Unhand the Lady!" (41, 47, 53, 69). Cries of self-destructive virtue (B2) ring throughout the play: "may the sweets of still-encreasing felicity be their portion, whatever becomes of me! . . . I have no will but her Ladyship's" (48, 61). But this attitude is ridiculed in the play. Instead of undeserved distress (B3) the distress in this play is "richly deserved" (34) because it derives from false delicacy. "Her delicacy is willing to be miserable" (58), Mrs. Harley says in a richly ambiguous aside that may in fact be the point of the play. And as we might expect from an essayist turned dramatist, the play is full of moralizing sentences (B4) of which the curtain line is probably the worst: "those who generously labour for the happiness of others, will, sooner or later, arrive at happiness themselves" (87).

As the curtain line implies, the play is about "delicacy" and "happiness." The word "happiness" with its synonyms and antonyms appears on nearly every page of the text. The theme of the play is not concealed. It is implied in every detail of the plot and stated explicitly at least three times: "I don't know any thing [this delicacy] does besides making people miserable" (20); "I'll . . . leave them to the consequences of their ridiculous delicacy" (59); "see the . . . lovers, who have . . . too much delicacy to be happy" (81). These must have been the "thoughts" in the play that Garrick found "worthy of an angel." They had long been in Kelly's mind. "An excess of sensibility," he wrote in a essay published the year after he arrived in London, "is perhaps one of the greatest misfortunes which the human mind can labour under."[18] The lesson of Kelly's "*Sermon*" in five acts, Ecclesiastes 8.15, is a popular one: "consult your own happiness" (39, 68). An audience likes to be told to remember what is due to itself (38).

The manifest satire on false delicacy, however, may have been less important to Kelly than the latent satire on marriage ritual in upper-class Britain. Without any stridency the play takes up the fact that women in this society were grossly undervalued. It was a society in which "the greatest proof which a woman can give of *her own worth*, is to entertain an affection for a man" (84, emphasis added). As a consequence "the common forms *impos'd* on [the] sex" (61, emphasis added) "the nice reserve" (46) that acquiesced in arranged marriages. Elizabeth Inchbald conceded that arranged marriages were "the order of society,"[19] but *False Delicacy* challenges this order: the "father has no right to force [his daughter's] inclinations; – 'tis equally cruel and unjust" (24). The play insists upon this point: "a treaty of marriage, should consult the *lady's* wishes" (73, emphasis added); "I rejoice that [Theodora's] inclinations are consulted" (85). Forced marriages are cruel because they are a form of "legal prostitution" (16). Kelly's propaganda against arranged marriage needs no sentimentality about the superiority of women; arranged marriages are unjust because they deny to both parties "that tenderness . . . necessary both for his happiness and my own" (51), as Hortensia says. If a man cannot make a woman happy, he should "scorn to make her miserable" (73). "There is something shocking," the hero says, "in a union with a woman whose affections we know to be alienated" (74).

Since it addresses itself to real problems of women in theatre-going society in Britain, it is not difficult to understand why the play was so popular upon its opening on 23 January 1768. "To sum up all in a word," as John Forster grudgingly admits, "*False Delicacy* became the rage." It was "acted with much applause," Thomas Davies said, "and continued to draw the public to the theatre near twenty nights successively." It was translated into Portuguese,

---

[18] *The Babler* 15 October 1761. This theme is so insistent in Kelly's work that one cannot help wondering whether it reflects a biographical incident, as it does in the case of Goldsmith.
[19] See below p. 107 note 22.

French, German, and Italian and acted with equal applause at the Théâtre de
la Comédie Italienne in Paris.[20] When the play was published on 2 February
1768, 3,000 copies were sold before 2:00 p.m. Four editions were required
within three weeks and 10,000 copies were sold before the end of the season.[21]
But the critics were as sharply divided as they had been in the case of *The
Conscious Lovers*. "The diction too is sufficiently pure and classical," wrote a
reviewer in *The Theatrical Monitor*, 30 January 1768, but his colleague in *The
Monthly Review*, February 1768, denied this: "The language," he said, "is by
no means pure." The "Fable ... is but very indifferently constructed,"
complained *The Theatrical Monitor*, but *The London Magazine*, February 1768,
found "The fable ... extremely interesting ... and the language easy, elegant
and characteristic." A hostile reviewer in *The Gentleman's Magazine*, February
1768, probably came closest to the truth when he insisted that *False Delicacy* is
"more a satire on true Delicacy than false." At least he deduced the idea of
satire, although he transposed the words "true" and "false."[22]

It is not hard to understand now why Garrick chose to produce *False
Delicacy* in January 1768. Two years later he wrote his friend, Charles Jenner
(who had just published a successful novel), commissioning a play:

I could wish that You would think of giving a Comedy of Character to the S[tage] –
One calculated more to make an Audience Laugh, than cry – the Comedie Lar-
moyante is getting too Much ground upon Us, & if those who can write the better
Species of the Comic drama don't make a Stand for the Genuine Comedy & vis
comic[a] the Stage in a few Years, will be (as Hamlet says) like Niobe all tears – pray
Sir Consider this.[23]

Oliver Goldsmith was not the only member of The Club to feel threatened by
the success of sentimental comedy.

[20] John Forster, *The Life and Adventures of Oliver Goldsmith* (London, 1848) 457; Davies 1780, II 136;
     Garrick 1831, I 264n.; *The Works of Hugh Kelly*, ed. Edward Thompson (London, 1778) vi.
[21] *The Whitehall Evening-Post* 2 February, 25 February 1768; James Prior, *The Life of Oliver
     Goldsmith*, 2 vols. (London, 1837) II 173. Despite its initial success on the stage and its huge
     sales in print, *False Delicacy* did not become part of the Drury Lane repertory. After the original
     run of twenty nights, it was played four times in 1768–9 and three times in 1769–70. After the
     third performance in the 1769–70 season Kelly "withdrew his comedy." There were single
     performances in April 1773 and October 1782, but so few tickets were sold in May 1783 that it
     was withdrawn before the performance and not revived again (*The London Stage*, part 4, III
     1459; part 5, I 614).
[22] After Goldsmith's *The Good Natur'd Man* opened at the Covent Garden theatre on 29 January
     1768, the two plays were frequently reviewed together, as in Hawkesworth's(?) long article in
     The Gentleman's Magazine February 1768, and the shorter notice in *The Whitehall Evening-Post* 4
     February 1768. In the latter it is observed that "If the Drury-lane comedy is more refined,
     correct, and sentimental, the Covent-garden performance is more bold, more comic, and more
     characteristic."
[23] Garrick 1963, II 690; cf. p. 30 above.

8

Richard Cumberland, *The West Indian* (1771)

In the spring of 1770 Richard Cumberland was thirty-eight years old (plate 5). He was a graduate of Trinity College, Cambridge, where his grandfather, the great Richard Bentley, had for too long been master. And although married and the father of three children, he did not depend upon the stage for a livelihood. He was clerk of reports to the Board of Trade at a salary of £200 a year. But since most of the work of this job was done by a clerk, Cumberland was left free to follow his real vocation, which was literature.[1]

By the spring of 1770 he had published a churchyard elegy, some blank verse upon the accession of George III, and three plays.[2] The first of the plays, *The Banishment of Cicero*, is a tragedy in blank verse. It was rejected out of hand by David Garrick and never acted, but published in 1761 "upon quarto paper in a handsome type" and pirated by George Faulkner in Dublin.[3] The second, *The Summer's Tale*, is the libretto for a musical comedy of which Johann Christian Bach may have written some of the music. It opened at Covent Garden on 6 December 1765 and ran for nine nights, but Cumberland called it "a tale about nothing and very indifferently told."[4] The third was *The Brothers*. It was produced not by David Garrick but by George Colman Sr. and opened at Covent Garden on 2 December 1769. It ran for twenty-two nights and was frequently revived for more than twenty years. On 6 February 1771 a theatregoer in London had his choice of *The West Indian* at Drury Lane or *The Brothers* at Covent Garden.[5]

Early in the year 1770 Cumberland took his family for an annual visit to Ireland, where his father was Bishop of Clonfert, on the banks of the Shannon in County Clare. There in a back room of "the episcopal residence, by courtesy called palace," "surrounded by an impassable bog" and "with no other prospect from [his] single window but that of a turf-stack," Cumberland

---

[1] Cumberland 1806, 18, 53, 122, 124.
[2] *An Elegy Written on Saint Mark's Day* (London, 1754). The panegyric to George III cannot now be identifed.
[3] Cumberland 1806, 99–104, 106.
[4] Stanley T. Williams, *Richard Cumberland His Life and Works* (New Haven: Yale University Press; London: Oxford University Press, 1917) 41–2 (where Johann Christian is called Johann Sebastian by mistake).
[5] *The London Stage*, part 4, III 1439–part 5, II 1345.

Plate 5   Richard Cumberland, an engraving by William Evans after the three-quarter figure by George Romney now in the National Portrait Gallery. Romney painted Cumberland shortly before Cumberland wrote *The West Indian* and before Rommey himself became famous; he asked eight guineas for the portrait and Cumberland paid him ten.

sat down to plan and compose *The West Indian*. With nothing to distract his attention from the turf-stack, his mind turned in upon itself and something very much like a religious experience occurred. Some of the excitement of this experience still remains in Cumberland's account of it written thirty-five years after the fact:

I perceived that I had fallen upon a time, when great eccentricity of character was pretty nearly gone by, but still I fancied there was an opening for some originality, and an opportunity for shewing at least my good will to mankind, if I introduced the characters of persons, who had been usually exhibited on the stage, as the butts for ridicule and abuse, and endeavoured to present them in such lights, as might tend to reconcile the world to them, and them to the world.

So far there is nothing new. The tendency of comedy from the beginning has been to include "the butts for ridicule and abuse," the clowns and the rustics, the impostors and the compulsives, in the final society in which heroes and heroines live happily ever after. But Cumberland goes on:

I thereupon looked into society for the purpose of discovering such as were the victims of its national, professional or religious prejudices;[6] in short for those suffering characters, which stood in need of an advocate, and out of these I meditated to select and form heroes for my future dramas.

Cumberland's project was nothing less than to make heroes and heroines out of "the butts for ridicule and abuse," or in Northrop Frye's language to make eirons out of *bomolochoi*.[7] This had not been done before and it constitutes a pure example of the sentimental attitude that upgrades inferiors in the social hierarchy (A6).

With this project in my mind, and nothing but the turf-stack to call off my attention [Cumberland recalls], I took the characters of an Irishman and a West Indian for the heroes of my plot, and began to work it out into the shape of a comedy.

What Cumberland did, in short, was to promote two of the most venerable butts of the English stage, the foreigner-immigrant-greenhorn and the stage Irishman, to the rank of comic hero. Cumberland's project was not complete until May 1794 when his comedy *The Jew* opened at Drury Lane and played thirty-four performances the first two seasons.[8]

Plot and subplot of *The West Indian* are generated by the impact of London on "a hot-brain'd headlong" young outlander who is also "very rich."[9] Belcour's response to the city is not very different from that of another recent visitor: "When we came upon Highgate hill and had a view of London," wrote James Boswell, "I was all life and joy."[10] Belcour came upon London from the

---

6 The intensity of the prejudice against the Irish that Cumberland hints at is made explicit in an anonymous pamphlet of 1711: "in *London* ... to use common Civility in speaking of those People, is ... look'd upon as Disaffection to the Government, and Dangerous to the Liberties of *England*" *(A Letter to the Eldest Brother of the Collegiate Church of St. Katherine* [London, 1711] 25; cf. Richard H. Popkin, *Studies in Eighteenth-Century Culture* 3 [1973], 245–62).

7 Cumberland 1806, 128, 135, 136; Frye 1957, 164–5, 172.

8 Cumberland 1806, 136; *The London Stage*, part 5, III 1645–1774.

9 An anonymous reviewer on the opening night noticed that it is "the ... nature of the young West Indian" that connects "the various characters ... into one plot" *(Lloyd's Evening Post* 21 January 1771); *The West Indian: A Comedy*, 2nd ed. (London, 1771), 5, 45; cited hereafter by page number. The second edition is a line-by-line resetting of the first.

10 Boswell 1950, 43.

other direction, from the Isle of Dogs and Limehouse Reach, but "For the first time in my life," he says, "here am I in England; at the fountain head of pleasure, in the land of beauty, of arts, and elegancies" (8). Both Boswell and Belcour suffered disillusionment.

Belcour is preceded onstage by negro slaves carrying "loads of trunks, boxes, and portmanteaus" and by a sailor in charge of the pets he could not leave behind: "two green monkies, a pair of grey parrots, a Jamaica sow and pigs, and a Mangrove dog" (5, 4). By this time the audience would have settled comfortably into a narrow range of attitudes between condescension and contempt: not even Belcour's dog is a recognized breed. And the carriages of rich West Indians were *known* to have blocked fashionable streets in London.[11]

But these are the comfortable attitudes that Cumberland had undertaken to disturb. "I would study to make such favourable and reconciliatory delineations," he said, "as might incline to spectators to look upon [Belcour] with pity, and receive [him] into their good opinion and esteem."[12] In the beginning, therefore, Belcour is made interesting for the audience by the mystery surrounding him. Even his name is unknown. "Belcour" was only lent to him by the generous Jamaican planter who had raised this foundling to be his heir (25). His father, one Stockwell, M.P., a most successful foreign trader who got his start as old Belcour's clerk, has never seen his son and prudently decides to withhold acknowledgment until he can learn his "real character" (4). Even the villain Fulmer, who is eager to exploit him, is puzzled. "I don't know what to make of this young man," he says, "but . . . I will find him out" (26).

Much of the play, therefore, goes into "finding out" the real character of Belcour. He is not a man whom Hamlet could have admired. "My passions are my masters," he says (8). Within minutes of landing he precipitates "a furious scuffle" in the streets (8) and within hours of his arrival he has fallen hopelessly in love with the first pretty girl he sees in the streets. The unscrupulous Mrs. Fulmer then convinces him that this virtuous girl, Louisa Dudley, is "an attainable wanton" (80), the mistress of an army officer. It is this "dark transaction" (82) that provides most of the complications of the plot, with its climax in which Belcour faces death in a duel at the London Tavern with Louisa's brother.

Since Belcour's outlandish behavior is always punished, the moral views assumed to be held by the audience are always satisfied. "I frequently do wrong," he says disarmingly, "but never with impunity" (57; cf. 50). But Belcour's outlandish behavior is carefully selected to make him more attrac-

---

[11] Wylie Sypher, *Studies in Philology* 36 (1939): 504. The intensity of the hatred of West Indians is well documented in this article.

[12] Cumberland 1806, 136.

tive because it is so natural.[13] When he catches up in the street with his "nimble-footed Daphne," he tries to lift up her hat to see her face (22, 21). When he runs into Louisa Dudley's father, the aristocratic and punctilious Captain Dudley, he pursues his questioning beyond the limits imposed by good manners. "Why so, pray?" he asks, and Captain Dudley replies indignantly, "Why so, Sir? 'Tis a home question for a perfect stranger to put" (28). But Belcour's impulsive questioning enables him to help the Captain in a way that would have been impossible without it. And because his behavior is natural, Belcour is "a great bungler at gallantry" (41), a highly developed system of unnatural behavior.

The hero of the subplot, Ensign Charles Dudley, is the reverse of Belcour. His origins are known and irreproachable. But he is desperately poor and so reserved that Charlotte Rusport, the girl who loves him, can only imagine that he has "brighter moments, and warmer spirits" (34), for she has never seen them. Belcour can let himself go, sometimes wrongly – "dispose of me as you think fit," he tells Mrs. Fulmer (49) – and sometimes rightly – "Mould me as you will," he begs Louisa (66). But Ensign Dudley always holds back. "I must beg to hear no more," he tells Charlotte Rusport just as she is about to "disclose" her love (35). Most of his excessive sensibility centers about money: "We, that are poor, shou'd be cautious," he tells his sister (65). And this excessive sensibility provides almost the only obstacle to the realization of the happiness of Charlotte Rusport and himself.

The comic heroine, Louisa Dudley, the ensign's sister has little more to do in the play than to attract Belcour's attention and keep him in a high stage of sexual excitement during most of the action. As object, she is either a goddess, a Daphne, an angel, a little devil (22, 23, 24, 47, 50) or a superlative mortal, indescribable, unique, uncommonly beautiful, exceedingly beautiful, the loveliest, the handsomest, a girl of most uncommon beauty (17, 18, 24, 43, 51, 80). But she is also a poor little poor girl (L102).

Her counterpart in the subplot, Charlotte Rusport, is a poor little rich girl in love with a poor boy (T91.5.1). Her character is more drawn out than Louisa's. She is "an ingenuous, worthy, animated girl" (41), capable of irony at the expense of her wicked step-mother (11) and, like Belcour, willing to risk her whole fortune to get what she wants (36; cf. 49). And as the "encouraging" heiress, frustrated in her attempts to "disclose" herself to her lover (33, 35), she becomes a stock comic figure, the forthputting woman (T55). Although she and her lover are of the same race, class, and religion, their economic standing is vastly disproportionate. Charlotte, soon to inherit £40,000, is reminded of the force of the taboo against economic exogamy by her penniless

---

[13] "Natural human instinct ... prompted Belcour's actions from the start" (Donohue 1970, 112). Aside from his assumption that exemplary comedy and sentimental comedy are identical, which I think is a mistake (p. 20 and note 64 above), Donohue's account of *The West Indian* is excellent.

lover. "To bring ... disgrace, reproach from friends, ridicule from all the world ... O Charlotte! dear, unhappy girl," he says, "it is not to be done" (75).

Aside from the heavy weight of this taboo, there is nothing to prevent the four lovers from leaping into marriage but their own weaknesses: Belcour's impetuosity, Louisa's conventionality, Charles Dudley's reserve, Charlotte Rusport's unconventionality. None of the six characters in the older generation function as blocking characters. Stockwell is a retreating parental eiron: "an older man, who begins the action of the play by withdrawing from it, and ends the play by returning. He is often a father with the motive of seeing what his son will do."[14] Captain Dudley is made to sound like an alazon. He is called "a Curmudgeon," "A close old fox," "An old absurd, incorrigible blockhead" (17, 18, 19, 20), but he is none of these. His major role in the play is to be the object of benevolence.

Lady Rusport, on the other hand, is a true impostor: an older woman who thinks she is still attractive to young men (11), who prides herself on her strict virtue, and who pretends to be indifferent to money. But the man with whom she coquettes calls her an "old cat" (95) and her puritan virtues turn out to be vices, notably the vice of avarice. In conspiring with a crooked lawyer to keep Charles Dudley from inheriting his grandfather's fortune, she appears to function as a blocking alazon, but in fact she has no influence on Charles and Charlotte (10). She is a wicked stepmother manquée, for she fails to hide the heroine from her suitor (T47) or to enchant her on her wedding day (T154).

The Fulmers are stock villains. Mr. Fulmer is a Catholic literary hack with a habit of absconding (16, 18). He seems to have acquired his tawdry Patty from a bordello in Boulogne (16). It is the "cursed machinations" (88) of Mrs. Fulmer, as she calls herself, that complicate the plot. But her role is that of eironic bawd or procuress (T452), bringing Belcour and Louisa together, rather than that of an alazon, keeping them apart.

Major Dennis O'Flaherty, pronounced O'Flarty, plays a similar role in the subplot. He is an unblocking eiron, like Emmy Harley in *False Delicacy*. By careful reconnoitering (eavesdropping), this major of grenadiers decorated with the Cross of St. Louis is able to outflank Lady Rusport and rescue Sir Oliver Roundhead's estate for the rightful heir, Charles Dudley. But this is only incidental. Major O'Flaherty's primary role is to "polarize the comic mood" in the play.[15] And as a clown he is very successful. The first words he speaks are a typical Irish bull: "I hope, madam, 'tis evidence enough, of my being present, when I've the honour of telling you so myself" (14). But there is a difference between bulls that reflect on the stage Irishman and bulls that reflect the other way.[16] Here is an example of the first. In Charles Macklin's

---

[14] Frye 1957, 174.   [15] Frye 1957, 172.

[16] "The art ... of finding language for the Irish character on the stage," Cumberland said, "consists not in making him foolish, vulgar or absurd, but on the contrary, whilst you furnish

farce, *Love à la Mode* (1759), the hero, Sir Callaghan O'Brallaghan, brags of his family, "which you are shensible is as ould as any in the three kingdoms, and oulder too." The audience laughs at him.[17] Major O'Flaherty's bulls make the audience laugh at his wit. "Now [Charles Dudley] can put you to death with a safe conscience," he tells Belcour before the duel, "And when he has done that job for you, let it be a warning how you attempt the sister of a man of honour" (81), which reduces to an absurdity the whole sorry business of "honour." Charles Dudley accounts for bulls in a manner very flattering. "If the Irish are not altogether so perfect in expression," he says in an aside, "'tis because they're not so practiced in deceit" (Larpent MS IV vii 9–11).

Major O'Flaherty's main role in the play is to transcend the role of stage Irishman and to be perceived as a superior human being (A6). Cumberland took advantage of his annual visits to Clonfert to study the Irish character "in its purest and most primitive state." He was "uncommonly delighted" with everything he found except the "Atrocities and violences, which set all law and justice at defiance."[18] Of this dark side of the Irish character there are residual traces in Major O'Flaherty: his five common-law wives (32), his threatening behavior to lawyer Varland (77, 94, 99), his eagerness to push Ensign Dudley and Belcour into a duel (85–6). For the rest the major is totally admirable. "I put him into the Austrian service," Cumberland said, "to impress upon the audience the melancholy and impolitic alternative, to which his religious disqualification had reduced a gallant and a loyal subject of his natural king: I gave him courage ... I endowed him with honour ... and I made him proud, jealous, susceptible, for such the exiled veteran will be, who lives by the earnings of his sword, and is not allowed to draw it in the service of that country, which gave him birth, and which of course he was born to defend."[19]

Cumberland was so successful in this project that O'Flaherty's lines, "Upon my soul I know but one excuse a person can have for giving nothing, and that is, like myself, having nothing to give" (32), had such "an astonishing Effect" on the audience that David Garrick was reminded of the effect that Terence's line, "Homo sum, humani nil a me alienum puto," is reported to have had on a Roman audience.[20]

The structure of the comedy that Cumberland worked out at Clonfert is a system of parallels and contrasts. "Contrast," he said much later, "is the very

---

him with expressions, that excite laughter, you must graft them upon sentiments that deserve applause" (Cumberland 1806, 137).

[17] The claim that Sir Callaghan O'Brallaghan is the model for Major Dennis O'Flaherty was given currency by Davies 1780, II 273 and rightly rejected by Cumberland himself: "I did not know the Irishman of the stage then existing," he said "whom I would wish to make my model" (Cumberland 1806, 137).

[18] Cumberland 1806, 128, 129.   [19] Cumberland 1806, 136–7.

[20] *The St. James's Chronicle* 14 February 1771. That Garrick wrote this review is hinted in Cumberland 1806, 146 and confirmed in Garrick 1831, I li.

essence of [the dramatist's] art."[21] The first one in *The West Indian* is strikingly visual. Stockwell's office in the first scene is an emblem of British order, security, industry, control. *"In an inner room, set off by glass doors, are discovered several clerks, employed at their desks."* Set off against this is the rich disorder, color, energy, and strangeness of Belcour's entrance, swinging his rattan, preceded by negro slaves carrying enough baggage for an ambassador and accompanied by his private menagerie. The cool, dry glass of the counting house contrasts with the hot, wet realities of the tropics in the hold of Belcour's ship: "Muscovado sugars, rum-puncheons, mahogany-slabs, wet sweetmeats, and green paroquets" (55).

Most of the contrasts, however, are not visual, but verbal. Louisa tells her brother that the stranger who accosted her in the street was "not ... absolutely rude ... but very importunate" (21). Fulmer tells Patty that his encounter with Captain Dudley was "not ... an absolute assault; but he threatened me" (25). By this parallel Belcour's behavior is favorably compared to that of Captain Dudley who is the very model of upper-class propriety in the play.

Charlotte Rusport exclaims, "O, Charles, give me your hand" (36). A moment later her wicked stepmother *"enters, leaning on Major O'Flaherty's arm"* (37). While this parallel sets up a flickering similarity between stepmother and stepdaughter (or perhaps only makes a point about *die eheliche Weiblichkeit*), another parallel serves to dissociate the two as widely as possible. Lady Rusport boasts to Varland, "I had enough before" [i.e. before inheriting Sir Oliver Roundhead's huge estate] (72). A moment later Charlotte Rusport is telling her lover, "I have enough [i.e. money for both of us]" (75). The difference, of course, is that Lady Rusport is lying. Her greed is insatiable. But Charlotte Rusport is telling the truth.

Belcour tells Louisa that he is "not worthy" of her (92). A moment later Louisa is telling her father that she is not worthy of Belcour (95), thus completing the parallelism that authenticates both of them as self-deprecating eirons.

Except to show how the play is constructed, these details are relatively unimportant. But the parallels and contrasts between England and Jamaica are thematically significant. They point directly to the presumed meaning of the play and constitute its sentimental heart (A11). London is "a damn'd good-for-nothing town," totally indifferent to Captain Dudley's necessities (26). England is "an awkward kind of a country" for a stranger to get acquainted in (32). "These latitudes are made for politics and philosophy," says the ingenuous Charlotte Rusport, "friendship has no root in this soil," but "the torrid zone ... quickens nature into ... benignity" (58). "What evil planet," Belcour asks, "drew me from that warm sunny region, where naked

[21] Cumberland 1806, 135.

nature walks without disguise, into this cold contriving artificial country?" (79). And even Stockwell, Member of Parliament for the City, finally acknowledges "the cunning and contrivances of this intriguing town" (82).

This is easily recognized as a version of cultural primitivism (A11) in which Jamaica is superior to England in its life-giving qualities and in its moral value. The play raises the question, Is there "charity, pure charity" apart from such self-regarding passions as "a certain anti-spiritual passion, called love?" (10). Confronted with the same problem in *A Sentimental Journey* (1768), Sterne had answered, No.[22] But the answer the play gives us is, Yes, but . . . The only examples of un-self-regarding charity in the play are those of a West Indian Creole (29) and an Irish Catholic mercenary (40). Belcour seems to understand the *principle* involved most clearly:

I am the offspring of distress [he says], and every child of sorrow is my brother; while I have hands to hold, therefore, I will hold them open to mankind.   (8)

O'Flaherty less clearly: "I am an Irishman, honey. Mine is not the country of dishonour" (78).

Cumberland does not generalize from these examples. He does not pretend that all Creoles or all Irish mercenaries are benevolent. But the conclusion of the play, which flows without interruption from these examples, *is* a generalization and one that has not lost its relevance today: "General conclusions [e.g. racial sterotypes] are illiberal" (79). Or, as Major O'Flaherty specifies it, "I think we shall be all related by and bye" (101).

Other sentimental attitudes in the play may be summarized very quickly. There is no trace of cosmic optimism (A1) and no trace of Pelagian heresy (A2), in spite of Goldsmith's sneer that Cumberland's "gallants are all faultless."[23] Belcour has "a thousand" faults (92); he is "fallible indeed" (102). But because he is a comedy hero, it can be said of him that "he would not be so perfect, were he free from fault" (44), which is certainly absurd and probably another example of sentimental paradox.

Shipping clerks are upgraded into friends (1, 89) and despised foreigners are set up as models for City merchants and country squires (A6). Money, of course, is dismissed as a trifle of no importance (29, 53) (A10). "So vile a thing as money must not come between us," says the heiress to her penniless lover (74).

Also present are all the secondary characteristics of the subgenre, from "tender melancholy Conversation" (B1): "Unhand me, Sir" (68), "Alas! my heart bleeds for him" (79), to barefaced moralizing (B4): "[Belcour] comes amongst you a new character, an inhabitant of a new world and both hospitality as well as pity recommend him to our indulgence" (90). One surprising detail in the play is the strength of the animus against the poor girl, Louisa Dudley (B3). She feels insulted by Belcour's improper advances and

[22] Sterne 1928, 173.   [23] Goldsmith 1966, IV 355.

she is insulted by her friend, Charlotte Rusport. "This little demure slut made up a face, and squeezed out three or four hypocritical tears," the rich girl tells Louisa's brother, "because I rallied her about [accepting gifts from Belcour]" (62). But none of this is true. Louisa puts it down to "the fatality of my condition" (66; cf. 92). Her "condition" is simply that of being poor, which degrades her as effectively as being Creole or Irish.

The success of *The West Indian* on the stage is also a story that can be recounted very quickly. In June 1770 the manuscript was submitted to David Garrick, with whom Cumberland had become acquainted after the success of *The Brothers* on the rival stage. Garrick accepted it at once but advised the addition of two scenes. "At Garrick's suggestion," Cumberland said, "I added the preparatory scene in the house of Stockwell, before the arrival of Belcour, where his baggage is brought in [I ii], and the domestics of the Merchant are setting things in readiness for his coming [I iii]. This insertion I made by his advice, and I punctually remember the very instant when he said to me in his chariot on our way to Hampton – 'I want something more to be announced of your West-Indian before you bring him on the stage to give eclat to his entrance, and rouse the curiosity of the audience; that they may say – Aye, here he comes with all his colour[s] flying.'"[24]

Garrick cast the temperamental John Moody as Major O'Flaherty, instead of the matinee idol, Spranger Barry, who "was extremely desirous to play the part." He gave the romantic leads to Thomas King and Sophia Baddeley, who had created the roles of Mr. Cecil and Hortensia Marchmont in *False Delicacy*. Then he wheedled Frances Abington, the original Lady Betty Lambton and now one of the most popular comediennes of the age, to play Charlotte Rusport, "and though she would not allow it to be any thing but a sketch, yet she made a character of it by her inimitable acting."[25] To make the part more attractive to Mrs. Abington, Garrick wrote a long epilogue for her to speak and ordered new costumes, sets, and "Decorations."

Garrick's gamble paid off and the opening night on Saturday 19 January 1771 was a prodigious success. "It is agreed by all," wrote the reviewer for *The St. James's Chronicle*, 24 January 1771, "that no Dramatick Piece in our Time ever met with such continued Bursts of Approbation." The published account is confirmed in William Hopkins's private diary: "This New Comedy written by Mr. Cumberland [is] receiv'd with the greatest applause imaginable particularly Mr Moody's part ... it will have a great run."[26]

It ran for "eight and twenty successive nights"[27] and was revived every

---

24 Cumberland 1806, 144. Garrick may have been thinking of Millamant's first entrance in *The Way of the World* II i.
25 Garrick 1963, II 697; Cumberland 1806, 144, 145. 26 *The London Stage*, part 4, III 1524.
27 But *not* "without the buttress of an afterpiece," as Cumberland thought he remembered (Cumberland 1806, 146). *The London Stage* confirms that there were twenty-eight performances of *The West Indian* that season (plus two more at Covent Garden "By Permission"), but (after the opening night) always with an afterpiece. Cumberland acknowledged his error in the

season until the end of the century. The printed play, published the end of January 1771, required seven editions in that year and the publisher, William Griffin, "boasted of having vended 12,000 copies."[28] The unsentimental Dr. Hoadly wept "twenty times in the reading" of it.[29] And years later even a hostile critic, who called himself Bossu, could testify to the civilizing influence of the play from which he was cut off by snobbery: "The crop-eared Barber's Boy invites his Trull to see the *West-Indian*, because, why, it is very pretty, and very *sentimental.*"[30]

Supplement to the Memoirs (London, 1807) 69. A recent critic calls *False Delicacy* and *The West Indian* "two of the most successful comedies of the period" (Cecil Price, *Theatre in the Age of Garrick* [Totowa: Rowman and Littlefield, 1973] 161).

[28] *The St. James's Chronicle* 31 January 1771; *Lloyd's Evening Post* 1 February 1771; Cumberland 1806, 147. The play was twice translated into German (1772, 1774) and once into Dutch (1794). In the French and Spanish translations it was renamed *L'Américain* (1822) and *El Americano* (n.d.) (*National Union Catalog Pre-1956 Imprints*, 685 vols. [London: Mansell, 1968–80] CXXIX 249, 263).

[29] Garrick 1831, I 420. [30] *The St. James's Chronicle* 11 March 1773.

9

Elizabeth Inchbald,
Every One Has His Fault (1793)

With even less education than Hugh Kelly and "an invincible impediment in her speech,"[1] it is incredible that Elizabeth Inchbald could have achieved success in London as an actress, dramatist, novelist, and critic. She was born in October 1753, the eighth of nine children of John Simpson, a Catholic tenant farmer in Standingfield, near Bury St. Edmunds, Suffolk. But she was as powerfully drawn to London as Samuel Johnson and once established there "could hardly bear to live out of it."[2]

Getting established there, however, was a long and painful process. In April 1772 she ran away from home to go on the stage. To a strikingly beautiful country girl of eighteen, "every lusty motherly-looking woman" in the streets around Covent Garden looked like "a Sinclair planning her destruction." And she may not have been far wrong, for James William Dodd, the star comedian of the Drury Lane company, offered her a job on the usual terms: that she become his mistress. Instead, in June 1772, she became the wife of a much less successful actor, Joseph Inchbald, who was twice her age and already the father of two byblows. For exactly seventeen years, the first seven with her husband and the last ten alone, Elizabeth Inchbald supported herself in the difficult and ill-paid profession of actress.[3]

She made her début as Cordelia in *King Lear* at Bristol in September 1772 and retired from the stage after playing Irene in her own farce, *A Mogul Tale*, at the Haymarket theatre in September 1789. In the provinces she played Indiana in *The Conscious Lovers* and Louisa Dudley in *The West Indian*, and other roles she did *not* like, such as Lady Sneerwell in *The School for Scandal*. But in London, where she made her début as Bellario in *Philaster, or Love Lies a-Bleeding* at Covent Garden in October 1780, she played supporting roles: Celia in *As You like It* and Olivia in *The Good-Natur'd Man*. In the intervals of rehearsing, playing, and travelling, she read voraciously. In January 1774 she began to study French. In June 1776, after Joseph Inchbald's performance

---

[1] Elizabeth Inchbald, *A Simple Story*, ed. J. M. S. Tompkins (London: Oxford University Press, 1967) 1; page references in the text are to this edition.

[2] Boaden 1833, I 6.

[3] Boaden 1833, I 21–2. Mrs. Inchbald was never paid more than £3 a week as an actress (*The London Stage*, part 5, II 1093) and sometimes as little as 30s., "Hay-makers' wages," as Boaden observed (Boaden 1833, I 203).

had precipitated a riot in the theatre at Edinburgh, the young couple decided to make a new start in Paris, he to study painting and she to write. But their money ran out after only three weeks and when they landed back in Brighton they walked out into the fields to eat turnips. Eventually they found work again at the theatre in Liverpool and in February 1777 in Manchester Elizabeth Inchbald began to outline the novel that became *A Simple Story*. By June 1778 she had written the first hundred pages.[4]

Into this nameless work Elizabeth Inchbald poured all the fantasies and frustrations of her buried life. The plot is a version of the guardian motif, like *The School for Lovers*. But Elizabeth Inchbald's guardian is Mr. Dorriforth, a Roman Catholic priest, whose enamourment with his ward, Miss Milner, takes on overtones of the Eloisa and Abelard motif (C160).[5] Miss Milner, like her creator, is strikingly beautiful (plate 6), with an irreverent wit and an indomitable will. But unlike her creator, she is rich, educated at an English boarding school, and the center of the unremitting attention of everyone else in the novel.

One of the main interests of *A Simple Story* is its style. Elizabeth Inchbald's prose has an edge to it like Jane Austen's:

Miss Milner ... meant to torment him by what she said ... and ... he harboured the same kind intent towards her.

(48)

"I hope they won't quarrel," said Mrs. Horton, meaning, she thought they would.

(54)

a common-place civility, such as is paid by one enemy to another every day.

(107)

Lady Matilda ... began to conceive [love] the instant she thought he would soon die.

(256)

As in all ironical works there are details in *A Simple Story* that can be interpreted literally or ironically, viz. "the thought that first occurs ... has generally truth on its side" (16). This might be a sentimental stroke in praise of impulsiveness (A8). Or it might be a sneer at intuition. Even the characters within the fiction are occasionally unsure whether a speech is to be taken "kindly, or ironically" (183).

And like Jane Austen, Elizabeth Inchbald delights to tease and mislead the reader. In one crisis in volume I, the heroine is so terrified that she reveals "for the first time her own sentiments," namely, that she loves Lord Frederick Lawnly (69), a fact that had been lovingly withheld. In another crisis in

---

[4] Boaden 1833, I 52, 68.
[5] The original of Dorriforth is John Philip Kemble, whom Mrs. Inchbald met at Manchester in January 1777, and whom, years later, the young widow would have "j-j-j-jumped at" if he had asked her to marry him (Frances Ann Kemble, *Records of a Girlhood*, 2nd ed. [New York, 1879] 213–14).

Plate 6   Elizabeth Inchbald, an engraving by J. Wooding after a drawing by
John Russell.

volume II, Miss Milner's footman reports that his lady attended a masquerade ball "in men's cloaths" (159). But George is wrong. What he had actually seen was Miss Milner entering a sedan chair in a long coat and buskins (part of her Diana-the-huntress costume) which he had mistaken for men's boots (160).[6]

From what has been said so far, one would not suppose that *A Simple Story* is a sentimental novel. But it is. Formally it is two successive comic romances. The first ends in the marriage of guardian and ward. After she suffers the most excruciating distress, to which Miss Milner, like all sentimental heroines, believes she is fated (72), all obstacles are removed. Dorriforth inherits the earldom of Elmwood, resigns his orders, breaks off his engagement with another woman. Miss Milner's mad pride is satisfied, and the lovers are united in marriage. But the marriage is an unhappy one.[7] Lady Elmwood is unfaithful and her daughter, Lady Matilda, is disinherited and banished from Elmwood Castle. The second comic romance recounts, after a lapse of seventeen years, the equally excruciating distress of Lady Matilda before she is reconciled with her father and engaged to be married to Harry Rushbrook, her cousin and Lord Elmwood's heir. The dénouement produces one of the finest moments in the sentimental literature of the eighteenth century:

> Lady Matilda ... put out her hand – which he knelt to receive, but did not raise it to his lips – he held the boon too sacred – and only looking upon it ["*passive observation*"], as it lay pale and wan in his, he breathed a sigh over it, and withdrew.[8]
>
> (312)

But this incandescent moment, worthy of *Werther*, also points to the trouble that Mrs. Inchbald has with sex in the novel.

This may indeed have been the subject of Mrs. Inchbald's deepest fears. Her mixed feelings about marriage are recorded in a letter she wrote to Joseph Inchbald a few months before they were married. "The bliss arising from

[6] This detail provides a good example of biographical irony. The reader who knows that Elizabeth Inchbald was "outrageously assailed" during the London season of 1781–2 for attending a masquerade in male attire – her costume as Bellario – and allowing herself to be admired by other women (Boaden 1833, I 140), experiences a surge of cognition that is denied the reader who is unaware of the biographical analogy.

[7] Katherine M. Rogers argues plausibly that Mrs. Inchbald was prevented from writing a realistic account of an incompatible marriage (like her own) by social pressures that denied any blame to the husband and by economic pressures exerted by publishers (*Eighteenth-Century Studies* 11 [1977]: 63–78). Treatment of two incompatible marriages in *Every One Has His Fault* is resolutely comical and unrealistic.

[8] Branfman 1954, 625. It seems correct to read this as if it were a detail from *The Man of Feeling* (1771) and *not* from *A Sentimental Journey* (1768). Mrs. Inchbald had prepared for this culmination through a series of hand-holdings (98, 184, 190, &c.). In addition, tears flow in *A Simple Story* at the rate of once every four or five pages, which is exactly the same rate as in *The Man of Feeling* (1771) and *The Mysteries of Udolpho* (1794), sentimental novels with and without the Gothic *frisson*. In her later career as a critic, Mrs. Inchbald would recommend that "The lavish use of 'tears,' both in 'showers' and 'floods,' should ... be scrupulously avoided" (*The Artist* 13 June 1807).

[marriage]," she said, "is superior to any other – but best not to be ventured for (in my opinion), till some little time have proved the emptiness of all other." She was convinced that Inchbald was unfaithful to her during their first year of marriage. He complained of her *"apathy"* and in her private devotions – which again recall Samuel Johnson – she confessed that she was guilty of "great coldness and imperfection in all [her] duties."[9]

In Miss Milner's professed "calendar of love . . . a devout archbishop ranks before a licentious king" (120). But in the deeper recesses of her mind, there is no ambivalence: "real, delicate, and restrained love, like that of Miss Milner's, was indulged in the sight of the object only" (81). Possession of the object, or enjoyment of the object, is unnecessary, or extraneous. When Dorriforth is forbidden to her by his vows of celibacy, Miss Milner can love him "with all the passion of a mistress, and with all the tenderness of a wife" (72). But when she becomes his wife, she is unfaithful to him.

Elizabeth Inchbald was only twenty-five when her husband died. But in spite of a long succession of suitors, she chose to live the rest of her life in *"virtue and a garret."* When asked why she had not remarried, she replied, "for wedlock, friendship was too familiar, and love too precarious."[10]

Before *A Simple Story* was published, Mrs. Inchbald won her freedom from the necessity of making her living by acting. She sold her first farce, *The Mogul Tale*, based on the balloon ascents that so much amused Samuel Johnson in the last months of his life, to George Colman Sr. for 100 guineas. It opened at the Haymarket in July 1784. For her first full-length comedy, *I'll Tell you What*, which opened a year later, Colman paid her £300. At the same time, she was earning £3 a week as an actress. After her ninth comedy had been produced in July 1789, she had saved enough to retire from the stage.[11]

One of these early plays, *Such Things Are* (February 1787), has a particular interest for the sentimental history of the eighteenth century. The central figure in the play, with the label name of Haswell, is John Howard the philanthropist. Howard was a rich man and an Anabaptist and, according to Bishop Burnet, "anabaptists were generally men of vertue, and of an universal charity."[12] Howard's philanthropies, which began with building model cottages on his estate in Bedfordshire and providing free education and vocational training for the cottagers, were channeled exclusively into prison reform in the 1770s. "Wrapt up in [his] long cloak,"[13] he soon became a familiar figure in the prisons of Europe (plate 7).

In 1777 Howard published *The State of Prisons in England and Wales, with Preliminary Observations and an Account of Some Foreign Prisons*, based on direct

9 Boaden 1833, I 15, 45, 78.   10 Boaden 1833, I 192; Taylor 1832, I 409.
11 Boaden 1833, I 185; *The London Stage*, part 5, II 1172. By this time Mrs. Inchbald's investments returned her £58 a year (Boaden 1833, I 261).
12 Gilbert Burnet, *History of His Own Time*, 2 vols. (London, 1724–34) I 702.
13 *Such Things Are; A Play, in Five Acts; By Mrs. Inchbald . . . with Remarks by the Author* (Inchbald 1808, XXIII 158).

Plate 7   *John Howard Visiting a Lazaretto,* pen with black ink and grey watercolour wash over traces of pencil, by George Romney.

personal observation of every prison in Britain and many of those on the Continent. What Howard discovered – chaos, filth, greed, and unbelievable cruelty – shocked a whole generation of readers.[14] In November 1785 Howard set out on a tour of inspection of the lazarettos of the Mediterranean and Near East to determine whether bubonic plague might be brought under control. From Smyrna he deliberately shipped aboard a plague-ridden vessel in order to be quarantined in Venice so that he could inspect the lazaretto there. It was this episode that led Sir Walter Scott a generation later to conclude that Howard's philanthropies had "risen to a pitch of insanity."[15] But at the time, Howard's contemporaries were raising monuments to him and money to finance his work.

It was Howard's trip to the Near East that suggested the setting as well as the central figure of *Such Things Are.* Mrs. Inchbald imagines that Howard has extended his researches to the Far East and has reached the island of Sumatra. Nearly a third of the action of the play takes place in prison,

[14] Second edition, 1780; third edition, 1784; fourth edition, 1792; reprinted as recently as 1973.
[15] *The Journal of Sir Walter Scott,* ed. D. Douglas, 2 vols. (Edinburgh, 1890; New York: Burt Franklin, 1970) II 126, quoted in Robert A. Cooper, *Eighteenth-Century Studies* 10 (Fall 1976): 75.

presumably in the capital city of Palembang. As Mrs. Inchbald said herself, her "ignorance was her protection ... There was novelty, locality, and invention" in the play and the audience overlooked the improbabilities in order to respond to the sentiments. In 1786 "When this play was written ... benevolence [was] the constant theme of enthusiastic praise" and John Howard was credible as a universally benevolent man, "a man of principle and sentiment," a true sentimental hero.[16]

During Haswell's first visit to the prison, his pocket is picked by a Javanese prisoner named Zedan. To throw off suspicion from himself, Zedan forces himself upon Haswell's attention as Haswell is leaving the prison. Unexpectedly he receives Haswell's sympathy and promises of help. And then, as James Boaden remembered the opening night, "Nature in a moment bursts through the villany ... [and Zedan] throws himself upon his knees before Haswell, and with convulsive emotion restores the pocket-book":

> ZEDAN (*shakes his Head, and holds his Heart*). 'Tis something that I never felt before – it makes me like not only you, but all the world besides. – The love of my family was confined to them alone – but this sensation makes me love even my enemies.

"The effect," in Boaden's words again, "was electric. [James] Fearon, a rough but valuable man [who played Zedan], struck it by his action into every heart, and Mrs. Inchbald must have trembled under the severe delight of applause that never was exceeded in a theatre." Besides this dramatic enactment of the essential goodness of man (A2), the play concludes quietly in another sentimental triumph, the heroine's engagement to marry a Eurasian (A6) upon whom her affections were said in the third act to have been "improperly" fixed.[17]

Every One Has His Fault may be the comedy on which Mrs. Inchbald had in July 1789 been "more than a year employed." If it is, it must have been set aside in March 1790, when *A Simple Story* was finally sold to the publisher John Robinson. For the next year Mrs. Inchbald was occupied with transcribing and proofreading two editions of her first novel, which appeared in February and April 1791. Only then could she return to the comedy that had been "laid ... up in store" after receiving the encouraging approbation of John Philip Kemble, the new manager at Drury Lane.[18]

When *Every One Has His Fault* was ready for the stage, however, Mrs. Inchbald submitted it, not to Kemble, but to Thomas Harris, the manager of the Covent Garden theatre, where it opened on 29 January 1793, with Alexander Pope, who had played Mr. Haswell in *Such Things Are*, playing opposite his wife in the role of Captain Irwin.

Mrs. Inchbald's new comedy was built around *four* pairs of lovers, one more than Hugh Kelly had attempted in *False Delicacy*. *Every One Has His Fault* also

[16] Inchbald 1808, XXIII [1]2–4, 24.   [17] Inchbald 1808, XXIII [1]34, 35; Boaden 1833, I 242.
[18] Boaden 1833, I 264, 273.

begins at a later stage of the boy-meets-girl, boy-wants-girl, boy-gets-girl formula of New Comedy.[19] All the boys have met all the girls. Three of them have wanted and got the girls. But none of them has lived happily ever after, as the formula promises. *Every One Has His Fault* provides a glimpse into the ever-after that comedy usually avoids.[20] And what is glimpsed is marriage in four lamentable states, broken, breaking, endangered, and avoided:

Sir Robert Ramble	Mr. Placid	Captain Irwin	Mr. Solus
↑	↑	↑	⋮
broken	breaking	endangered	avoided
↓	↓	↓	⋮
Lady Maria	Mrs. Placid	Lady Eleanor	Miss Spinster

All four couples are domiciled in the West End of London: "The Squares ... part of Piccadilly, down St. James's-street, and so home by Pall Mall"[21] – that fashionable but inhospitable enclave where to visit a friend or to leave a card "is all the same" (II i 196). Sir Robert Ramble, Bart. is typical of the "dissipated, unthinking, unprincipled men" (IV i 54) who adorn this society. But he is also the only character in the play of any complexity: he is a man of fashion and a heavy gambler (II i 47–8), but he also writes verse (III ii 27) (cf. p. 63 above). And now that he is divorced, he says, he has more time to devote to his wife (IV i 61). Seven years before the time of the play a brilliant marriage had been arranged for him in Scotland with Maria Wooburn, a ward of the "rich and proud" Lord Norland (II i 272) and an heiress worth £3,000 a year (III ii 22).[22] But Sir Robert did not even pretend to love his wife and after a year of marriage he told her frankly that he was tired of her and wanted a divorce (II i 60–1). His open infidelities – he even made love to other women in his wife's presence – provided grounds for divorce under Scottish law, and Lady Maria, very reluctantly, sued in "that excellent institution the Commissary Court," as J. G. Lockhart called it, and was awarded title to her entire estate and the right to retain her married name (II i 184–5; III i 98–9, 185–6). Her reluctance to sue has stemmed from her love for Sir Robert, which she acknowledges now to have been "an imprudent passion" (III i 250–1). Her surviving "secret affection" for Sir Robert is, ironically, sufficiently well known for him to ridicule her for it (III i 177). Lady Maria is saved from being nothing *more* than a patient Griselda (H461) by a fine sense of comedy (IV ii 54–6) and "a little sparkle ... out of the corner of one eye" (II i 92–3) supplied originally by Harriet Esten, whose large eyes were captivating London in the 1790s.

---

[19] Frye 1957, 44.   [20] Frye 1957, 169.

[21] II i 173–4. The play is quoted by act, scene, and line number of the text in the appendix below.

[22] Lord Norland explains to his ward that for an heiress an arranged marriage is "the order of society" (III i 275). Although by this time Mrs. Inchbald had become a Jacobin and a *de facto* feminist, she does not question this custom; cf. note 30 below.

The remaining pairs of lovers, however, are all types. Mr. Placid is the browbeaten husband – the stock figure of the cuckold in a less-inhibited age – and Mrs. Placid is splendid as the shrewish wife (T251): "I don't approve of people lending their money," she tells Mr. Placid, "I desire you will hear what I say . . . I insist on your being hungry" (I i 81–5, 120). Not surprisingly, the Placids "are in the fairest way for a separation" (III ii 174).

Captain Irwin is "worthy, but . . . ill-fated" (V iii 136), the man-pursued-by-misfortune type (N251). As a young army officer with no prospects, he made an "indiscreet" (I i 53) marriage with the daughter of Lord Norland, who was promptly disowned and disinherited (V i 91). Now after nine years of garrison duty in America (I i 89; I iii 23), Captain Irwin's regiment has been broken and he has come home to London to try to support a large family "without friends, without money, without credit" (I iii 68–9). His mind is broken by these deficiencies (II i 230) and he is close to suicide (II i 263–4). His wife, however, has surmounted all these blows. Born and educated in "the luxury of wealth and splendour" (I iii 64), Lady Eleanor married for love, "never murmured at the change of fortune" (I iii 64–5) that she has suffered, and remains "the most tender, anxious, and affectionate [of] wives" (II ii 31–2), the stock figure of the faithful wife (T210.1). The unconcern with which she contemplates suicide comes as something of a shock: "[To leave the world] in company with you," she tells her husband, "would make the journey pleasant" (II ii 101–2). But faithfulness to marriage in death is, of course, another folklore motif (T211). Taken out of fairy-land and subjected to real economic and social pressures during the crisis years of the French Revolution, it is not surprising that the Irwins' marriage is close to dissolution.

The remaining couple, or anti-couple who have avoided marriage, are Mr. Solus, "An old [and] ugly" (III ii 181) bachelor who wishes he had married thirty years ago (I i 9), and Miss Spinster, a "peevish, fretful and tiresome" old maid (I ii 57).

Into this bear-garden of blocked marriages, Mrs. Inchbald releases her one unblocking eiron, Mr. Harmony. Like Mrs. Inchbald herself and Mr. Haswell in *Such Things Are*, Mr. Harmony is unmarried, but his "whole life is passed in endeavouring to make people happy" (V ii 8). To unsentimental people like Lord Norland and Miss Spinster it appears only that Mr. Harmony – again like Mr. Haswell – "take[s] the criminal's part" (I ii 25) and has compassion for "none but the wicked" (IV i 185). But the truth is that Mr. Harmony is universally benevolent. Since childhood he has "felt the most unbounded affection for all [his] fellow creatures" (I ii 10–11).

Mr. Harmony's secret, like that of the philosophic beggar in *A Sentimental Journey*, is flattery:

Delicious essence! how refreshing art thou to nature! how strongly are all its powers and all its weaknesses on thy side! how sweetly dost thou mix with the blood, and help it through the most difficult and tortuous passages to the heart.[23]

23 Sterne 1928, 203.

In the case of Sir Robert and Lady Maria, Mr. Harmony is helped (1) by a magic gesture on the part of Lady Maria (III i 229–33) that is more surprising than that of Sir John Dorilant in *The School for Lovers* (p. 76 above) and (2) by a conversion on the part of Sir Robert (IV ii 63–6) that is more surprising (and less convincing) that that of Sir Charles Easy in *The Careless Husband* (V v 45).[24] But it is only Mr. Harmony's flatteries that reconcile Lord Norland and Sir Robert to each other (III i 109–16; III ii 91–6).

A little more flattery at strategic moments (V ii 27–34; V iii 82–5) is enough to reconcile the Placids. But stronger measures are needed to reconcile Lord Norland to Captain Irwin. Mr. Harmony does not hang back. He pretends that Captain Irwin has committed suicide (V iii 135–7). With Lord Norland's pride thus shaken, Mr. Harmony then leads in the supposed suicide surrounded by his wife and ten-year-old son for a tearful reconciliation (V iii 176) at the final curtain.

Very little flattery is needed to reconcile Mr. Solus and Miss Spinster (I ii 82–8), whose entrance in V iii in their white wedding clothes sets up the climactic reconciliation scene.

Mrs. Inchbald does not shy away from the fact that the four marriages are reconstituted, preserved, created, by lies. Miss Spinster tells Mr. Harmony quite frankly that his methods "stigmatize [him] with the character of deceit" (I ii 30–1). This cannot have been a moot point for Mrs. Inchbald. Her own response to flattery may be reflected in Mr. Haswell's words in *Such Things Are*:

Flattery! – a vice that renders you not only despicable, but odious … Never let the honest, plain, blunt, English [language] be degraded by so mean a vice.

The strength of the animus in these words suggests that they may convey something of the personal feelings of Elizabeth Inchbald.[25]

Even Mr. Harmony confesses that flattery is "a weakness," "a species of falsehood and deceit" (I ii 32, 35–6). The overt theme of the play, of course, is that no one is perfect. Mr. Harmony's fault is flattery.[26] Less obviously, the play is also saying that happiness in marriage may be based on lies and deception. "We should never have known half how well we all love one another," Sir Robert tells Mr. Harmony, "if you had not told us" (V iii

[24] Mr. Harmony plays on Lady Maria's sympathies by pretending that Sir Robert has been seriously wounded in a duel with Lord Norland (V ii 14–16), but this contributes nothing to reconciling the estranged couple. It leads to a scene of low farce (V iii) in which Sir Robert is discovered by Lady Maria in drunken carousing. This scene, a parody of the "true" discovery scenes that come before and after it in Act V, may betray Mrs. Inchbald's restlessness under the constraints of sentimental comedy.

[25] Inchbald 1808, XXIII ¹73–4. Mrs. Inchbald "had a perfect contempt for all praise not combined with censure" (Boaden 1833, II 166).

[26] Mr. Harmony recalls Goldsmith's universally benevolent Will Honeywood in *The Good Natur'd Man* (1768). But unlike Will Honeywood, Mr. Harmony is not exposed and converted in the last act to prudence and self-regard. Thomas Holcroft, however, in his review of *Every One Has His Fault* calls Mr. Harmony immoral (*The Monthly Review* March 1793).

195–6). But what Mr. Harmony tells is lies. It is difficult to read the play without sensing some ambivalence about sentimentality.

Part of the difficulty may be that Mrs. Inchbald never decided whether this was to be realistic comedy or a morality play like her second novel, *Nature and Art* (1796). The title, *Every One Has His Fault*, which flatly contradicts the sentimental attitude toward man (A2), is proverbial (Tilley M116), and all the characters but one or two are pure folklore types. Part of the time, therefore, *Every One Has His Fault* reads like *Everyman* with Mr. Harmony in the role of Good-dedes. But *Everyman* is a tragedy, as Thomas Percy pointed out, "not without some rude attempts to excite terror and pity," and terminating in death,[27] whereas *Every One Has His Fault* is a comedy terminating in marriages. There seem, however, to be elements of *Every One Has His Fault* that are incompatible with comedy.

There can be no doubt that generically *Every One Has His Fault* is a sentimental comedy. Anna Margaretta Larpent concluded correctly that although it was "rather out of the Rules," it was still "une *Comedie Larmoyante*."[28] And despite the title of the play, it *is* sentimental about women (A3) (IV ii 58; V iii 64), parents (A4) (I iii 24–5; V i 101–2), children (A5) (IV i 162–5; V i 120–2), emotion (A8) (I ii 39–40; V iii 188),[29] crime (A9) (I ii 24–6; IV i 187), money (A10) (III i 231–5; III ii 85–7), and the elsewhere (A11) (I iii 6–11; II i 198–9).[30]

Also in evidence are three of the four secondary characteristics of sentimental comedy:

"*Tender melancholy Conversation*" (B1): "what has Lord Norland to do with souls as free as ours … Who let this woman in?" (IV ii 49; V i 103);

Heroic virtue (B2): "obliging myself … was never one of my considerations … though his frown should kill me, yet must I thank him for his care" (III i 146–7; V i 97–8);

Undeserved distress (B3): "Now I have not a friend on earth … Do not let me see her hardly treated – Indeed I cannot bear it" (I iii 44; V i 104–5).

Explicit moralizing (B4) is reserved for the prologue and epilogue, neither

---

27 Thomas Hawkins, *The Origin of the English Drama*, 3 vols. (Oxford, 1773) I sig. B8v. Thomas Holcroft thought that "The story of Lady Eleanor Irwin, and … her husband … [is] of a tragical kind" (*The Monthly Review* March 1793). James Boaden called the play a "tragicomedy" (Boaden 1825, 302).

28 L. W. Conolly, *Huntington Library Quarterly* 35 (November 1971), 54.

29 A French critic has observed that Mrs. Inchbald "conserva pour sa part un culte réel à 'l'intelligence du cœur' " (Françoise Moreux, *Elizabeth Inchbald et la comédie "sentimentale" anglaise à XVIIIe siècle* [Paris: Aubier-Montaigne, 1971] 131).

30 As a dramatist Mrs. Inchbald supposed that she was "the very slave of the audience." She felt that she must have their tastes and prejudices in view, not to correct, but to humour them (*The Artist* 13 June 1807). But "the … idealizing of the moral views assumed to be held by the audience" is the business, not of comedy, but of melodrama (Frye 1957, 47).

of which Mrs. Inchbald wrote. Ironies and paradoxes are much more Mrs. Inchbald's style than moral sentences: "now that I am single," says Sir Robert Ramble of his divorced wife, "I shall have leisure to pay her more attention" (IV i 62).

The sentimentality about marriage in *Every One Has His Fault* contrasts sharply with cynicism about marriage in *Love's Last Shift*:

> NARCISSA. . . . then you take Marriage to be a kind of Jesuit's Powder, that infallibly cures the Fever of Love?
> YOUNG WORTHY. 'Tis indeed . . .
>
> (II i 390).

If *Love's Last Shift* is an example of one subgenre, Restoration comedy of manners, that was falling out of fashion in 1696, perhaps *Every One Has His Fault* is an example of another subgenre, sentimental comedy, that was falling out of fashion in 1793.

There is, in any case, a stratum in *Every One Has His Fault* that is not comic at all. Here is a test boring:

> CAPTAIN IRWIN (*opens the letter hastily . . . Reads, and drops the letter*). Now I have not a friend on earth . . . What am I to do? I must leave you! I must go, I know not where! I cannot stay to see you perish.
>
> (*Takes his hat, and is going*).
> LADY ELEANOR (*holding him*). Where would you go? 'Tis evening. 'Tis dark. Whither would you go at this time?
> CAPTAIN IRWIN (*distractedly*). I must consider what's to be done. And in this room my thoughts are too confined to reflect . . .
> LADY ELEANOR. You are not well. Your health has been lately impaired. Your temper has undergone a change too: I tremble lest any accident –
>
> (I iii 41–58)

Captain Irwin's next scene (II i) in which he tries to borrow money from Sir Robert, is kept comic by Sir Robert's conflicting needs to refuse the loan and to maintain an impression of great prosperity (II i 49–50, 143, 174–5, 181). But then, "His mind deranged by his misfortunes" (II i 230), Captain Irwin holds up his father-in-law in the street (III i 81–3; V i 7–10) and brings home the loot to Lady Eleanor, thrusting banknotes into her hands:

> *She looks at them, then screams.*
> LADY ELEANOR. Ah! 'Tis money. (*Trembling*) These are Bank notes.
> CAPTAIN IRWIN. . . . What alarms you thus? . . .
> LADY ELEANOR. A sight so new has frightened me.
>
> (II ii 82–8)

By this time, it may be feared, a modern audience would be helpless with laughter. But there is no cue for laughter in the play, which by this time has passed over the line into pure melodrama. With deadly seriousness Mrs. Inchbald is making a *moral* judgment of a conventionally comic deformity in the social structure. The alazonic Lord Norland is "rich and proud" (II i 272), while the eirons, the Captain and his lady, are poor (they keep only one servant) (I iii 33–4; II ii 15–16) and self-deprecating.

In the last act the first scene is pure melodrama. Lady Eleanor is accidentally reunited with a lost child (N730), who tearfully chooses to leave his grandfather, Lord Norland, and cleave unto his mother (V i 120–1). Scenes ii and iii are comic until the reconciliation scene that ends the play:

> LORD NORLAND (*runs to* IRWIN and embraces him). My son! (IRWIN *falls on his knees*)
> I take a share in all your offences ... My heart is softened, and receives you all.
> (*Embraces Lady* ELEANOR, *who falls on her knees*) ...
>
> (V iii 176–88)

But the happy ending is brought about "with a self-righteous tone that most comedy avoids."[31]

Every One Has His Fault wavers between comedy and melodrama and in so doing presents another paradigm for the breakdown of a subgenre. *The Careless Husband* is a Restoration comedy of manners in the process of becoming sentimental, *sentimentalisante. Every One Has His Fault* is a sentimental comedy in the process of becoming melodrama, *mélodramatisante.*

"On its first appearance" at the Covent Garden in January 1793 *Every One Has His Fault* was a huge success. It ran "near thirty nights; during which, some of the audience were heard to laugh, and some were seen to weep," Mrs. Inchbald said, and it was "productive [*i.e.* profitable] both to the manager and the writer."[32] The success was helped along by a foolish attack on it in a ministerial paper designed to find sedition everywhere in those anxious days while Britain waited for a declaration of war by republican France. *The True Briton* of 31 January 1793 found, or purported to find, that "the moral tendency" of *Every One Has His Fault* was subversive. This was followed the next day by an acknowledgement that Mrs. Inchbald had expunged "The exceptionable parts" (*The True Briton* 1 February 1793). Mrs. Inchbald fired off a crackling letter to the editor of *The Diary*, an opposition paper, assuring the public "that not one line, or one *word*, [had] been altered or omitted since the first night [29 January 1793]."[33] This exchange may have helped create a demand for copies, for it has long been known that "the way ... to have a Book sell, is, to make an Interest to get it burn'd."[34] But this exchange does not explain why the play survived the demise of sentimental comedy.

In his prologue to the play the Reverend Edward Nares had wondered whether "The Comic Muse perhaps is growing old." Fifteen years later, in her "Remarks" for a new edition of *Such Things Are*, Mrs. Inchbald had to point

---

[31] Frye 1957, 167.
[32] Inchbald 1808, XXIII 24. The play ran exactly 32 nights (*The London Stage*, part 5, III 1480, 1516–29). Mrs. Inchbald earned £700 (Boaden 1833, I 309).
[33] Boaden 1833, I 311.   [34] [William Pittis], *The Whipping-Post* 2 November 1705.

out th it "benevolence [was] no longer the constant theme of enthusiastic praise as [it was] when this drama was first produced [February 1789]."[35] By 1820 John Bernard could see that "the taste and feeling" of what he called the "English 'age of sentiment'" had long been forgotten.[36] "This style of writing has fallen into disrepute," said another critic in 1822, but *Every One Has His Fault*, he added quickly, "has escaped the general doom."[37] In December 1841, when the comic muse was beginning to show surprising signs of life, not on the stage but in serialized novels, Charles Dickens found time amid the incredible hurly-burly of his departure for America, to enjoy a performance of *Every One Has His Fault.*[38]

[35] Inchbald 1808, XXIII ¹4.

[36] John Bernard, *Retrospections of the Stage*, 2 vols. (Boston, 1832) I 86, 88. Boaden observes that "This rage of sentiment ended in the massacres of the French revolution" (Boaden 1825, I 195).

[37] *Every One Has His Fault. A Comedy; by Mrs. Inchbald. With Prefatory Remarks* (London, 1822) i–ii.

[38] *The Pilgrim Edition of the Letters of Charles Dickens*, ed. Madeline House *et al.*, 3 vols. (Oxford: Clarendon, 1969) II 455.

Aftermath

10

Conclusions

The first and most obvious conclusion to be drawn from the foregoing evidence is that sentimental comedy exists. It is not "a construct of Mr. Sherbo's devising," nor an oxymoron, nor "a many-branching upas tree" the sap of which is deadly poison. This will be particularly good news for anyone rehearsing a production of *The Critic* (1771), which ridicules sentimental comedy, or for graduate students writing dissertations on sentimental comedy.[1]

Neither is sentimental comedy a single thing. It is not narcissism, "avoidance of impropriety," solipsism, exemplary comedy, nor genteel comedy. Nothing, of course, can be defined by saying what it is not: avoidance of satire or avoidance of impropriety cannot define sentimental comedy. If it exists, it has to be a particular thing. The thing that sentimental comedy is most frequently confused with is moral comedy. But the only connection between the two is simultaneity. The great shift in public morality that occurs in the reigns of William III and Queen Anne (1689–1714) could not fail to be reflected on the London stage. Colley Cibber and Richard Steele were preternaturally sensitive to this vector shift – more so perhaps than Pope and Swift. But without this shift neither the Societies for Reformation of Manners nor Steele's efforts to "Moralize the Stage" could have made much headway. How much headway was made is evident from Garrick's letter to Marie Jeanne Riccoboni of September 1768, the year he produced *False Delicacy*. "Our taste at present," he complained, "cannot endure any indecency." Garrick meant public indecency, of course, for Boswell's journals provide ample evidence that there had been no vector shift in private morality.

The truth seems to be that sentimental comedy as such is morally neutral. Ernest Bernbaum observes that sentimental comedy lacks "clearly conceived ethical ... principles." The sentimental attitudes are value judgments, not moral judgments. After seeing a performance of Steele's sentimental comedy,

---

[1] John Loftis, review of Arthur Sherbo, *English Sentimental Drama* (1957), *Modern Language Notes* 74 (1959): 449; Havens 1945, 184. Two recent dissertations are: Anne Elizabeth Boeckx Parker, *A Glass for the World: The Witty and the Sentimental Modes in British Drama 1660–1900*, University of Manitoba Ph.D. Dissertation, 1980, and Mark H. Burch, *Eighteenth Century Sentimentality: A Study of Literature and its Contexts*, University of Texas Ph.D. Dissertation, 1984.

The Tender Husband, Pamela observes, "It looks to me . . . as if the Author had forgot the Moral all the way; and being put in mind of it by some kind Friend (Mr. *Addison* perhaps) was at a Loss to draw one from such Characters and Plots." It is also true, as one critic has said that "no single element identifies a sentimental comedy."[2] This is true because a sentimental comedy is a congeries of specifically defined attitudes or beliefs implanted – the fashionable word is "embedded" – in a comedy.

The best evidence for the existence of sentimental comedies is the fact that some of them are adaptations of unsentimental comedies. Steele's *The Conscious Lovers* is an adaptation of Terence's *Andria*. Whitehead's *The School for Lovers* is an adaptation of Fontenelle's *Le Testament*. "The very scenes which render [Philippe Destouches's] *Le Trésor caché* a sentimental comedy," Bernbaum says, "are absent in [Plautus's] *Trinummus*." In all three of these cases the sentimental details are literally stuck in. And having been stuck in, by Whitehead for example, they can be taken out, by Kelly in satirizing *The School for Lovers*. Sticking things in and taking things out may seem too mechanical for platonizing critics, but this is one way at least that comedies are sentimentalized and desentimentalized. Even "the most sentimental play ever written," Diderot's *Le Père de famille* (1758), was made more sentimental in Charles Jenner's adaptation of it, *The Man of Family. A Sentimental Comedy* (1771), by adding a line for which there is no counterpart in the original: "my heart," the heroine boasts, "never deceived me" (A8).[3]

The critics who were willing to discard the term "sentimental comedy" either because it means too much ("fuzzy omnibus categories like . . . 'sentimental comedy'") or because it means too little ("oversimplifications like . . . 'Sentimental Comedy'") may now agree that it has been brought within compass, like Falstaff's guts. When other critics say that "There is no such genre as 'sentimental comedy'" and that sentimental comedy is not "a definable genre," one is forced, perversely, to agree with them. "Anything that exists," Elder Olson says, "is not merely a particular thing but also a thing of a certain determinate kind, even if it is only one of its kind." Sentimental comedy is not *sui generis*; there are many examples of it. Nor is it a genre, like satire or romance; it exists on a different level of generalization. It is "a certain determinate kind" of comedy, a subgenre of comedy, like comedy of manners or romantic comedy.[4]

---

2 Waterhouse 1907, 288–9; I. R. Titunik, in *Semiosis. Semiotics and the History of Culture In Honorem Georgii Lotman*, ed. Morris Halle *et al.*, Michigan Slavic Contributions No. 10 (Ann Arbor: University of Michigan Press, 1984) 230–1; Kovach 1986, 50; Steele, *The Conscious Lovers* (London, 1723) sig. A8r; Bernbaum 1915, 95; Pamela IV 87–8; Garrick 1963, II 628; Bevis 1980, 50.

3 Bernbaum 1915, 16; Alan R. Thompson, *The Anatomy of Drama* (Berkeley and Los Angeles: University of California Press, 1946) 230.

4 David M. Vieth, *Criticism* 19 (1977): 262; J. M. Armistead, *South Atlantic Quarterly* 76 (1977): 254; John Loftis, *Comedy and Society from Congreve to Fielding* (Stanford: Stanford University Press, 1959) 127; Hume 1981, 12; Olson 1968, 26; Frye 1957, 166–7.

Robert D. Hume rightly complains about the laughing/weeping dichotomy that Goldsmith introduced into the debate about eighteenth-century comedy. "No such dichotomy can validly be drawn," Hume says. And he is right for two reasons: (1) Goldsmith uses laughing/weeping to differentiate literary subgenres, but subgenres are differentiated on the basis of intrinsic features, not on the basis of audience reaction (comedy is not a kind of catalyst), and (2) the best passages of sentimental comedy, such as the discovery scene in *The Conscious Lovers* and certain sequences in Charlie Chaplin films, elicit laughing and weeping at the same time. James Beattie thought that this was "impossible." "Can pity ... and risibility, be excited by the same object, and at the same time?" he asks. But Thomas Holcroft knew better. "Perhaps, of all the delights which comedy can give," he says, "that of exciting tears and laughter by the same thought is the supreme." And the first reviewer of *The West Indian* gave assurance that the play "so blended the pathetic and ridiculous, that if the spectator or reader has sensibility and discernment, he will be kept almost continually laughing with tears in his eyes." Since he had joked about recognition by tokens in his last play, *The Tender Husband*, Steele knew that the discovery scene in *The Conscious Lovers* was funny and he also knew that "Tears ... were shed on that Occasion." The audience reaction to the discovery scene may be described in Dr. Branfman's phrase, *"passive observation."* "This is the way things should be," we can imagine the first-night audience saying as the curtain went down. A month later, with most of the same cast and before some of the same audience, *The Man of Mode* was played at the same theatre. On this occasion we can imagine the audience turning into cynical, disenchanted observers, saying, "This is the way things really are," in yet another instance of the Augustan Quest.[5]

It seems that the major English writers who "deal in *sentimentals"* (in Garrick's phrase),[6] Fielding, Sterne, Goldsmith, Sheridan, Jane Austen, without exception satirize sentimentality. It is only the lesser figures, Steele, Cumberland, Henry Mackenzie, Henry Brooke, who take it seriously or play it straight. Samuel Richardson is "The glory, jest, and riddle" of eighteenth-century sentimental writing because one does not know what to make of him. It would be unthinkable to rank him with Henry Brooke and Ann Radcliffe, so he must be the exception that proves the rule. Only the genius of Sterne could consistently and repeatedly make his readers laugh and cry at the same time.

Another obvious conclusion to be drawn from the foregoing evidence is the intermittent nature of the sentimentality in sentimental comedies. Osborn

---

[5] Hume 1981, 4; Goldsmith 1966, III 210–13; James Beattie, *Essays on Poetry and Music* (Edinburgh, 1778) 424; Thomas Holcroft, *The Monthly Review* March 1793, quoted in Sherbo 1957, 164; cf. "La Chaussée voulait ... provoquer à la fois le rire et les larmes" (Gustave Larroumet, *Marivaux sa vie et ses oeuvres* (Paris, 1882) 301; *The Monthly Review* February 1771; Steele, *The Conscious Lovers* (London, 1723) sig. A6r; Branfman 1954, 625; *The London Stage*, part 2, II 694, 699; *Swift vs. Mainwaring*, ed. Frank H. Ellis (Oxford: Clarendon, 1985) 412n.

[6] Goldsmith 1966, V 102.

Waterhouse observes that "the sentimental scenes [in *A Sentimental Journey*] are rarely ... prolonged." Other critics say the same thing: "The sentimental elements which are to be found in [eighteenth-century] plays did not involve a more than partial or momentary espousal of the sentimental *idea*;" "The sentimentality found in Cibber is sporadic and accidental." Another way of putting this is to say that – apart from the flagrant moments that induce tears and laughter simultaneously – the sentimental elements in a sentimental comedy alternate with comic elements. This fact was known and clearly stated in the eighteenth century and the evidence of this book only confirms it. The alternation between *l'attendrissement* and laughter in sentimental comedies (*Comédies attendrissantes*) has been criticized, Voltaire says, "mais ce passage ... n'en est pas moins naturel aux hommes ... c'est ainsi malheureusement que le genre humain est fait" (but this change ... is nonetheless inherent in man ... It is unfortunately the way man is made). "La comédie," Voltaire adds, "peut donc ... attendrir, pourvu qu'ensuite elle fasse rire les honnêtes gens" (Comedy can draw tears as long as it also ... makes the audience laugh). Both of Voltaire's ideas found their way to England. "The mind has been shewn to be capable of sadness and mirth in very sudden transitions," John Hawkesworth says. "Uninterrupted scenes of tenderness and sensibility (*Comedie Larmoyante*) may please the very refined," added the dramatist John Burgoyne, "but the bulk of an English audience ... go to a comic performance to laugh."[7]

Unfortunately the evidence of the foregoing pages does not provide an answer to the question of proportion, or How much sentimentality is required to make a comedy sentimental? *The Conscious Lovers*, *The School for Lovers*, and *Every One Has His Fault* are loaded with sentimental ore. *The West Indian* has less, but is still without doubt a sentimental comedy. *Love's Last Shift* has almost none, but the insistence upon the goodness of human nature (A2) is so obtrusive that the play almost certainly qualifies as sentimental comedy. It is repeatedly cited as marking a signal departure from the characteristic plays of the previous generation, and goodness of human nature is the assumption that Vanbrugh challenges in *The Relapse, or Vertue in Danger* (1696). *The Foundling*, on the other hand, with only one sentimental detail, with almost equal certainty does not qualify as sentimental comedy. The problem of proportion therefore must be added to the list of emergent desiderata below.[8]

Nothing remains but to say what remains to be done. Most writers about sentimental literature have been more interested in the origins and history than in the nature of sentimental literature. "The history of the drama of

---

[7] Waterhouse 1907, 143; Bateson 1928, 11; James E. Cox, *The Rise of Sentimental Comedy* (Springfield, Missouri, 1926) 187; Voltaire, *Nanine, comedie en trois actes* (Paris, 1749) viii–ix; John Hawkesworth, *The Monthly Review* February 1769, quoted in Sherbo 1957, 74; John Burgoyne, *Lord of the Manor* (London, 1780) xviii, quoted in Sherbo 1957, 84.

[8] Bernbaum 1915, 1–2; Bateson 1928, 20; Sherbo 1957, 104–5.

sensibility begins with the year 1696;" "about fourteen years ago [1767], the French *Comédie Larmoyante*, or as we call it, Sentimental Comedy, was introduced;" "After Richardson came Rousseau." Since it was never determined exactly what it was the origins and history of which were being investigated, the results have not been conclusive. George W. Stone, for example, compiled a useful list of the most popular comedies of the period 1747–76 based on the number of London performances and divided into subgenres. *The Conscious Lovers* and *The West Indian* fall into the sentimental category, but so do *The Provok'd Husband* (1728) and *The Suspicious Husband* (1747), neither of which is sentimental. We are no closer now to knowing the origins of sentimental comedy than we were in 1748 when Edmund Burke confessed that he could not tell "Who were the first Inventors of this Weeping Comedy." Is it true, as Varro says, that "*Trabea, Attilius* and *Caecilius* excelled in *sentimental . . . comedy*"? Is Terence really more sentimental than Plautus? Is Nivelle de la Chaussée really the inventor of *comédie larmoyante*? Can Fielding be taken seriously when he says that "Charity is in fact the very Characteristic of this Nation at this Time [1752]"? Is it true that sentimental attitudes were propagated in the sermons of latitudinarian divines (as R. S. Crane and Frans DeBruyn have said) or not (as Donald Greene has said)?[9]

Peter Burra's observation that "Sentimentalism is the product of an irregular alliance between Tragedy and Comedy" is witty, but the truth may be that sentimental comedy is the product of an irregular alliance between Comedy and Restoration heroic plays, with the Cambridge Platonists in attendance as *accoucheurs*. Alternatively, sentimental comedy may be the product of a *mésalliance* between Comedy and Romance, as Ernest Bernbaum and Maximillian Novak have suggested. Edward Revet's *The Town Shifts, or The Suburban Justice* (1671), produced a whole generation before *Love's Last Shift* (1696), has been called a sentimental comedy. It may be true, as C. M. Scheurer claims, that "all the conventional features of sentimental comedy had been for generations the common property of English playwrights," but the "features of sentimental comedy" are not specified and *The Town Shifts* is devoid of sentimentality. One character is graced with a sentimental compulsion to give away money, but only in order to establish him as a fool. *The Winter's Tale*, which has also been called "thoroughly sentimental," is equally devoid of sentimentality. It appears therefore that a history of sentimental comedy, not only in England, but in Spain, France, Germany, and Italy, is a major desideratum. The tradition that sentimental comedy originated in the

---

9 Johannes H. Harder, *Observations on some Tendencies of Sentiment and Ethics chiefly in Minor Poetry and Essay in the Eighteenth Century until the Execution of Dr. W. Dodd in 1777* (Amsterdam: Portielje, 1933) 76; Thomas Holcroft, *Duplicity: A Comedy* (London, 1781) iv; Smith 1899, 451; Edmund Burke, *The Reformer* 31 March 1748; Richard Cumberland, *The Choleric Man. A Comedy* (London, 1775) xi; Kovach 1986, 44; Henry Fielding, *The Covent Garden Journal* 2 June 1752; R. S. Crane, *English Literary History* 1 (1934): 205–30; Donald J. Greene, *Modern Philology* 75 (1977): 159–83; Frans DeBruyn, *Journal of English and Germanic Philology* 80 (1981): 349–68.

years 1689–1714, when Societies for Reformation of Manners were springing
up like weeds and Jeremy Collier was terrorizing Drury Lane like Senator
Joseph McCarthy, may be true, but it remains to be demonstrated.[10]

More research on sentimentality is obviously needed. It is a shame that
there has been no sequel to Dr. Branfman's challenging article in 1954. Since
that time sentimentality has become a topic in analytical philosophy.[11] But
none of the articles in the philosophy journals cite Dr. Branfman, even while
treating sentimentality as a disease. And this would seem to be a mistake.
Clinical sentimentality may make people like Dr. Branfman's patient "unable
to deal with the real world," in Mary Midgeley's phrase (385), but ordinary
demotic sentimentality can turn people like Steele, Cumberland, and Inchbald into propagandists for humanitarian causes. And mass sentimentality
can reform prisons, outlaw child labor, and abolish slavery. Mark Jefferson's
very engaging study concludes that the moral objection to sentimentality
"arises from the special character of the fiction sentimentality employs"
(529). Jefferson's mistake, it seems to me, lies in thinking that sentimentality
employs one particular fiction, which he calls "a fiction of innocence" (527,
529). Sentimental comedy employs a different fiction for each object of
sentimentality:

> Women are superior to men (A3).
> Children are wiser than parents (A5).
> Emotions are less fallible than reason (A8).
> The past is better than the present (A11).

"Sentimentality is distinguished and objectionable," Jefferson concludes,
"simply because it is a form of emotional indulgence that depends upon a
distortion of the way things are" (529). But the assumption that "the way
things are" is the way things should be cannot be true. And "distortion" is the
word that Aristotle used to describe the comic mask. Jefferson partly accepts
Mary Midgeley's claim that sentimentalism "misrepresent[s] the world in
order to indulge our feelings" (521), but it seems more accurate to say that
sentimentalism re-represents the world. Cumberland re-represents the rich-
American and Irish-mercenary-soldier stereotypes. The operative fiction in
The West Indian is this:

> Rich Americans and Irish mercenaries are superior to reserved and
> prudent Englishmen (A6).

[10] Peter Burra, *Baroque and Gothic Sentimentalism* (London: Duckworth, 1931) 4; Bernbaum 1915,
76; Maximillian Novak, *Modern Language Studies* 9 (1979): 55; C. M. Scheurer, *Anglia* 37 (1913):
125; George Williams, *Rice University Studies* 51 (1965): 131.

[11] Mary Midgeley, *Philosophy* 54 (1979): 385–9; Michael Tanner, *Proceedings of the Aristotelian
Society* n.s. 77 (1976–7): 127–47; Mark Jefferson, *Mind* 92 (1983): 519–29; all three of these
works cited hereafter by page number.

Such an outrageous "distortion of the way things are" in 1771 could only be understood as a joke. But this "distortion of the way things are," by the "High Priest of all the Tragic-comic sect," as Thomas Tickell called Cumberland, is a fiction of great social utility. It is in this example that the two faces of sentimental comedy finally come into a single focus. Cumberland may have written *The West Indian* in order to indulge his feelings of superiority or self-righteousness, but we shall never know. And who cares? "Sentimentality," as Michael Tanner says, "deserves to be taken more seriously" (146). The evolution of a species mentality, "pity for all humanity" (A2), may be man's last chance on this ravaged planet (A7).

Appendix

Included in the appendix are the texts of two of the plays discussed above. The copy-text for the first of these, *The School for Lovers*, called "the model of the sentimental branch of the modern Comedy" (1793 ed., sig. B1r), is the Yale copy of the first edition (1762). The Larpent manuscript has not survived. Although Whitehead made desultory emendations of the text for his collected *Plays and Poems* (2 vols., 1774) the first edition represents most nearly the original conception of the play.

The copy-text for *Every One Has His Fault* is the Indiana University copy of the first edition (1793) supplemented by more than 150 unique readings of the Larpent manuscript (in the Huntington Library) that seem authorial.

The format of both plays has been modernized and normalized, (1) to make every sentence end with a full stop of some kind and the succeeding sentence begin with a capital letter, and (2) to eliminate the dash, to which eighteenth-century playwrights and compositors alike were lazily addicted. Swift observed in 1710 that "The first thing that strikes your Eye" about the new way of writing, "is the *Breaks* at the End of almost every Sentence, of which I know not the Use, only that it is a Refinement, and very frequently practis'd."

WILLIAM WHITEHEAD

The School for Lovers,
A Comedy
1762

PROLOGUE. As it was intended to have been SPOKEN

Success makes people vain. The maxim's true,
We all confess it – and not over new.
The veriest clown who stumps along the streets,
And doffs his hat to each grave cit he meets,
Some twelvemonths hence, bedaub'd with livery lace,   5
Shall thrust his saucy flambeau in your face.
Not so our Bard: tho' twice[1] your kind applause
Has, on this fickle spot, espous'd his cause:
He owns, with gratitude, th'obliging debt;
Has twice been favour'd, and is modest yet.   10
Plain Tragedy, his first adventurous care,
Spoke to your hearts, and found an echo there.
Plain Comedy to-night, with strokes refin'd,
Would catch the coyest features of the mind:
Would play politely with your hopes and fears,   15
And sometimes smiles provoke, and sometimes tears.
     Your giant wits, like those of old, may climb
Olympus high, and step o'er space and time;
May stride with seven-leagu'd boots, from shore to shore,
And, nobly by transgressing, charm you more.   20
Alas! our Author dares not laugh at schools,
Plain sense confines his humbler Muse to rules.
Form'd on the classic scale his structures rise,
He shifts no scenes to dazzle and surprize.
In one poor garden's solitary grove,   25

---

[1] *twice*: Whitehead's two earlier plays were tragedies. The first, *The Roman Father*, a free adaptation of Corneille's *Horace* (1639), was also his most successful. It opened at Drury Lane on 24 February 1750 with Garrick in the role of Horace's father, became part of the repertory, and was played regularly until 1795. Whitehead's second play, *Creusa, Queen of Athens*, was an adaptation of Euripides' *Ion*. It opened at Drury Lane on 20 April 1754 with Garrick in the role of Aletes, but only nine performances were required and after 1758–9 it was never revived. Horace Walpole, however, called it "the only new tragedy that I ever saw, and really liked" (*Horace Walpole's Correspondence with John Shute [et al.]*, ed. W. S. Lewis et al., New Haven: Yale University Press, 1973, p. 79).

Like the primaeval pair, his lovers rove.
And in due time with each transaction pass,
– Unless some hasty critic shakes the glass.[1]

[1] *glass*: hour glass.

Persons Represented

Sir JOHN DORILANT, a Man of Nice Honour, Guardian to Caelia.   Mr. GARRICK

MODELY,   Men of the Town.   Mr. PALMER

BELMOUR,   Mr. OBRIEN

An old Steward to Sir John Dorilant.   Mr. CASTLE

Footman to Sir John Dorilant.   Mr. FOX

Lady BEVERLEY, a Widow Lady, Mother to Caelia.   Mrs. CLIFF

CAELIA, Daughter to Lady Beverley, and Ward to Sir John.   Mrs. CIBBER

ARAMINTA, Sister to Sir John Dorilant.   Mrs. YATES

SCENE, a Garden belonging to Sir John Dorilant's House in the Country, with an Arbour, Garden Chairs, &c.

THE SCHOOL FOR LOVERS

ACT I [Scene i]

SCENE, *the Garden*

Enter ARAMINTA *with an affected Carelessness, and knotting,* MODELY *following*
MODELY. But madam!¹

ARAMINTA. But Sir! what can possibly have alarmed you thus? You see me quite
unconcerned. I only tell you in a plain simple narrative manner – (this plaguy
thread²) – and merely by way of conversation, that you are in love with
Caelia; and where is the mighty harm in all this?   5
MODELY. The harm in it, madam! Have I not told you a thousand and a
thousand times that you were the only woman who could possibly make me
happy?
ARAMINTA. Why aye, to be sure you have, and sworn a thousand and a
thousand oaths to confirm that affection.   10
MODELY. And am not I here now expressly to marry you?
ARAMINTA. Why that *too* is true. But – You are in love with Caelia.
MODELY. Bless me, madam, what can I say to you? If it had not been for my
attendance upon you, I had never known Caelia or her mother either, though
they are both my relations. The mother has since, indeed put some kind of   15
confidence in me; she is a widow you know –
ARAMINTA. And wants consolation! The poor orphan too, her daughter. Well,
charity is an excellent virtue. I never considered it in that light before. You are
vastly charitable, Mr. Modely.
MODELY. It is impossible to talk with you. If you will not do *me* justice, do it to   20
yourself at least. Is there any comparison betwixt you and Caelia? Could any
man of sense hesitate a moment? She has yet no character. One does not know
what she is, or what she will be; a chit, a green girl of fourteen or fifteen.
ARAMINTA. Seventeen³ at least. (I cannot undo this knot.)
MODELY. Well, let her be seventeen. Would any man of judgment attach himself   25

---

¹ Lines 1–64: these lines translate Fontenelle, *Le Testament*, I i quite literally, but with a
few changes noted below.
² *thread*: Araminta's difficulties in "knitting of knots for fancy-work" (*OED*), which
Samuel Johnson also failed to master, are Whitehead's invention.
³ *Seventeen*: Fontenelle's Caelia is fifteen.

to a girl of that age? O' my soul, if one was to make love to her, she would hardly understand what one meant.

ARAMINTA. Girls are not quite so ignorant as you may imagine, Mr. Modely. Caelia will understand you, take my word for it, and does understand you. As to your men of judgment and sense, here is my brother now. I take him to be full as reasonable as yourself, and somewhat older; and yet with all his philosophy, he has brought himself to a determination at last, to fulfill the father's will, and marry this green girl. I am sorry to tell you so, Mr. Modely, but he will certainly marry her.

MODELY. Let him marry her. I should perhaps do it myself, if I was in his place. He was an intimate friend of her father's. She is a great fortune,[1] and was given to him by will. But do you imagine, my dear Araminta, that if he was left to his own choice, without any bias, he would not rather have a woman nearer his own years? He might almost be her father.

ARAMINTA. That is true. But you will find it difficult to persuade me, that youth in a woman is so insurmountable an objection. I fancy, Mr. Modely, it may be got over. Suppose I leave you to think of it. (I cannot get this right.)   *Going*

MODELY. Stay, dear Araminta. Why will you plague me thus? Your own charms, my earnestness, might prove to you –

ARAMINTA. I tell you I don't want proofs.

MODELY. Well, well, you shall have none then. But give me leave to hope, since you have done me the honour to be a little uneasy on my account –

ARAMINTA. Uneasy! I uneasy! What does the man mean? I was a little concerned indeed to give you uneasiness by informing you of my brother's intended marriage with Caelia. But – (This shuttle bends so abominably.)

MODELY. Thou perplexing tyrant! Nay, you shall not go. May I continue to adore you! You must not forbid me that.

ARAMINTA. For my part I neither command nor forbid any thing. Only this I would have you remember: I have quick eyes. Your servant. (I wish this knotting had never come in fashion.)   *Exit* ARAMINTA

MODELY. Quick eyes indeed![2] I thought my cunning here had been a master piece. The girl cannot have told sure! And the mother is entirely on my side. They certainly were those inquisitive eyes she speaks of, which have found out this secret. Well, I must be more cautious for the future, and act the lover to Araminta ten times stronger than ever. One would not give her up till one was sure of succeeding in the other place.

Enter BELMOUR *from behind with a Book in his Hand*

BELMOUR. Ha! ha! ha! well said Modely!

MODELY (*starting*). Belmour! How the duce came you here?

BELMOUR. How came I here? How came you here, if you come to that? A man can't retire from the noise and bustle of the world, to admire the beauties of

---

[1] *a great fortune*: Fontenelle's Caelia is penniless. By endowing her with a fortune, Whitehead imposes a heavier burden on Sir John Dorilant's "delicacy" (II i 17) and makes the money itself block the course of true love (IV i 107–10).
[2] Lines 56–175: although it retains the plot outline (Modely to exploit Sir John's delicacy to win Caelia), this scene is entirely rewritten. No further notice will be taken of scenes that are entirely rewritten or entirely original.

the spring, and read pastoral in an arbour, but impertinent lovers must disturb his meditations. Thou art the errantest hypocrite, Modeley.

Throwing away the book

MODELY. Hypocrite! My dear friend, we men of gallantry must be so. But have a care, we may have other listeners for aught I know, who may not be so proper for confidantes.   *Looking about*   70

BELMOUR. You may be easy on that head. We have the garden to ourselves. The widow and her daughter are just gone in, and Sir John is busy with his steward.

MODELY. The widow, and her daughter! Why, were they in the garden?

BELMOUR. They just came into it, but upon seeing you and Araminta together,   75
they turned back again.

MODELY. On seeing me and Araminta? I hope I have no jealousies there too. However I am glad Caelia knows I am in the garden, because it may probably induce her to fall in my way, by chance, you know, and give me an opportunity of talking to her.   80

BELMOUR. Do you think she likes you?

MODELY. She does not know what she does.

BELMOUR. Do you like her?

MODELY. Why faith, I think I do.

BELMOUR. Why then do you pursue your affair with Araminta, and not find   85
some honourable means of breaking off with her?

MODELY. That might not be so expedient. I think Araminta the finest woman, and Caelia the prettiest girl I know. Now they are both good fortunes, and one of them I am resolved to have. But which?

BELMOUR. Your great wisdom has not yet determined. Thou art undoubtedly   90
the vainest fellow living. I thought you brought me down here now to your wedding?

MODELY. 'Egad I thought so too, but this plaguy little rustic has disconcerted all my schemes. Sir John, you know, by her father's will, may marry her if he pleases, and she forfeits[1] her estate if she marries any one else. Now I am   95
contriving to bring it about, that I may get her, and her fortune too.

BELMOUR. A very likely business, truly. So you modestly expect that Sir John Dorilant should give up his mistress, and then throw her fortune into the bargain, as an additional reward to the obliging man who has seduced her from him.   100

MODELY. Hum! Why I don't expect quite that. But you know, Belmour, he is a man of honour, and would not force her inclinations tho' he loved her to distraction. Come, come, he is quite a different creature from what you and I are.

BELMOUR. Speak for yourself, good Sir. Yet why should you imagine that her   105
inclinations are not as likely to fix upon him as you? He has a good person, and is scarce older than yourself.

MODELY. That shews your ignorance. I am ten years younger than he is. My dress and the company I keep, give a youth and vivacity to me, which he must always want. An't I a man of the town? O that town, Belmour! Could I but   110
have met these ladies there, I had done the business.

---

[1] *forfeits*: On the evidence of I i 98–9 it is Sir John who gets Caelia's estate if she refuses to marry him, but IV 1 9–11 throws doubt on this.

BELMOUR. Were they never there?

MODELY. Never. Sir Harry Beverley, the father of this girl, lived always in the country, and divided his time between his books and his hounds. His wife and daughter seldom mixed with people of their own rank, but at a horse-race, or a   115
rural visit. And see the effects! The girl, tho' she is naturally genteel, has an air of simplicity.

BELMOUR. But does not want sense.

MODELY. No, no! She has a devilish deal of that kind of sense which is acquired by early reading. I have heard her talk occasionally, like a queen in a tragedy,   120
or at least like a sentimental lady in a comedy, much above your misses of thirty in town, I assure you. As to the mother – But she is a character, and explains herself.

BELMOUR. Yes, yes, I have read her. But pray how came it to pass, that the father, who was of a different way of thinking in regard to party, should have   125
left Sir John guardian to his daughter, with the additional clause too, of her being obliged to marry him.

MODELY. Why that is somewhat surprizing. But the truth of the case was, they were thoroughly acquainted, and each considered party as the foible of the other. Sir Harry thought a good husband his daughter's best security for   130
happiness, and he knew it was impossible Sir John Dorilant should prove a bad one.

BELMOUR. And yet this prospect of happiness would you destroy.

MODELY. No, no, I only see farther than Sir Harry did, and would increase that happiness, by giving her a better husband.   135

BELMOUR. O! your humble servant, Sir.

MODELY. Besides, the mother is entirely in my interest, and by the by has a hankering after Sir John herself. "He is a sober man, and should have a woman of discretion for his wife, not a hoydening girl." 'Egad, Belmour, suppose you attacked the widow? The woman is young enough, and has an   140
excellent jointure.

BELMOUR. And so become your father-in-law.

MODELY. You will have an admirable opportunity tonight. We are going to have the fiddles you know, and you may dance with her.

       When musick softens, and when dancing fires![1]   145
Eh! Belmour!

BELMOUR. You are vastly kind to Sir John, and would ease him I find, of both his mistresses. But suppose this man of honour should be fool enough to resign his mistress, may not another kind of honour oblige him to run you through the body for deserting his sister?   150

MODELY. Why faith, it may. However, it is not the first duel I have fought on such an occasion, so I am his man. Not that it is impossible but he may have scruples there too.

BELMOUR. You don't think him a coward?

MODELY. I know he is not. But your reasoning men have strange distinctions.   155
They are quite different creatures, as I told you, from you and me.

BELMOUR. You are pleased to compliment. But suppose now, as irrational as you think me, I should find out a means to make this whole affair easy to you?

---

[1] Modely quotes Pope, *The Rape of the Lock* (1714), I 76.

MODELY. How do you mean?
BELMOUR. Not by attacking the widow, but by making my addresses in good   160
earnest to Araminta.
MODELY. I forbid that absolutely.
BELMOUR. What, do you think it possible I should succeed after the
accomplished Mr. Modely?
MODELY. Why faith, between you and me, I think not, but I don't chuse to   165
hazard it.
BELMOUR. Then you love her still?
MODELY. I confess it.
BELMOUR. And it is nothing upon earth but that insatiable vanity of yours,
with a little tincture of avarice, that leads you a gadding thus?   170
MODELY. I plead guilty. But be it as it will, I am determined to pursue my
point. And see where the little rogue comes most opportunely. I told you she
would be here. Go, go, Belmour, you must not listen to all my love scenes.
(*Exit* BELMOUR) Now for a serious face, a little upon the tragic. Young girls are
mighty fond of despairing lovers.   175

Enter CAELIA

CAELIA (*with an affected surprize*). Mr. Modely! Are you here?[1] I am come to meet
my mama. I did not think to find you here.
MODELY. Are you sorry to find me here, madam?
CAELIA. Why should I be sorry, Mr. Modely?
MODELY. May I hope you are pleased with it?   180
CAELIA. I have no dislike to company.
MODELY. But is all company alike? Surely one would chuse one's companions.
Would it have been the same thing to you, if you had met Sir John Dorilant
here?
CAELIA. I should be very ungrateful if I did not like Sir John Dorilant's   185
company. I am sure I have all the obligations in the world to him, and so
had my poor papa.   *Sighing*
MODELY. Whatever were your papa's obligations, his gratitude I am sure was
unbounded. O that I had been his friend!
CAELIA. Why should you wish that, Mr. Modely? You would have had a great   190
loss in him.
MODELY. I believe I should. But I might likewise have had a consolation for
that loss, which would have contained in it all earthly happiness.
CAELIA. I don't understand you.
MODELY. He might have left his Caelia to me.   195
CAELIA. Dear, how you talk!
MODELY. Talk, madam! O I could talk for ever, would you but listen to my
heart's soft language, nor cruelly affect to disbelieve when I declare I love
you.
CAELIA. Love me, Mr. Modely? Are you not in love with Araminta?   200
MODELY. I once thought I was.

[1] Lines 176–236. The scene follows Fontenelle closely, but Whitehead rearranges and
omits many lines. Fontenelle's Caelia is much more responsive to Modely's love-making
and much more suspicious of him: "Ecoutés," she says, "je vous crois. Vous seriés
inexcusable si vous me trompiés" ("It would be inexcusable for you to fool me, for I trust
you") (I iii).

CAELIA. And do lovers ever change?

MODELY. Not those who feel a real passion. But there are false alarms in love, which the unpractised heart sometimes mistakes for true ones.

CAELIA. And were yours such for Araminta?   205

MODELY (*looking earnestly at her*). Alas, I feel they were.

CAELIA. You don't intend to marry her then, I hope.

MODELY. Do you hope I should not marry her?

CAELIA. To be sure I do. I would not have the poor lady deceived, and I would willingly have a better opinion of Mr. Modely than to believe him capable of   210 making false protestations.

MODELY. To you he never could.

CAELIA. To me? I am out of the question. But I am sorry for Araminta, for I believe she loves you.

MODELY. If you can pity those who love in vain, why am not I an object of   215 compassion?

CAELIA. Dear Mr. Modely, why will you talk thus? My hand, you know, is destined to Sir John Dorilant, and my duty there does not even permit me to think of other lovers.

MODELY. Happy, happy man! Yet give me leave to ask one question, madam. I   220 dread to do it, tho' my last glimpse of happiness depends upon your answer.[1]

CAELIA. What question? Nay, pray speak, I entreat it of you.

MODELY. Then tell me, lovely Caelia, sincerely tell me, were your choice left free, and did it depend upon you only to determine who should be the master of your affections, might I expect one favourable thought?   225

CAELIA (*after some hesitation*). It – It does not depend on me.

MODELY. I know it does not, but if it did?

CAELIA. Come, come, Mr. Modely, I cannot talk upon this subject. Impossibilities are impossibilities. But I hope you will acquaint Araminta instantly with this change in your inclinations.   230

MODELY. I would do it, but I dare not.

CAELIA. You should break it first to Sir John.

MODELY. My difficulty does not lie in the breaking it. But if I confess my passion at an end, I must no longer expect admittance into this family, and I could still wish to talk to Caelia as a friend.   235

CAELIA. Indeed, Mr. Modely, I should be loath myself to lose your acquaintance; but – O here comes my mama, she may put you in a method.

Enter LADY BEVERLEY

LADY BEVERLEY. In any method, my dear, which decency and reserve will permit. Your servant, cousin Modely. What, you are talking strangely to this girl now? O you men!   240

MODELY. Your ladyship knows the sincerity of my passion here.

CAELIA (*with surprize*). Knows your sincerity?

LADY BEVERLEY. Well, well, what signifies what I know. You was mentioning some method I was to put you in.

CAELIA. Mr. Modely, madam, has been confessing to me that he no longer loves   245 Araminta.

---

[1] *one question*: This detail, for which there is no counterpart in Fontenelle, recalls Cibber, *Love's Last Shift*, V ii 110–14.

LADY BEVERLEY. Hum! Why such things may happen, child. We are not all able to govern our affections. But I hope if he breaks off with her, he will do it with decency.

MODELY. That, madam, is the difficulty.   250

LADY BEVERLEY. What! Is it a difficulty to be decent? Fie, fie, Mr. Modely.

MODELY. Far be it from me even to think so, madam, before a person of your ladyship's reserved behaviour. But considering how far I have gone into the affair –

LADY BEVERLEY. Well, well, if that be all, I may perhaps help you out, and   255
break it to Sir John myself. Not that I approve of roving affections, I assure you.

MODELY. You bind me ever to you. But there is another cause which you alone can promote, and on which my eternal happiness –

LADY BEVERLEY. Leave us, leave us, cousin Modely. I must not hear you talk   260
in this extravagant manner. (*Pushing him towards the scene, and then aside to him*) I shall bring it about better in your absence. [*To him*] Go, go, man, go. (*Exit* MODELY) [*Aside*] A pretty kind of fellow really. [*Aloud*] Now, Caelia,[1] come nearer, child: I have something of importance to say to you. What do you think of that gentleman?   265

CAELIA. Of Mr. Modely, madam!

LADY BEVERLEY. Ay, Mr. Modely, my cousin Modely.

CAELIA. Think of him, madam?

LADY BEVERLEY. Ay, think of him, child. You are old enough to think sure, after the education I have given you. Well, what answer do you make?   270

CAELIA. I really don't understand your ladyship's question.

LADY BEVERLEY. Not understand me, child? Why I ask you how you like Mr. Modely? What should you think of him as a husband.

CAELIA. Mr. Modely as a husband! Why surely madam, Sir John –

LADY BEVERLEY. Fiddle faddle Sir John! Sir John knows better things than to   275
plague himself with a wife in leading strings.

CAELIA. Is your ladyship sure of that?

LADY BEVERLEY. O ho! Would you be glad to have me sure of it?

CAELIA. I don't know what I should be glad of. I would not give Sir John a moment's pain to be mistress of the whole world.   280

LADY BEVERLEY. But if it should be brought about without giving him pain. Hey! Caelia –   *Patting her cheek with her fan*

CAELIA. I should be sorry for it.

LADY BEVERLEY. Hey day!

CAELIA. For then he must think lightly of me.   285

LADY BEVERLEY. What does the girl mean? Come, come, I must enter roundly into this affair. Here, here, sit down, and tell me plainly and honestly without equivocation or reservation, is Modely indifferent to you? Nay, nay, look me in the face. Turn your eyes towards me. One judges greatly by the eyes, especially in a woman. Your poor papa used to say that my eyes reasoned   290
better than my tongue. Well, and now tell me without blushing, is Modely indifferent to you?

---

[1] Lines 262–339: this scene retains only the plot outline and a few phrases (I i 330–4) of *Le Testament*, I v.

CAELIA. I fear he is not, madam, and it is that which perplexes me.
LADY BEVERLEY. How do you feel when you meet him?
CAELIA. Fluttered.
LADY BEVERLEY. Hum! While you are with him?   295
CAELIA. Fluttered.
LADY BEVERLEY. Hum! When you leave him.
CAELIA. Fluttered still.
LADY BEVERLEY. Strong symptoms truly!   300
CAELIA. When Sir John Dorilant talks to me, my heart is softened but not
perplexed. My esteem, my gratitude overflows towards him. I consider him as
a kinder father, with all the tenderness without the authority.
LADY BEVERLEY. But when Mr. Modely talks?
CAELIA. My tranquility of mind is gone. I am pleased with hearing what I   305
doubt[1] is flattery, and when he grasps my hand –
LADY BEVERLEY. Well, well, I know all that. Be decent, child. You need say no
more. Mr. Modely is the man.
                                                             Rising
CAELIA. But, dear madam, there are a thousand obstacles. I am afraid Sir John
loves me. I am sure he esteems me, and I would not forfeit his esteem for the   310
universe. I am certain I can make him an affectionate and an humble wife,
and I think I can forget Mr. Modely.
LADY BEVERLEY. Forget a fiddle! Don't talk to me of forgetting. I order you on
your duty not to forget. Mr. Modely is, and shall be the man. You may trust
my prudence for bringing it about. I will talk with Sir John instantly. I know   315
what you are going to say, but I will not hear a word of it. Can you imagine,
Caelia, that I shall do anything but with the utmost decency and decorum?
CAELIA. I know you will not, madam. But there are delicacies –
LADY BEVERLEY. With which I am unacquainted to be sure, and my daughter
must instruct me in them. Pray, Caelia, where did you learn this nicety of   320
sentiments? Who was it that inspired them?
CAELIA. But the maxims[2] of the world –
LADY BEVERLEY. Are altered, I suppose, since I was of your age. Poor thing,
what world hast thou seen? Notwithstanding your delicacies and your
maxims, Sir John perhaps may be wiser than you imagine, and chuse a wife of   325
somewhat more experience.
CAELIA. May he be happy wherever he chuses. But dear madam –
LADY BEVERLEY. Again. Don't make me angry. I will positively not be
instructed. Ay, you may well blush. Nay, no tears. Come, come, Caelia, I
forgive you. I had idle delicacies myself once. Lard![3] I remember when your   330
poor papa – He, he, he – But we have no time for old stories. What would you
say now if Sir John himself should propose it, and persuade the match, and yet
continue as much your friend as ever, nay more so, a nearer friend.
CAELIA. In such a case, madam –
LADY BEVERLEY. I understand you, and will about it instantly. B'ye Caelia.   335
O how its little heart flutters.   *Exit* LADY BEVERLEY

---

[1] *doubt:* fear (archaic and dialectical) (*OED*).
[2] *maxims:* Caelia's "maxims of the world" are not the worldly wisdom of *Le Testament*, II iii,
but "those delicate strokes of sentimental morality" (B4).
[3] *Lard:* appropriately recalling such unregenerate characters as Lady Graveairs (Cibber,
The Careless Husband, III i 158 above).

CAELIA. It does indeed. A nearer friend? I hardly know whether I should wish her success or not. Sir John is so affectionate. Would I had never seen Mr. Modely. Araminta too! What will she say? O I see a thousand bad consequences. I must follow her, and prevent them.   340

ACT II [Scene i]
SCENE *continues*

LADY BEVERLEY *and* MODELY

LADY BEVERLEY. Prithee don't teize me so. I vow, cousin Modely, you are
almost as peremptory as my daughter. She truly was teaching me decorum
just now, and plaguing me with her delicacies, and her stuff. I tell you Sir
John will be in the garden immediately. This is always his hour of walking:
and when he comes, I shall lay the whole affair before him, with all its   5
concatenation of circumstances, and I warrant you bring it about.
MODELY. I have no doubt, madam, of the transcendency of your ladyship's
rhetorick; it is on that I entirely rely. But I must beg leave to hint, that
Araminta already suspects my passion, and should it be openly declared,
would undoubtedly prevail that instant with her brother to forbid me the   10
house.
LADY BEVERLEY. Why, that might be.
MODELY. And tho' I told your daughter I did not care how soon it came to an
eclaircisment, yet a woman of your ladyship's penetration and knowledge of
the world, must see the necessity of concealing it, at least for a time. I beg   15
pardon for offering what may have even the distant appearance of instruction.[1] But it is Sir John's delicacy which must be principally alarmed with
apprehensions of her disregard for him. And I am sure your ladyship's
manner of doing it, will shew him where he might much better place his
affections, and with an undoubted prospect of happiness.   20
LADY BEVERLEY. Ay, now you talk to the purpose. But stay, is not that Sir John
coming this way? It is I vow, and Araminta with him. We'll turn down this
walk, and reason the affair a little more, and then I will come round the
garden upon him. (MODELY *takes her hand to lead her out*) You are very gallant,
cousin Modely.   *Exeunt*   25
Enter SIR JOHN DORILANT *and* ARAMINTA
ARAMINTA. What do you drag me into the garden for? We were private enough
where we were. And I hate walking.
SIR JOHN. Forgive me, my dear sister. I am restless everywhere. My head and
heart are full of nothing but this lovely girl.

---

[1] *offering ... instruction*: This suggests that Modely overheard I i 319–20, 327–8 and may
have been eavesdropping since his exit at I i 261.

141

ARAMINTA. My dear, dear brother, you are enough to spoil any woman in the   30
universe. I tell you again and again, the girl is a good girl, an excellent girl,
and will make an admirable wife. You must trust one woman in her
commendation of another. We are not apt to be too favourable in our
judgments, especially when there is beauty in the case.
SIR JOHN. You charm me when you talk thus. If she is really all this, how happy   35
must the man be who can engage her affections. But alas! Araminta, in
everything which regards me, it is duty, not love, which actuates her
behaviour. She steals away my very soul by her attentions, but never once
expresses that heart-felt tenderness, those sympathetic feelings.
ARAMINTA. Ha, ha, ha! O my stars! Sympathetic feelings! Why would you have   40
a girl of her age have those sympathetic feelings, as you call them! If she had,
take my word for it, she would coquet it with half the fellows in town[1] before
she had been married a twelvemonth. Besides, Sir John, you don't consider
that you was her father's friend; she has been accustomed from her infancy to
respect you in that light. And our father's friends, you know, are always old   45
people, grey beards, philosophers, enemies to youth, and the destruction of
gayety.[2]
SIR JOHN. But I was never such.
ARAMINTA. You may imagine so; but you always had a grave turn. I hated you
once myself.   50
SIR JOHN. Dear Araminta!
ARAMINTA. I did as I hope to live. For many a time has your aversion to dancing
hindered me from having a fiddle. By the by, remember we are to have the
fiddles to-night. But let that pass: As the case now stands, if I was not already
so near akin to you, you have the temper in the world which I should chuse in   55
a husband.
SIR JOHN. That is obliging, however.
ARAMINTA. Not so very obliging perhaps neither. It would be merely for my
own sake. For then would I have the appearance of the most obedient
sympathetic wife in the universe, and yet be as despotic in my government as   60
an eastern monarch. And when I grew tired, as I probably should do, of a
want of contradiction, why, I should find an easy remedy for that too. I could
break your heart in about a month.
SIR JOHN. Don't trifle with me. 'Tis your serious advice I want. Give it me
honestly as a friend, and tenderly as a sister.   65
ARAMINTA. Why I have done it, fifty times. What can I say more? If you will
have it again you must. This then it is in plain terms. But are you sure you are
heartily in love with her?
SIR JOHN. Pshaw!
ARAMINTA. Well then, that we will take for granted. And now you want to know   70
what is right and proper for you to do in the case. Why, was I in your place, I
should make but short work with it. She knows the circumstances of her
father's will. Therefore, would I go immediately to her, tell her how my heart

---

[1] *town*: the local market town. Caelia has "lived always in the country" (I i 113–14).
[2] *old people, grey beards, philosophers, enemies to youth, and the destruction of gayety*: This fine
definition of *alazon* expands one word, "un barbon," in *Le Testament*, II iii.

stood inclined, and hope she had no objections to comply, with what it is not
in her power to refuse.   75
SIR JOHN. You would not have me talk thus abruptly to her?
ARAMINTA. Indeed I would. It will save a world of trouble. She will blush
perhaps at first, and look a little aukward, (and by the by so will you too); but
if she is the girl I take her for, after a little irresolute gesture, and about five
minutes conversation, she will drop you a curtesy with the demure humility of   80
a Vestal, and tell you it shall be as you and her mama pleases.
SIR JOHN. O that it were come to that!
ARAMINTA. And pray what hinders it? Nothing upon earth but your consum-
mate prudence and discretion.
SIR JOHN. I cannot think of marrying her, till I am sure she loves me.   85
ARAMINTA. Lud, Lud! Why what does that signify? If she consents, is not that
enough?
SIR JOHN. Her gratitude may induce her to consent, rather than make me
unhappy.
ARAMINTA. You would absolutely make a woman mad.   90
SIR JOHN. Why, could you think of marrying a man who had no regard for you?
ARAMINTA. The case is widely different, my good casuistical brother; and
perhaps I could not – unless I was very much in love with him.
SIR JOHN. And could you then?
ARAMINTA. Yes I could. To tell you the truth I believe I shall.   95
SIR JOHN. What do you mean?
ARAMINTA. I shall not tell. You have business enough of your own upon your
hands.
SIR JOHN. Have you any doubts of Modely?
ARAMINTA. I shall keep them to myself if I have. For you are a wretched   100
counsellor in a love case.
SIR JOHN. But dear Araminta –
ARAMINTA But dear Sir John Dorilant, you may make yourself perfectly easy,
for you shall positively know nothing of my affairs. As to your own, if you do
not instantly resolve to speak to Caelia, I will go and talk to her myself.   105
SIR JOHN. Stay, Lady Beverley is coming towards us.
ARAMINTA. And has left my swain yonder by himself.
SIR JOHN. Suppose I break it[1] to her?
ARAMINTA. It is not a method which I should advise; but do as you please.
(*Aside*). I know that horrid woman's sentiments very exactly, and I shall be   110
glad to have her teized a little. [*To him*]. I'll give you an opportunity by leaving
you. And so adieu, my dear sentimental brother! (*To* LADY BEVERLEY *as she
enters*) We'll change partners if you please, madam.   *And then exit to* MODELY
LADY BEVERLEY (*aside, and looking after* ARAMINTA). Poor mistaken creature!
How fond the thing is! [*Aloud*] Your servant, Sir John.   115
SIR JOHN. Your ladyship's most obedient.
LADY BEVERLEY (*after some irresolute gesture on both sides*). I – I – have wanted an
opportunity of speaking to you, Sir John, a great while.
SIR JOHN. And I, madam, have long had an affair of consequence to propose to
your ladyship.   120

---

[1] *it*: Sir John's "resolve to speak to Caelia" (II i 104).

LADY BEVERLEY. An affair of consequence to me! O Lud! You will please to speak, Sir.

SIR JOHN. Not till I have heard your ladyship's commands.

LADY BEVERLEY (*looking languishingly*). What, must women speak first? Fie, Sir John! Well then, the matter in short is this. I have been long thinking how to 125 dispose of my girl properly. She is grown a woman you see, and tho' I who am her mother say it, has her allurements.

SIR JOHN. Uncommon ones indeed.

LADY BEVERLEY. Now I would willingly consult with you how to get her well married, before she is tainted with the indecorums of the world. 130

SIR JOHN. It was the very subject which I proposed speaking to you upon. I am sorry to put your ladyship in mind of a near and dear loss, but you remember Sir Harry's will.

LADY BEVERLEY. Yes, yes, I remember it very well. Poor man! It was undoubtedly the only weak thing he was ever guilty of. 135

SIR JOHN. Madam!

LADY BEVERLEY. I say, Sir John, we must pardon the failings of our deceased friends. Indeed his affection for his child excuses it.

SIR JOHN. Excuses it!

LADY BEVERLEY. Yes indeed does it. His fondness for her might naturally make 140 him wish to place her with a person of your known excellence of character. For my own part, had I died, I should have wished it myself. I don't believe you have your equal in the world. Nay, dear Sir John, 'tis no compliment. This I say might make him not attend to the impropriety of the thing, and the reluctance a gentleman of your good sense and judgment must undoubtedly 145 have to accede to so unsuitable a treaty. Especially as he could not but know there were women of discretion in the world, who would be proud of an alliance where the prospect of felicity was so inviting and unquestionable.

SIR JOHN (*who had appeared uneasy all the time she was speaking*). What women, madam? I know of none. 150

LADY BEVERLEY. Sir John! That is not quite so complaisant methinks, to our sex, I mean.

SIR JOHN. I beg your pardon, madam; I hardly know what I say. Your ladyship has disconcerted every thing I was going to propose to you.

LADY BEVERLEY. Bless me, Sir John! I disconcerted every thing? How pray? I 155 have been only talking to you in an open friendly manner, with regard to my daughter. Our daughter indeed I might call her, for you have been a father to her. The girl herself always speaks of you as such.

SIR JOHN. Speaks of me as a father?

LADY BEVERLEY. Why, more unlikely things have happened, Sir John. 160

SIR JOHN. Than what, madam?

LADY BEVERLEY. Dear Sir John! You put such peremptory questions. You might easily understand what one meant methinks.

SIR JOHN. I find, madam, I must speak plain at once. Know then, my heart, my soul, my every thought of happiness is fixed upon that lovely girl. 165

LADY BEVERLEY. O astonishing! Well, miracles are not ceased, that's certain. But every body, they say, must do a foolish thing once in their lives. And can you really and seriously think of putting Sir Harry's will in execution?

SIR JOHN. Would I could!

LADY BEVERLEY. To be sure the girl has a fine fortune.   170
SIR JOHN. Fortune! I despise it. I would give it with all my soul to any one who could engage me her affections. Fortune! Dirt.
LADY BEVERLEY. I am thunderstruck!
SIR JOHN (*turning eagerly to her*). O madam, tell me, sincerely tell me, what method can I possibly pursue to make her think favourably of me! You know   175
her inmost soul, you know the tender moments of address, the easy avenues to her unpractised heart. (*Grasping her hand*) Be kind, and point them out.
LADY BEVERLEY. I vow, Sir John, I don't know what to say to you. Let go my hand. You talked of my disconcerting you just now. I am sure you disconcert me with a witness. (*aside*) I did not think the man had so much rapture in   180
him. He squeezed my hand with such an emphasis! I may gain him perhaps at last.
SIR JOHN. Why will you not speak, madam? Can you see me on the brink of desperation, and not lend a friendly hand to my assistance?
LADY BEVERLEY (*aside*). I have it. [*Aloud*] Alas, Sir John, what signifies what I   185
can do! Can I answer for the inclinations of a giddy girl?
SIR JOHN. You know she is not such. Her innocent mind is yet untainted with the follies of her sex. And if a life devoted to her service, without a wish but what regards her happiness, can win her to be mine –
LADY BEVERLEY. Why that might go a great way with an unprejudiced mind.   190
But when a first passion has taken place.
SIR JOHN (*with amazement*). What do you mean?
LADY BEVERLEY. To tell you the truth, I am afraid the girl is not so untainted as you imagine.
SIR JOHN. You distract me. How? When? Whom can she have seen?   195
LADY BEVERLEY. Undoubtedly there is a man.
SIR JOHN. Tell me who, that I may – No, that I may give her to him, and make her happy whatever becomes of me.
LADY BEVERLEY (*aside*). That is generous indeed. So, so.
SIR JOHN. But 'tis impossible. I have observed all her motions, all her   200
attentions, with a lover's eye incapable of erring. Yet stay, has any body written to her?
LADY BEVERLEY. There are no occasions for letters, when people are in the same house together.
SIR JOHN. Confusion!   205
LADY BEVERLEY. I was going to offer some proposals to you, but your strange declaration stopped me short.
SIR JOHN. Your proposals? You? Are you her abetter in the affair? O madam, what unpardonable crime have I committed against you, that you should thus conspire my ruin? Have not I always behaved to you like a friend, a brother? I   210
will not call you ungrateful.
LADY BEVERLEY. Mercy on us! The man raves. How could it possibly enter into my head, or the girl's either, that you should have any serious thoughts of marrying her? But I see you are too much discomposed at present, to admit of calm reasoning. So I shall take some other opportunity. Friend! Brother!   215
Ungrateful! Very fine, truly! I hope, at least, you will not think of forcing[1] the

---

[1] *not think of forcing*: cf. I i 102.

poor girl's inclinations! Ungrateful indeed!   *Exit in a passion*
SIR JOHN. Not for the universe. Stay, madam. She is gone. But it is no matter. I
am but little disposed for altercation now. Heigh ho! Good heaven! Can so
slight an intercourse have effected all this? I have scarce ever seen them   220
together. O that I had been born with Belmour's happy talents of address.
Address! 'Tis absolute magick, 'tis fascination. Alas! 'Tis the rapidity of real
passion. Why did Modely bring him hither to his wedding? Every thing has
conspired against me. He brought him, and the delay of the lawyers has kept
him here. Had I taken Araminta's advice a poor fortnight ago, it had not been   225
in the power of fate to have undone me. And yet she might have seen him
afterwards, which would at least have made her duty uneasy to her. Heigh ho!
                        Enter ARAMINTA *and* MODELY
ARAMINTA (*entering*). I tell you, I heard them very loud! And I will see what is
the matter. O! here is my brother alone.
SIR JOHN (*taking her tenderly by the hand*). O Araminta! I am lost beyond   230
redemption.
ARAMINTA. Dear brother, what can have happened to you?
SIR JOHN (*turning to* MODELY). Mr Modely, you could not have intended it, but
you have ruined me.
MODELY (*alarmed*). I Sir John?   235
SIR JOHN. You have brought a friend with you, who has pierced me to the very
soul.
MODELY. Belmour!
SIR JOHN. He has stolen my Caelia's affections from me.
ARAMINTA (*looking slyly at* MODELY). Belmour!   240
MODELY (*aside*). This must be a mistake, but I'll humour it. [*Aloud*] It cannot be.
Who can have told you so?
SIR JOHN. Her mother has been this instant with me, to make proposals on the
subject.
MODELY. For Belmour!   245
SIR JOHN. She did not absolutely mention his name, but I could not mistake it.
For she told me the favoured lover was under the same roof with us.
MODELY (*a little disconcerted*). I could not have believed it of him.
ARAMINTA (*looking slyly again at* MODELY). Nor do I yet.
MODELY. There must certainly be some mistake in it. At the worst, I am sure I   250
can prevail so far with Belmour, as to make him drop his pretensions.
SIR JOHN (*sighing*). You cannot make her cease to love him.
MODELY. Time may easily get the better of so young a passion.
SIR JOHN. Never, never. She is too sincere, too delicately sensible.
MODELY. Come, come, you must not think so. It is not gone so far, but that it   255
may be totally forgotten. (*Aside*) Now for a master-stroke to clench the whole.
[*Aloud*] In the mean time, Sir John, I have the satisfaction of acquainting you,
that my affair, with Araminta's leave, draws very near a conclusion. The
lawyers have finished their papers, and I only now wait for perusal of them.
ARAMINTA (*aside*). Well said!   260
MODELY. I ordered the writings[1] to be laid upon your table.
ARAMINTA. (*aside*) What does he mean?

---

[1] *the writings*: the contract of marriage between Modely and Araminta.

SIR JOHN. Dear Mr. Modely, you shall not wait a moment for me. I will dispatch
them instantly. I feel the want of happiness too severely myself, to postpone it
in others. I leave you with my sister. When she names the day, you may   265
depend upon my concurrence.   *Exit* SIR JOHN

MODELY *and* ARAMINTA *look at one another for some time, then he speaks*

MODELY. I hope, madam, you are now convinced of my sincerity.
ARAMINTA. I am absolutely struck dumb with your assurance.
MODELY (*with an affected surprize*). Madam!
ARAMINTA. You cannot mean all this.   270
MODELY. Why not, madam?
ARAMINTA. Why, don't you know that I know –
MODELY. I cannot help a lady's knowledge or imaginations. All I know is, that it
is in your power to make me either the happiest or most miserable man in the
whole creation.   275
ARAMINTA. Well, this is astonishing.
MODELY. I am sorry, madam, that any unguarded behaviour of mine, any little
playful gallantries, should have occasioned surmises, which –
ARAMINTA. Serious, as I hope to live.
MODELY. Is it not enough to make one serious, when the woman one has   280
pursued for years, almost with adoration, is induced by mere appearances to
doubt the honourableness of one's intentions? Have you not heard me this
moment apply to your brother, even in the midst of his uneasiness? I little
expected where the difficulty would lie.
ARAMINTA. Well, well, poor thing. I won't teize it any longer. Here, there, take   285
my hand.
MODELY (*aside*). Duped, by Jupiter.[1] [*To her*] O my ever-lasting treasure! And
when – And when shall I be happy?
ARAMINTA. It shall depend upon yourself.
MODELY. To-morrow, then, my angel, be the day. O Araminta, I cannot speak   290
my transport. And did you really think that I was in love with Caelia?
ARAMINTA. Why, as a proof of my future sincerity, I must confess I did.
MODELY. I wonder how you could.
ARAMINTA. Come, come, there were grounds enough for a woman in love to go
upon.   295
MODELY (*taking her by the hand*). But you are now perfectly easy?
ARAMINTA (*pulling her hand from him*). Why, yes, I think I am. But what can my
brother mean about Belmour?
MODELY. It is some trick of the widow's.
ARAMINTA. I dare say she meant you.   300
MODELY. Possibly she might. You know her motives.
ARAMINTA. Yes, yes, her passion for my brother is pretty notorious. But the
wretch will be mistaken. To-morrow, you say?
MODELY. To-morrow, my adorable.
ARAMINTA. It shall be as you please. But my situation is so terribly aukward,   305
that I must break from you. Adieu!   *Exit* ARAMINTA
MODELY. Upon my soul she is a fine woman; and loves me to distraction. And

---

by Jupiter: Modely's counterpart in Garrick's *The Guardian*, London, 1759, p. 51, also
swears "by Jupiter."

what is still more, I most undoubtedly love her. I have a good mind to take her. Yet not to have it in my power to succeed in the other place, would call my parts in question. No, no; I must not disparage my parts neither. In order   310 to be a great character, one should go as near being a rogue as possible. I have a philosopher's[1] opinion on my side in that, and the practice of half the heroes and politicians in Europe.

[1] *philosopher*: Niccolò Machiavelli, whose formula for greatness is this: "those princes have done great things who have valued their promises little, and who have understood how to addle the brains of men with trickery" (Machiavelli, *The Chief Works*, trans. Allan Gilbert, 3 vols., Durham NC: Duke University Press, 1965, I 64).

ACT III [Scene i]
SCENE *continues*

BELMOUR (*alone*). Caelia in love with me! Egad the thing is not impossible. My friend Modely may have been a little mistaken. Sir John was very serious when he told me of it. And though I protested to him that I had never made the least advances, he still persisted in his opinion. The girl must have told him so herself. Let me recollect a little. She is always extremely civil to me; but   5 that indeed she is to every body. I do not remember any thing particular in her looks; but I shall watch them more narrowly the next time I see her. She is very handsome; and yet in my opinion, notwithstanding Modely's infidelity, Araminta is much the finer woman. Suppose – No, that will not do.

Enter MODELY

MODELY. So, so, Mr. Belmour, I imagined I should find you here. This is the   10 lover's corner. We have all had our reveries in it. But why don't you talk louder, man? You ought, at least, to give me my revenge in that. My soliloquies, you know, are easily over-heard.

BELMOUR. I never designedly over-heard them, Mr. Modely; nor did I make any improper use of the accident.   15

MODELY. Grave, very grave, and perfectly moral! And so this is all I am to have for the loss of my mistress. Heigh ho!

> Then I must be content to see her bless
> Yon happier youth.

BELMOUR. Your raillery is a little unseasonable, Mr. Modely. For to speak   20 plainly, I begin to suspect that this is some trick of yours, to dupe me as well as Sir John Dorilant.

MODELY. Upon my honour, no, if we must be serious. It may be a mistake, but not intended on my side, I can assure you. Come, come, if the girl really likes you, take her. If I should prove the happy man, give me joy, and there's an   25 end of it.

BELMOUR. I fancy you are used to disappointments in love, they sit so easy upon you. Or rather I should suppose, in this case, you are pretty sure of your ground.

MODELY. Neither, upon my soul; but a certain *Je ne scai quoy*,[1] a *Gayete de Coeur*,   30 which carries me above misfortunes. Some people call it vanity –

BELMOUR. And are not absolutely mistaken. But what becomes of Araminta all this while.

MODELY (*yawning*). I shall marry her, I believe, to-morrow.
BELMOUR. Marry her?   35
MODELY. Yes. Sir John is at this very moment looking over the settlements.
BELMOUR. I don't understand you.
MODELY. And yet it is pretty plain, methinks. I tell you I am to be married
    to-morrow. Was it not time to make sure of one mistress, when you was
    running away with the other?   40
BELMOUR. You know I have no such intentions. But are you really serious?
    Have you laid aside your designs upon Caelia?
MODELY. Not so, neither.
BELMOUR. What do you mean then by your marriage with Araminta? Why
    don't you unriddle this affair to me?   45
MODELY. Because it is at present a riddle to myself, and I expect Lady Beverley
    here every moment to resolve the enigma.
BELMOUR. Was it a scheme of her's?
MODELY. Certainly, and I partly guess it, but will not unbosom till I know it
    fully. Come, come, with all that gravity of countenance and curiosity, you   50
    must leave me instantly. The lady will be here, and the plot unravelled, and
    then –
BELMOUR. I shall expect to be satisfied.   *Exit*
MODELY. Ha! ha! ha! Or else you will fight me, I suppose. Why, so you may; and
    so may Sir John Dorilant too, and faith with some colour of reason. But my   55
    comfort is, that I have experience on my side, and if I survive the rencounter, I
    shall be a greater hero than ever amongst the ladies, and be esteemed in all
    companies as much a man of honour as the best of you.
                        Enter LADY BEVERLEY
LADY BEVERLEY. Dear cousin Modely, I am all over in an agitation. We shall
    certainly be discovered. That devil Araminta –   60
MODELY. What of her, madam?
LADY BEVERLEY. Is now with her brother talking so eagerly. Oh! I saw the
    villainous changes in her countenance. I would have given the world to have
    over-heard their conversation. Come, come, you must advise me instantly.
MODELY. Your ladyship must first let me into the secret. I am absolutely in a   65
    wood with regard to the whole affair. What is all this of Caelia and Belmour?
LADY BEVERLEY. Nothing, nothing at all; an errant dilemma of the foolish
    man's own making, which his impertinent sister will immediately clear up to
    him, and then all must out.
MODELY. But how came Belmour ever to be mentioned in the case?   70
LADY BEVERLEY. Dear, dear, he never was mentioned. I must confess that I
    was so provoked with Sir John's unnatural behaviour, that I could not help
    telling him that Caelia had a lover, and in the house too. Your situation with
    regard to Araminta made him never dream of you, and consequently all his
    suspicions turned on Belmour.   75

---

[1] *Je ne scai quoy*: Whitehead published a song entitled *The Je ne scai Quoi* in *A Collection of
Poems*, 3 vols., London: Robert Dodsley, 1748, II 260:

> Yes, I'm in love, I feel it now,
>   And *Caelia* has undone me;
> And yet I'll swear I can't tell how
>   The pleasing plague stole on me.

MODELY. But you did not say that that lover had made his addresses to Caelia?
LADY BEVERLEY. I don't know what I might say; for he used me like a Turk. But whatever I said I can unsay it again.
MODELY. Why, if I might venture to advise¹ a person of your ladyship's sagacity.
LADY BEVERLEY. O ay, with all my heart, cousin Modely. For though I say it   80
without vanity, that nobody has a more clear apprehension of things when the mental faculty is totally undisturbed; yet, when I am in a trepidation, nobody upon earth can be more glad of advice.
MODELY. Why, then, madam, to speak with reverence, I should hope your ladyship would see the necessity of keeping me as concealed as possible. It is   85
the young lady's passion, not mine, which must have the principal influence. Sir John Dorilant's peculiarity of temper is such –
LADY BEVERLEY. Yes, yes, he has peculiarity enough, that's certain.
MODELY. And it is there, madam, as the weakest part, that our attack will be the surest. If she confesses an inclination for me, not both the Indies, added to her   90
fortune, could induce him to marry her.
LADY BEVERLEY. That is honourable, however, cousin Modely. But he is a horrid creature, notwithstanding.
MODELY. I grant it, madam; but a failure in an improper suit may recall his reason, and, as he does not want understanding, teach him to search for   95
happiness where only it is to be expected.
LADY BEVERLEY. He! he! I am so angry with him at present, that I really believe I should refuse him.
MODELY. Your ladyship must not be too cruel.
LADY BEVERLEY. Why, I confess it is not in my nature; but bless me, here   100
they come. Let us run down this walk directly, for they must not see us together.   *Exeunt*

Enter ARAMINTA *and* SIR JOHN DORILANT

ARAMINTA. Come along, I say. You dragged me into the garden just now, and I will command in my turn. Talk to her you must, and shall. The girl has sense and spirit when she is disengaged from that horrid mother of her's; and I have   105
told her you wanted her, and in this very spot.
SIR JOHN. You cannot feel, Araminta, what you make me suffer. But sooner or later it must come to this, and therefore I will assume a resolution, and be rid of all my doubts at once.
ARAMINTA. I tell you, this nonsense about Belmour is merely a phantom of her   110
mother's own raising, to sound your intentions, and promote her own.
SIR JOHN. Thus far is certain, that Belmour disclaims all knowledge of the affair, and with an appearance of sincerity. But even that is doubtful. Besides, they are not his, but her inclinations² which give me any concern. It is the heart I require. The lifeless form, beauteous as it is, would only elude my grasp; the   115
shadow of joy, not the reality.
ARAMINTA [*aside*]. Dear, dear, that men had but a little common sense; or that one could venture to tell them what one knows of one's own sex! I have a good mind to be honest. [*Aloud*] As I live, the girl is coming. I'll speed her on the way. Courage, brother, Voila!   *Exit*   120
SIR JOHN. How shall I begin with her? What ideots are men when they have a

---

venture to advise: cf. II i 15–16.
not his, but her inclinations: cf. III i 84–5 above.

real passion! Ridiculous, beneath contempt. (*Walks about the stage*) Suppose – I will not suppose. The honest heart shall speak its faithful dictates, and if it fails – Why, let it.

Enter CAELIA

CAELIA (*with timidity*). Araminta tells me, Sir, that you had something to say to   125
me.

SIR JOHN. I have, madam. Come forward, Miss Beverley. Would you chuse to sit (*They sit down. After some irresolute gesture*[1]) You are not afraid of catching cold?

CAELIA. Not in the least, Sir.   130

SIR JOHN. I know sitting in the open air has that effect upon some people, but your youth and constitution – Did my sister say anything concerning the subject I would speak to you upon?

CAELIA. She only told me, Sir, that it was of moment.

SIR JOHN. It is of moment, indeed, Caelia. But you must not think that I am   135
angry.

CAELIA. Angry, Sir!

SIR JOHN. I don't mean angry. I am a little confused; but I shall recover myself presently. (*Rises, and* CAELIA *rises too*) Nay, pray sit, Miss Beverley. Whatever I feel myself, I would not disturb you. (*Returns to his seat, then after a pause, goes on*)   140
The affair I would speak to you upon is this: You remember your father perfectly?

CAELIA. And ever shall.

SIR JOHN. Indeed he was a good man, Miss Beverley, a virtuous man, and felt tenderly for your happiness. Those tears become you, and yet, methinks, I   145
would not provoke them. When he died, he left you to my care.

CAELIA. Which alone made his loss supportable.

SIR JOHN. Are you sincere in what you say?

CAELIA. I should be ungrateful indeed, if I was not.

SIR JOHN (*turning towards her*). Nay, you are sincerity itself. (*Taking her by the*   150
hand) O Caelia – But I beg your pardon. I am assuming a liberty I have no right to take, till you allow it.

CAELIA. Sir!

SIR JOHN. I see I have alarmed you. Retire Miss Beverley. I'll speak to you some other time. (*She is going*) Caelia, Miss Beverley, pray come back, my dear. I   155
am afraid my behaviour is rather too abrupt. Perhaps, too, it may displease you.

CAELIA. I can be displeased with nothing from you, Sir; and am ready to obey you, be your commands what they will.

SIR JOHN. Command, Caelia! That's a hard word.   160

CAELIA. I'm sorry it offends you.

SIR JOHN. You know best, Caelia, whether it ought to offend me. Would I could read the sentiments of your heart! Mine are but too apparent. In short, my dear, you know the purport of your father's will? Dare you fulfil it?

---

[1] irresolute gesture: cf. II i 79 above.

CAELIA. To the minutest circumstance. It is my duty.[1]   165
SIR JOHN. Ah, Caelia, that word *duty* destroys the obligation.
CAELIA. Sir!
SIR JOHN. I don't know how it is, but I am afraid to ask you the only question,[2]
which sincerely answered, could make me happy (*half aside*) or miserable.
CAELIA. Let me beg of you, Sir, to ask it freely.   170
SIR JOHN. Well then, is your heart your own? O Caelia, that hesitation confirms
my fears. You cannot answer in the affirmative, and have too much humanity
for what I feel, to add to my torments. Good God! And is it possible, that an
acquaintance of a few days, should entirely obliterate the attentive assiduity,
the tender anxieties which I have shewn for years! But I understand it all too   175
well. Mine were the aweful, though heart-felt attentions of a parent; his, the
sprightly address of a presuming lover. His easy assurance has won upon your
affections, and what I thought *my* greatest merit, has undone me.
CAELIA. You were so good, Sir, a little while ago, to pity my confusion; pity it
now, and whilst I lay my heart open before you, be again that kind, that   180
generous friend, which I have always found you.
SIR JOHN. Go on.
CAELIA. It is in vain for me to dissemble an ignorance of your meaning, nor
would I if I could. I own I have been too much pleased with Mr. Modely's
conversation.   185
SIR JOHN. Modely's?
CAELIA. Let me go on. His intended marriage with Araminta, gave him a
freedom in this family which it was not my business to restrain. His attentions
to my mother, and the friendly manner in which he executed some commis-
sions of consequence to her, gave him frequent opportunities of talking to me.   190
I will confess too, that his appearance and his manner struck me. But I was so
convinced of his real passion for Araminta, that I never dreamt of the least
attachment to me, till –
SIR JOHN. Till what? When? Modely? Why, he is to be married to my sister
to-morrow or next day.   195
CAELIA. I know it was so intended, but his behaviour this morning, and the
intercession of my mother, had, I own, won upon me strangely, and induced
me to believe that I only was the object of his pursuits.
SIR JOHN. I am thunderstruck!
CAELIA. My mother made me clearly perceive that the complexion of his   200
marriage would be an injury to Araminta. She told me too, sir, that you
yourself would be my adviser in the affair, and even persuade me to accept it.
SIR JOHN. O the malicious woman!
CAELIA. In that indeed I perceive she greatly erred. And I only mean this as a

---

[1] *It is my duty*: Fontenelle's Caelia is more articulate: "non, monsieur," she says, "j'avoue
qu'il ne falloit rien de plus que mon devoir pour me soumettre à vos volontés. Je croirois
désobéir à mon pere lui-même, si je vous désobéissois" ("Sir, I confess that duty alone
would make me responsive to your wishes. To disobey you would be like disobeying my
father himself") (III v).
[2] *only question*: cf. I i 219–20 above.

confession of what is past, and of what is now at an end for ever. For the   205
future, I give myself to your guidance alone, and am what you direct.
                                                        Giving her hand to him
SIR JOHN. Thou amiable softness! No, Caelia, however miserable I may be
myself, I will not make you so. It was your heart, not your hand I aspired to.
As the former has been seduced from me, it would be an injustice to us both to
accept of the latter. As to Mr. Modely, and Lady Beverley, I have not   210
deserved this treachery from them, and they shall both feel my resentment.
CAELIA. Sir!
SIR JOHN. She told me indeed there was a favoured lover, and my suspicions fell
very naturally upon Belmour. Nay, even now, nothing but that lovely
sincerity, which undoes me,[1] could make me credit this villainy of Modely. O   215
Caelia! What a heart have I lost!
CAELIA. You cannot, shall not lose it. Worthless as it is, 'tis yours, and only
yours, my father, guardian, lover, husband!   *Hangs upon him weeping*
                        Enter ARAMINTA
ARAMINTA. Hey day! What a scene[2] is here! What is the matter with ye both.
SIR JOHN. O sister! That angel goodness, that mirror of her sex, has ruined me.   220
ARAMINTA. Ruined you! How?
SIR JOHN. Nay, I am not the only sufferer. Modely is as false to you, as her
mother is to all of us.
ARAMINTA. I don't understand you.
SIR JOHN. You will too soon. My suspicions of Belmour were all a chimaera. It is   225
your impious Modely who has possession of her heart. To me she is lost
irrecoverably.   *Going*
ARAMINTA. Stay, brother.
SIR JOHN. I cannot, my soul's too full.   *Exit*
ARAMINTA. Pray, Miss Beverley, what is the meaning of all this?   230
CAELIA. I cannot speak.   *Throwing herself into a chair*
ARAMINTA. I'll be hang'd if this fellow Modely has not talked you into an
opinion, that he is in love with you. Indeed, my dear, your youth and
inexperience may lead you into strange scrapes. And that mother of yours is
enough to turn any girl's head in the universe. Come, come, unriddle this   235
affair to me.
CAELIA. Alas! madam, all I know is, that the only man I ever did, or ever can
esteem, despises me, and, I fear, hates me.
ARAMINTA. Hates you! He doats upon you to distraction. But pray, did Modely
ever make any serious addresses to you?   240
CAELIA. Alas! but too often.
ARAMINTA. The hypocrite! But I'll be even with him. And your mother, I
suppose, encouraged him? An infamous woman! But I know her drift well
enough.
                        Enter LADY BEVERLEY
LADY BEVERLEY. Where is my poor girl? I met Sir John Dorilant in such a   245

---

[1] *that ... sincerity ... undoes me*: Sir John's counterpart in *Le Testament* complains in the
same terms: "cette sincérité ... dussai-je en mourir" ("this sincerity could be fatal")
(III v).
[2] *What a scene*: Has Araminta been eavesdropping since III i 119?

furious way, that he seems to have lost all common civility. What have they done to you, child?

ARAMINTA. Done to her? What has your ladyship done to her? I knew your little artifices long ago, but –

LADY BEVERLEY. My artifices! Mrs. Araminta.   250

ARAMINTA. Your artifices, Lady Beverley; but they are all to no purpose. The girl has too good an understanding to be imposed upon any longer. And your boasted machinations are as vain and empty in their effect, as in their contrivance.

LADY BEVERLEY. What does the woman mean? But the loss of a lover, I   255
suppose, is an excuse for ill-breeding! Poor creature! If the petulancy of thy temper would let me, I could almost pity thee. The loss of a lover is no agreeable thing; but women at our time of life, Mrs. Araminta, must not expect a lasting passion.

ARAMINTA. Scarce any at all I believe, if they go a wooing themselves. For my   260
part, I have had the satisfaction of being sollicited however. And I am afraid my rustic brother never gave your ladyship's sollicitations even the slightest encouragement. How was it? Did you find him quite hard-hearted? No bowels of compassion for so accomplished a damsel?

CAELIA (*interposing*). Dear madam! Dear Araminta!   265

LADY BEVERLEY. Stand away, child. Desert, madam, is not always attended with success, nor confidence neither. There are some women so assured of their conquest, as even to disgust a lover on the very day of marriage.

ARAMINTA. Was my behaviour ever such?

LADY BEVERLEY. I really cannot say, Mrs. Araminta. But the world, you know,   270
is censorious enough, when a match is broken off so near its conclusion, as generally to charge the inconstancy of the lover on some defect in his mistress.

ARAMINTA. I defy him to produce any.

LADY BEVERLEY. And yet he has certainly left you, "Never, ah never to return."[1]   275

ARAMINTA. Insolent!

CAELIA (*interposing again*). Dear Araminta!

ARAMINTA. But your ladyship may be mistaken even in that too. I may find him at his sollicitations again; and if I do –

LADY BEVERLEY. You'll take him.   280

ARAMINTA. Take him! Daggers and poison sooner.

LADY BEVERLEY. Poor creature! Come, Caelia, words do but aggravate her misfortune. We only disturb her. You see, my dear, what are the effects of too violent a passion. It may be a lesson for your future conduct.

ARAMINTA. Look you, Lady Beverley, don't provoke me.   285

LADY BEVERLEY. Why, what will you do?

CAELIA (*interposing*). For heaven's sake, madam –

LADY BEVERLEY. I fancy, Mrs. Araminta, instead of quarrelling, we had better join forces. If we could but get this girl out of the way, we might both succeed.

ARAMINTA. You are a wicked woman.   290

LADY BEVERLEY. Poor creature! Shall I say any thing to my cousin Modely for you? You know I have great weight with him.

---

[1] "*Never . . . return*": Lady Beverley quotes [John Gay?], *The Quidnuncki's* (1724), where the words are spoken about a monkey (Gay, *Poetry and Prose*, ed. Vinton A. Dearing and Charles E. Beckwith, 2 vols., Oxford: Clarendon Press, 1974, I 286).

ARAMINTA. Yes, madam; you may tell him that his connections with you, have rendered him ridiculous; and that the revenge[1] of an injured woman is never contemptible.   *Exit* ARAMINTA   295

LADY BEVERLEY (*leading off* CAELIA *on the other side*). Poor creature! Come along, child.

[1] *revenge*: cf. Cibber, *Love's Last Shift*, IV i 105.

ACT IV [Scene i]
SCENE *continues*

SIR JOHN DORILANT (*alone*). This fatal spot, which draws me to it almost involuntarily, must be the scene of another interview. Thank heaven I have recovered my self. Nor shall any misery which I may suffer, much less any prospect of a mean revenge, make me act unbecoming my character.

Enter ARAMINTA

ARAMINTA. Well, brother, I hope you are resolved to marry this girl. 5

SIR JOHN. Marry her, my dear Araminta? Can you think it possible, that I should have so preposterous a thought? No, my behaviour shall deserve her, but not over-rule her inclinations. Were I to seize the tender opportunity of her present disposition, the world would ascribe it to her fortune. And I am sure my deceased and valuable friend, however kindly he meant to me in the 10 affair, never intended that I should make his daughter unhappy.

ARAMINTA. But I tell you she loves you: and you must and shall marry her.

SIR JOHN. Ah sister, you are willing to dispose of her any way. That worthless lover of yours still hangs about your heart, and I have avoided seeing him on your account, as well as Caelia's. 15

ARAMINTA. To shew how mistaken you are in all this, I have given him up totally. I despise and hate him. Nay I am upon the brink of a resolution to give myself to another. (SIR JOHN *shakes his head*) I am, I assure you. His friend, Mr. Belmour is by no means indifferent on my subject.

SIR JOHN. And is this revenge on yourself a proof of your want of passion for 20 him? Ah Araminta! Come, come, my dear, I own I think him unworthy of you, and would resent his usage to the utmost, did not I clearly perceive that it would appear mercenary in my self, and give real pain both to you and Caelia.

ARAMINTA. I actually don't know what to say to you. 25

SIR JOHN. You had better say nothing. Your spirits at present are too much alarmed. I have sent for Caelia hither. A short hour may determine the fates of all of us. I know my honourable intentions will give her great uneasiness. But it is my duty which exacts them from me. You had better take a turn or two in some other part of the garden. I see my steward coming this way. I may want 30 your assistance but too soon. *Exit* ARAMINTA

Enter STEWARD

157

SIR JOHN. Have you brought those papers I bade you look out?

STEWARD. Yes, Sir. But there is the gentleman within to wait upon your honour, concerning the estate you intended to purchase. It seems a mighty good bargain.   35

SIR JOHN. I cannot speak to him now.

STEWARD. Your honour always used to be punctual.

SIR JOHN. Alas! Jonathan, I may be punctual again to-morrow. Give me the papers. Did Miss Beverley say she would come to me?

STEWARD. Immediately, Sir. But I wish your honour would consider. Such   40
bargains as these do not offer every day.

SIR JOHN. Heigh ho!

STEWARD. It joins so conveniently too to your honour's own estate, within a hedge as I may say.

SIR JOHN. Prithee don't plague me.   45

STEWARD. Nay, 'tis not my interest, but your honour's. Tho' that indeed I may call my interest, for I am sure I love your honour.

SIR JOHN. I know thou dost, Jonathan, and I am too hasty, but leave me now. If the gentleman will do me the favour of staying all night, I may satisfy him in the morning. My head and heart are too full now for any business which   50
concerns my fortune.

STEWARD. Something goes very wrong with my poor master. Some love nonsense or other I suppose. I wish all the women were in the bottom of the sea, for my part.   *Exit* STEWARD

Enter LADY BEVERLEY *and* CAELIA

LADY BEVERLEY. I thought it requisite, Sir John, as I heard you had something   55
of importance to transact with my daughter, to wait upon you with her.

SIR JOHN. Was that necessary, madam? I begged the favour of Miss Beverley's company only.

LADY BEVERLEY. But a mother, you know, Sir John, who has a tender concern for her child –   60

SIR JOHN. Should shew it upon every occasion.

LADY BEVERLEY. I find, Sir John, there is some misunderstanding at present, which a woman of prudence and experience might be much better consulted upon, than a poor young thing, whose –

SIR JOHN. Not at all, madam. Caelia has all the prudence I require, and our   65
present conversation will soon be over.

LADY BEVERLEY. Nay, Sir John, to be sure I am not afraid of trusting my daughter alone with you. A man of your discretion will undoubtedly be guilty of no impropriety. But a third person sometimes, where the parties concerned are a little too much influenced by their passions, has occasioned very   70
substantial, and very useful effects. I have known several instances of it, in the course of my experience.

SIR JOHN. This, madam, will not be one of them. (*Walking aside*) How teizing!

LADY BEVERLEY. I find, Sir John, that you are determined to have your own way, and therefore I shall shew you by my behaviour that I know what good   75
manners require, tho' I do not always meet with the same treatment from other people.   *Exit* LADY BEVERLEY

SIR JOHN. Now, Caelia, we are alone, and I have many excuses to make to you for the impassioned sallies of our late conversation; which I do most sincerely. Can you pardon them?

CAELIA. Alas! Sir, 'tis I who ought to intreat for pardon.

SIR JOHN. Not in the least, madam. I have no blame to cast upon you for any part of your conduct. Your youth and inexperience, joined to the goodness of your heart, are sufficient apologies for any shadow of indiscretion which might appear in your behaviour. I am afraid mine was not so irreproachable. However, Caelia, I shall endeavour to make you all the amends in my power; and to shew you that it is your happiness, not my own, which is the object of my anxiety.

Your father's will is but too clear in its intentions. But the purity of his heart never meant to promote my felicity at the expence of yours. You are therefore, madam, entirely at liberty from this moment, to make your choice where you please. This paper will entitle you to that authority, and this will enable you to bestow your fortune where you bestow your hand. Take them, my dear! Why are you so disturbed? Alas, Caelia, I see too plainly the cause of these emotions. You only wish the happy man to whom your have given your heart, loved you as I do!

But I beg pardon; and will only add one caution, which my duty demands of me, as your guardian, your protector, and your father's friend. You have been a witness of Modely's transactions with my sister. Have a care therefore, Caelia. Be sure of his firm attachment before you let your own hurry you into a compliance. These papers give you up all power on my part; but as an adviser, I shall be always ready to be consulted.

CAELIA. My tears and my confusion have hitherto hindered me from answering, not the invidious suggestion which you have so cruelly charged me with. What friend, what lover have I, to engross my attentions? I never had but one, and he has cast me off for ever. O, Sir, give me the papers, and let me return them where my soul longs to place them.

SIR JOHN. No, Caelia, to accept them again, would impeach the justice of my whole proceeding. It would make it look like the mean artifice of a mercenary villain, who attempted to gain by stratagem what his merits did not entitle him to. I blush to think of it. I have performed my office. Be mistress of yourself, and let me fly from a combat to which I find myself unequal.   *Exit* SIR JOHN

CAELIA sits down, leaning her head upon her hand
Enter MODELEY *and* BELMOUR

MODELY. Hist! hist! He has just left her, and in a fine situation for my approaches. If you are not yet satisfied, I will make up all differences with you another time. Get into the arbour, and be a witness of my triumph. You shall see me, like another Caesar, Come, See, and Overcome.

                                      BELMOUR *goes into the arbour*
MODELY *comes forward, walks two or three turns by her, bowing as he passes, without being taken notice of, then speaks*

MODELY. If it is not an interruption, madam, when I find you thus alone –

CAELIA (*rising*). I would chuse to be alone.

MODELY. Madam!

CAELIA (*after a little pause*). In short, Mr. Modely, your behaviour to me of late is what I can by no means approve of. It is unbecoming your character as a man

of honour, and would be a stain to the ingenuous modesty of my sex for me to
suffer it.

MODELY. You surprize me, madam. Can the adoration of an humble love, the   125
timid advances of a man whom your beauty has undone, be such unpardonable offences?

CAELIA looks at him with indignation, and is going off

MODLEY (*catching hold of her, and falling upon his knees*). Nay, madam, you must not
leave me!

CAELIA. Rise, Sir, or I am gone this moment. I thought of flying from you, but   130
my soul disdains it. Know then, Sir, that I am mistress of myself, mistress of
my fortune, and may bestow my hand wherever my heart directs it.

MODELEY (*coming eagerly up to her*). My angel!

CAELIA. What do you mean?

MODELY. That you may make the most sincere of lovers, the happiest of   135
mankind. The addition of your fortune[1] will add splendor to our felicity; and
the frowns of disappointed love, only heighten our enjoyments.

CAELIA. Oh thou vile one! How does that cruel generous man who has rejected
me, rise on the comparison!

MODELY. Rejected you? Sir John Dorilant?   140

CAELIA. Yes, Mr. Modely, that triumph at least is yours. I have offered myself,
and been refused. My hand and fortune equally disdained. But may perpetual
happiness attend him, where'er his honest, honest heart shall fix!

MODELY. O, madam, your inexperience deceives you. He knows the integrity of
your mind, and trusts to that for recompence. His seeming disinterestedness is   145
but the surer method of compleating his utmost wishes.

CAELIA. Blasphemer, stop thy tongue. The purity of his intentions is as much
above thy malice, as thy imitation.

She walks to one side of the stage, and MODELY *stands disconcerted on the other*

Enter LADY BEVERLEY

LADY BEVERLEY. Well, child, what has the man said to thee? Cousin Modely,
your servant. You find our plot would not take. They were too quick upon us.   150
Hey day! What has been doing here?

MODELY. O, madam, you are my only refuge. A wretch on the brink of despair
flies to you for protection. That amiable creature is in full possession of herself
and fortune, and yet rejects my tenderest sollicitations.

LADY BEVERLEY. Really! What is all this? Tell me, Caelia, has the man actually   155
given up all right and title to thee, real and personal? Come, come, I must be a
principal actress, I find, in this affair. Decency and decorum require it. Tell
me, child, is it so?

CAELIA. Sir John Dorilant, madam, with a generosity peculiar to himself, (cruel
generosity!) has cancelled every obligation which could confine my choice.   160
These papers confirm the freedom he has given me, and rob me of all future
comfort.

LADY BEVERLEY. Indeed! I did not expect this of him; but I am heartily glad of
it. Give *me* the papers, child.

CAELIA. No, madam! Useless as they are, they are yet my own.   165

---

[1] *fortune*: cf. I i 96 above.

LADY BEVERLEY. Useless? What do you mean? Has the base man laid any other embargo on thee, child.

CAELIA. I cannot bear, madam, even from you, to hear Sir John Dorilant treated with disrespect. Useless! Yes, they shall be useless. Thus, thus I tear them into atoms, and disdain a liberty which but too justly reproaches *my* 170 conduct. Your advice, madam, has already made me miserable, but it shall not make me ungrateful or unjust.   *Exit* CAELIA

LADY BEVERLEY. I am astonished. I never saw the girl in such a way before. Why this is errant disobedience, cousin Modely. I must after her, and know the bottom of it. Don't despair.   *Exit* LADY BEVERLEY 175

BELMOUR (*coming out of the arbour*). Come, See, Overcome! O poor Caesar!

MODELY (*humming a tune*). You think I am disconcerted now?

BELMOUR. Why really I should think something of that kind.

MODELY. You never were more mistaken in your life. Egad 'tis a spirited girl. She and Sir John Dorilant were certainly born for one another. I have a good 180 mind to take compassion of them, and let them come together. They must and shall be man and wife, and I will e'en go back to Araminta.

BELMOUR. Thou hast a most astonishing assurance.

MODELY. Hush! She is coming this way. Get into your hole again and be dumb. Now you shall see a scene of triumph indeed.   185

BELMOUR. Have a care, Caesar, you have the Britons to deal with.   *Retires*
                          Enter ARAMINTA

ARAMINTA [*aside*]. What, are they gone, and my wretch here by himself? O that I could dissemble a little! I will, if my heart bursts for it. [*Aloud*] O, Mr. Modely, I am half ashamed to see you; but my brother has signed those odious writings.[1]   190

MODELY. Then thus I seize my charmer.

ARAMINTA. Agreeable rascal! Be quiet, can't you. You think one so forward now.

MODELY. I cannot, will not be restrained, when the dear object of my wishes meets me with kind compliance in her eyes and voice! To-morrow. 'Tis an age. 195 Why should we wait for that?

> To-night, my angel, to-night may make us one,
> And the fair prospect of our halcyon days
> Even from this hour begin.

ARAMINTA [*aside*]. Who would not think this fellow, with his blank verse now, 200 was in earnest? But I know him thoroughly. [*Aloud*] Indeed Mr. Modely, you are too pressing. Marriage is a serious thing. Besides, you know, this idle bustle betwixt my brother and Caelia, which you seem to think me ignorant of, and which you, in some measure, tho' undesignedly I dare say, have occasioned, may obstruct us a little.   205

MODELY. Not at all, my dear; an amusement *en passant*; the meer raillery of gallantry on my side, to oblige her impertinent mother (who, you know, has a *penchant* for Sir John herself) was the whole insignificant business. Perhaps, indeed, I was somewhat blameable in it.

ARAMINTA. Why really I think so, in your situation.[2] But are you sure it went no 210 farther? Nothing else passed between you?

---

[1] *writings*: cf. II i 262 above.   [2] *in your situation*: engaged to marry Araminta.

MODELY. Nothing in nature.

ARAMINTA. Dear me, how mistaken people are. I cannot say that I believed it; but they told me, that you had actually proposed to marry her, that the girl was near consenting, and that the mother was your friend in the affair.   215

MODELY. The mere malice, and invention of Lady Beverley.

ARAMINTA. And there is not a word of truth in it then?

MODELY. Not a syllable. You know my soul is yours.

ARAMINTA. O thou villain! I thought to have kept my temper, and to have treated you with the contempt you deserve; but this insolence is intolerable.   220
Can you imagine that I am a stranger to your proceedings, a deaf, blind ideot? O I could tear this foolish heart, which, cheated by its passion, has encouraged such an insult. How, how have I deserved this treatment?

Bursting into tears

MODELY (*greatly alarmed*). By holy faith, by every power above, you, and you only are the passion of my soul! May every curse –   225

ARAMINTA. Away, deceiver. These tears are the tears of resentment. My resolution melts not in my eyes. 'Tis fixed, unalterable! You might imagine from the gayety of my temper, that it had its levity too. But know, Sir, that a woman who has once been duped, defies all future machinations.

MODELY. Hear me, madam. Nay, you shall hear me.   230

ARAMINTA. Shall! Insufferable insolence! Go, Sir. For any thing which regards me, you are as free as air, free as your licentious principles.[1] Nor shall a thought of what I once esteemed you, disturb my future quiet. There are men who think me not contemptible, and under whose protection I may shelter my disgrace. Unhand me. This is the last time I shall probably ever see you; and I   235
may tell you in parting, that you have used me cruelly; and that Caelia knows you as perfectly as I do. *Exit* ARAMINTA. MODELY *stands confounded*

Enter BELMOUR

BELMOUR. Caesar shamed! And well he may i'faith. Why, man, what is the matter with you? Quite dumb? Quite confounded? Did not I always tell you that you loved her?   240

MODELY. I feel it sensibly.

BELMOUR. And I can tell you another secret.

MODELY. What's that?

BELMOUR. That she loves you.

MODELY. O that she did!   245

BELMOUR. Did! Every word, every motion of passion through her whole conversation betrayed it involuntarily. I wish it had been otherwise.

MODELY. Why?

BELMOUR. Because I had some thoughts of circumventing you. But I find it will be vain. Therefore pursue her properly, and she is yours.   250

MODELY. O never, Belmour, never. I have sinned beyond a possibility of pardon. That she did love me, I have a thousand proofs, which like a brainless ideot I wantonly trifled with. What a pitiful rascal have I made myself?

BELMOUR. Why in that I agree with you. But don't despair, man. You may still be happier than you deserve.   255

MODELY. With what face can I approach her? Every circumstance of her former

---

[1] *licentious principles*: cf. Cibber, *The Careless Husband*, III i 536–7.

affection, now rises in judgment against me. O Belmour! She has taught me to blush.

BELMOUR. And I assure you it becomes you mightily.

MODELY. Where can I apply? How do I address her? All that I can possibly do,   260
will only look like a mean artificial method, of patching up my other disappointment.

BELMOUR. More miracles still! She has not only taught you to blush, but has absolutely made a man of honour of you!

MODELY. Raillery is out of season.   265

Enter a SERVANT

SERVANT. Mrs. Araminta, Sir, desires to speak with you.

MODELY (*eagerly*). With me?

SERVANT. No, Sir, with Mr. Belmour.

BELMOUR. With me?

SERVANT. Yes, Sir.   270

BELMOUR. Where is she?

SERVANT. In the close walk by the house, Sir.

BELMOUR. And alone?

SERVANT. Entirely, Sir.

BELMOUR. I wait upon her this instant.   275

MODELY. Belmour, you shall not stir.

BELMOUR. By my faith but I will, Sir.

MODELY. She said there were men to whom she could fly for protection. By my soul she intends to propose herself to you.

BELMOUR. And if she does, I shall certainly accept her offer.   280

MODELY. I'll cut your throat if you do.

BELMOUR. And do you think to fright me by that? I fancy I can cut throats as well as other people. Your servant. If I cannot succeed for myself, I'll speak a good word for you.   *Exit* BELMOUR

MODELY. What can this mean? I am upon thorns till I know the event. I must   285
watch them. No, that is dishonest. Dishonest! How virtuous does a real passion make one! Heigh ho! (*Walks about in disorder*) He seems in great haste to go to her. He has turned into the walk already. That abominable old fashioned cradle work[1] makes the hedges so thick, there is no seeing through them. An open lawn has ten thousand times the beauty, and is kept at less   290
expence by half. (*Stumbling against one of the garden chairs*) These cursed unnatural chairs are always in the way too. What a miserable dog am I? I would give an arm to know what they are talking about. We talk of female coquettes! By my soul we beat them at their own weapons! Stay. One stratagem I may yet put in practice, and it is an honest one. The thought was   295
lucky. I will about it instantly. Poor Modely! How has thy vanity reduced thee?[2]

---

[1] *cradle work*: "a garden walk over-arched with clipped yew" (*OED*).
[2] *vanity reduced thee*: cf. Cibber, *The Careless Husband*, IV i 179–80.

ACT V [Scene i]

ARAMINTA *and* BELMOUR

ARAMINTA. You find, Mr. Belmour, that I have seen your partialities, and like a woman of honour I have confessed my own. You behaviour to your friend is generous beyond comparison, and I could almost join in the little stratagem you propose, merely to see if he deserves it.

BELMOUR. Indeed, madam, you mistake him utterly. Vanity is his ruling vice.   5
An idle affectation of success among the ladies, which makes fools admire, and boys envy him, is the master passion of his giddy heart. The severe checks he has met with to-day, have sufficiently opened his understanding; and the real possession of one valuable woman, whom he dreads to lose, will soon convince him how despicable his folly has made him.   10

ARAMINTA. I am afraid, Mr. Belmour, a man who has half his life been pursuing bubbles, without perceiving their insignificance, will be easily tempted to resume the chace. The possession of one reality will hardly convince him that the rest were shadows. And a woman must be an ideot indeed, who thinks of fixing a man to herself after marriage, whom she could not secure before it.   15
To begin with insensibility, O fie, Mr. Modely.

BELMOUR. You need not fear it, madam; his heart —

ARAMINTA. Is as idle as our conversation on the subject. I beg your pardon for the comparison; as I do, for having sent for you in this manner. But I thought it necessary that both you and Mr. Modely should know my real sentiments,   20
undisguised by passion.

BELMOUR. And may I hope you will concur in my proposal?

ARAMINTA. I don't know what to say to it. It is a piece of mummery which I am ill suited for at present. But if an opportunity should offer, I must confess I have enough of the woman in me, not to be insensible to the charms of an   25
innocent revenge. But this other intricate business, if you can assist me in that, you will oblige me beyond measure. There are two hearts, Mr. Belmour, worthy to be united! Had my brother a little less honour, and she a little less sensibility — But I know not what to think of it.

BELMOUR. In that, madam, I can certainly assist you.   30

ARAMINTA. How, dear Mr. Belmour?

BELMOUR. I have been a witness, unknown to Caelia, to such a conversation,[1] as will clear up every doubt Sir John can possibly have.

[1] *conversation*: cf. IV i 117–71.

164

ARAMINTA. You charm me when you say so. As I live, here comes my brother.
Stay. Is not that wretch Modely with him? He is actually. What can his   35
assurance be plotting now? Come this way, Mr. Belmour. We will watch them
at a distance, that no harm may happen between them, and talk to the girl
first! The monster!   *Exeunt*

Enter SIR JOHN DORILANT *and* MODELY

MODELY (*entering and looking after* ARAMINTA *and* BELMOUR). They are together
still! But let me resume my nobler self.   40
SIR JOHN. Why will you follow me, Mr. Modely? I have purposely avoided you.
My heart swells with indignation. I know not what may be the consequence.
MODELY. Upon my honour, Sir John –
SIR JOHN. Honour, Mr. Modely! 'tis a sacred word. You ought to shudder when
you pronounce it. Honour has no existence but in the breast of truth. 'Tis the   45
harmonious result of every virtue combined. You have sense, you have
knowledge; but I can assure you, Mr. Modely, tho' parts and knowledge,
without the dictates of justice, or the feelings of humanity, may make a bold
and mischievous member of society even courted by the world, they only in
my eye, make him more contemptible.   50
MODELY. This I can bear, Sir John, because I have deserved it.
SIR JOHN. You may think, perhaps, it is only an idle affair with a lady, what half
mankind are guilty of, and what the conceited wits of your acquaintance will
treat with raillery. Faith with a woman! Ridiculous! But let me tell you, Mr.
Modely, the man who even slightly deceives a believing and trusting woman,   55
can never be a man of honour.
MODELY. I own the truth of your assertions. I feel the aweful superiority of your
real virtue. Nor should any thing have dragged me into your presence, so
much I dreaded it, but the sincerest hope of making you happy.
SIR JOHN. Making me happy, Mr. Modely! You have put it out of your own   60
power. (*Walks from him, then turns to him again*) You mean, I suppose, by a
resignation of Caelia to me.
MODELY. Not of Caelia only, but her affections.
SIR JOHN. Vain and impotent proposal!
MODELY. Sir John, 'tis not a time for altercation. By all my hopes of bliss here   65
and hereafter, you are the real passion of her soul. Look not so unbelieving: by
heaven 'tis true. And nothing but an artful insinuation of your never intending
to marry her, and even concurring in our affair, could ever have made her
listen one moment to me.
SIR JOHN. Why do I hear you? O Mr. Modely, you touch my weakest part.   70
MODELY. Cherish the tender feelings, and be happy.
SIR JOHN. Is it possible that amiable creature can think and talk tenderly of me?
I know her generosity; but generosity is not the point.
MODELY. Believe me, Sir, 'tis more; 'tis real unaffected passion. Her innocent
soul speaks through her eyes the most honest dictates of her heart. In our last   75
conference, notwithstanding her mother's commands; notwithstanding, what
I blush to own, my utmost ardent solicitations to the contrary, she persisted in
her integrity, tore the papers which left her choice free, and treated us with an
indignation which added charms to virtue.
SIR JOHN. O these flattering sounds! Would I could believe them!   80
MODELY. Belmour, as well as myself, and Lady Beverley, was a witness to the

truth of them. I thought it my duty to inform you, as I knew your delicacy
with regard to her. And indeed I would in some measure endeavour to repair
the injuries I have offered to your family, before I leave it for ever. O Sir John,
let not an ill-judged nicety debar you from a happiness, which stands with   85
open arms to receive you. Think what my folly has lost in Araminta; and,
when your indignation at the affront is a little respited, be blest yourself, and
pity me. (*As he goes out, he still looks after* ARAMINTA *and* BELMOUR) I don't see
them now; but I will go round that way to the house.   *Exit* MODELY
SIR JOHN. What can this mean? He cannot intend to deceive me; he seems too   90
sincerely affected. I must, I will believe him. The mind which suffers[1]
injustice, is half guilty of it itself. Talks tenderly of me? Tore the papers?
Treated them with indignation? Heavens! What a flow of tender joy comes
over me! Shall Caelia then be mine? How my heart dances! O! I could be
wondrous foolish! Well, Jonathan.   95
                           Enter STEWARD
STEWARD. The gentleman, Sir –
SIR JOHN. What of the gentleman? I am ready for any thing.
STEWARD. Will wait upon your honour to-morrow, as you are not at leisure.
SIR JOHN. With all my heart. Now or then, whenever he pleases.
STEWARD. I am glad to see your honour in spirits.   100
SIR JOHN. Spirits! Jonathan! I am as light as air. Make a thousand excuses to
him. But let it be to-morrow, however, for I see Lady Beverley coming this
way.
STEWARD. Heavens bless his good soul! I love to see him merry. *Exit* SERVANT
                           Enter LADY BEVERLEY
LADY BEVERLEY. If I don't interrupt you, Sir John –   105
SIR JOHN. Interrupt me, madam? 'Tis impossible.
LADY BEVERLEY. For I would not be guilty of an indecorum, even to you.
SIR JOHN. Come, come, Lady Beverley, these little bickerings must be laid
aside. Give me your hand, lady. (*Kissing it*) Now we are friends. How does
your lovely daughter?   110
LADY BEVERLEY. You are in mighty good humour, Sir John. Perhaps every
body may not be so.
SIR JOHN. Every body must be so, madam, where I come: I am joy itself.

          The jolly god that leads the jocund hours!

LADY BEVERLEY (*aside*). What is come to the man? Whatever it is, I shall damp   115
it presently. [*To him*] Do you chuse to hear what I have to say, Sir John?
SIR JOHN. You can say nothing, madam, but that you consent, and Caelia is my
own. Yes, you yourself have been a witness to her integrity. Come, indulge
me, Lady Beverley. Declare it all, and let me listen to my happiness.
LADY BEVERLEY. I shall declare nothing, Sir John, on that subject. What I   120
have to say is of very different import. In short, without circumlocution, or
any unnecessary embarrassment to entangle the affair, I and my daughter are
of an opinion, that it is by no means proper for us to continue any longer in
your family.

---

[1] *suffers*: allows to exist, puts up with (archaic and dialectal) (*OED*).

SIR JOHN. Madam!   125
LADY BEVERLEY. This is what I had to declare, Sir John.
SIR JOHN. Does Caelia, madam, desire to leave me?
LADY BEVERLEY. It was a proposal of her own.
SIR JOHN. Confusion.
LADY BEVERLEY. And a very sensible one too, in my opinion. For when people   130
are not easy together, as might be expected, I know no better remedy than
parting.
SIR JOHN (aside). Sure, this is no trick of Modely's, to get her away from me? He
talked too, himself, of leaving my family. I shall relapse again.
LADY BEVERLEY. I find, Sir John, you are somewhat disconcerted: but, for my   135
part –
SIR JOHN. O torture!
LADY BEVERLEY. I say, for my part, Sir John, it might have been altogether as
well, perhaps, if we had never met.
SIR JOHN. I am sorry, madam, my behaviour has offended you, but –   140
          Enter ARAMINTA, CAELIA, *and* BELMOUR
ARAMINTA (to CAELIA as she enters). Leave the house indeed! Come, come, you
shall speak to him. What is all this disorder for? Pray, brother, has any thing
new happened? (Aside to BELMOUR) That wretch has been before-hand with us.
LADY BEVERLEY. Nothing at all, Mrs. Araminta. I have only made a very
reasonable proposal to him, which he is pleased to treat with his and your   145
usual incivility.
SIR JOHN. You wrong us, madam, with the imputation. (After a pause, and some
irresolution,[1] he goes up to CAELIA) I thought, Miss Beverley, I had already given
up my authority, and that you were perfectly at liberty to follow your own
inclinations. I could have wished, indeed, to have still assisted you with my   150
advice. And I flattered myself that my presence would have been no restraint
upon your conduct. But I find it is otherwise. My very roof is grown irksome to
you, and the innocent pleasure I received in observing your growing virtues, is
no longer to be indulged to me.
CAELIA. O Sir, put not so hard a construction upon what I thought a blameless   155
proceeding. Can it be wondered at, that I should fly from you, who has twice[1]
rejected me with disdain?
SIR JOHN. With disdain, Caelia?
CAELIA. Who has withdrawn from me even his parental tenderness, and driven
me to the hard necessity of avoiding him, lest I should offend him farther.   160
   I know how much my inexperience wants a faithful guide. I know what cruel
censures a malicious world will pass upon my conduct; but I must bear them
all. For he who might protect me from myself, protect me from the insults of
licentious tongues, abandons me to fortune.
SIR JOHN. O Caelia! Have I, have I abandoned thee? Heaven knows my inmost   165
soul, how did it rejoice but a few moments ago, when Modely told me that
your heart was mine!
ARAMINTA. Modely! Did Modely tell you so? Do you hear that, Mr. Belmour?
SIR JOHN. He did, my sister, with every circumstance which could increase his
own guilt, and her integrity.   170

---

[1] *some irresolution*: cf. III i 127 above.   [2] *twice*: III i 206; IV i 107.

ARAMINTA. That was honest, however.

SIR JOHN. I thought it so, and respected him accordingly. O he breathed comfort to a despairing wretch! But now a thousand thousand doubts crowd in upon me. He leaves my house this instant; nay, may be gone already. Caelia too is flying from me, perhaps to join him, and with her happier lover, 175 smile at my undoing!

CAELIA. I burst with indignation! Can I be suspected of such treachery? Can you, Sir, who know my every thought, harbour such a suspicion? O madam,[1] this contempt have you brought upon me. A want of deceit was all the little negative praise I had to boast of, and that is now denied me. 180

Leans on LADY BEVERLEY

LADY BEVERLEY. Come away, child.

CAELIA. No, madam. I have a harder task still to perform. (*Comes up to Sir John*). To offer you my hand again[1] under these circumstances, thus despicable as you have made me, may seem an insult. But I mean it not as such. O Sir, if you ever loved my father, in pity to my orphan state, let me not leave you. Shield 185 me from the world, shield me from the worst of misfortunes, your own unkind suspicions.

ARAMINTA. What fooling is here? Help me, Mr. Belmour. There, take her hand. And now let it go if you can.

SIR JOHN (*grasping her hand*). O Caelia. May I believe Modely? Is your heart 190 mine?

CAELIA. It is, and ever shall be.[1]

SIR JOHN (*turning to* CAELIA). Transporting extacy!

LADY BEVERLEY. I should think, Sir John, a mother's consent – Tho' Mrs. Araminta, I see, has been so very good to take that office upon herself. 195

SIR JOHN. I beg your pardon, madam. My thoughts were too much engaged. But may I hope for your concurrence?

LADY BEVERLEY. I don't know what to say to you. I think you have bewitch'd the girl amongst you.

ARAMINTA. Indeed, Lady Beverley, this is quite preposterous. Ha! He here 200 again! Protect me, Mr. Belmour.

Enter MODELY

MODELY. Madam, you need fly no where for protection: you have no insolence to fear from me. I am humbled sufficiently, and the post-chaise is now at the door to banish me for ever. My sole business here is, to unite that virtuous man with the most worthy of her sex. 205

ARAMINTA (*half aside*). Thank you for the compliment. [*Aloud*] Now, Mr. Belmour.

LADY BEVERLEY. You may spare yourself that trouble, cousin Modely. The girl is irrecoverably gone already.

---

[1] *madam*: Lady Beverley.   [2] *again*: cf. III i 205.

[3] *ever shall be*: Again Fontenelle's Caelia is more articulate: "Ah!" she says, "que je serois bien plus heureuse & plus contente de moi, si je pouvois vous apporter un coeur qui n'eût jamais été un seul instant occupé que de vous seul! C'étoit-là le prix que méritoient vos vertus & votre amour, & je ne puis les payer dignement" ("Oh how much prouder and happier would I have been, if I could have brought you a heart that had never belonged to anyone but yourself! That would have been a reward worthy of your virtues and your love, but now I have no adequate way to repay you") (V vi).

MODELY. May all the happiness they deserve attend them. (*Going, then looks back*   210
at ARAMINTA) [*aside*] I cannot leave her.

SIR JOHN. Mr. Modely, is there no body here besides, whom you ought to take
leave of?

MODELY. I own my parting from that lady (*to* ARAMINTA) should not be in silence;
but a conviction of my guilt stops my tongue from utterance.   215

ARAMINTA. I cannot say I quite believe that; but as our affairs may make some
noise in the world, for the sake of my own character, I must beg of you to
declare before this company, whether any part of my conduct[1] has given even
a shadow of excuse for the insult I have received. If it has, be honest and
proclaim it.   220

MODELY. None by heaven. The crime was all my own, and I suffer for it justly
and severely. With shame I speak it, notwithstanding the appearances to the
contrary, my heart was ever yours, and ever will be.

ARAMINTA. I am satisfied; and will honestly confess, the sole reason of my
present appeal was this, that where I had destin'd my hand, my conduct   225
might appear unblemish'd.   *Gives her hand to* BELMOUR

MODELY. Confusion! Then my suspicions were just.

SIR JOHN. Sister!

CAELIA. Araminta.

ARAMINTA. What do ye mean? What are ye surprized at? The insinuating Mr.   230
Modely can never want mistresses any where. Can he, Mr. Belmour? You
know him perfectly.

MODELY. Distraction! Knows me? Yes, he does know me. The villain, though he
triumphs in my sufferings, knows what I feel! You, madam, are just in your
severity. From you I have deserved every thing. The anguish, the despair   235
which must attend my future life comes from you like heaven's avenging
minister! But for him – (SIR JOHN *interposes*) O for a sword! But I shall find a
time, and a severe one. Let me go, Sir John.

ARAMINTA. I'll carry on the farce no longer. Rash inconsiderate madman! The
sword which pierces Mr. Belmour's breast, would rob you of the best of   240
friends. This pretended marriage, for it is no more, was merely contrived by
him, to convince me of your sincerity. Embrace him as your guardian angel,
and learn from him to be virtuous.

BELMOUR. O madam, let me still plead for him. Surely when a vain man feels
himself in the wrong, you cannot desire him to suffer a greater punishment.   245

ARAMINTA. I have done with fooling. You told me[2] today, Lady Beverley, that
he would never return to me.

LADY BEVERLEY. And I told you at the same time, madam, that if he did, you
would take him.[3]

ARAMINTA. In both you were mistaken. Mr. Modely, your last behaviour to   250
Caelia and my brother, shews a generosity of temper I did not think you
capable of, and for that I thank you. But to be serious on our own affair,
whatever appearance your present change may carry with it, your transactions of to-day have been such, that I can never hereafter have that respect
for you, which a wife ought to have for her husband.   255

---

[1] *conduct*: cf. III i 271 above.   [2] *told me*: cf. III i 273 above.
[3] *take him*: cf. III i 279 above.

SIR JOHN. I am sorry to say it, Mr. Modely, her determination is, I fear, too
just. Trust to time however. At least let us part friends, and not abruptly. We
should conceal the failings of each other, and if it must come to that,
endeavour to find out specious reasons for breaking off the match, without
injuring either party.   260

ARAMINTA. To shew how willing I am to conceal every thing, now I have had
my little female revenge, as my brother has promised us the fiddles this
evening, Mr. Modely, as usual, shall be my partner in the dance.

MODELY. I have deserved this ridicule, madam, and am humbled to what you
please.   265

ARAMINTA. Why then, brother, as we all seem in a strange dilemma, why
mayn't we have one dance in the garden? It will put us in good humour.

SIR JOHN. As you please, madam. Call the fiddles hither. (*Half aside to him*).
Don't despair Mr. Modely.

LADY BEVERLEY. I will not dance, positively   270

BELMOUR. Indeed but you shall, madam. Do you think I will be the only
disconsolate swain who wants a partner? Besides, you see there are so few of
us, that we must call in the butler and the ladies maids even to help out the
figure.

SIR JOHN. Come, Lady Beverley, you must lay aside all animosities. If I have   275
behaved improperly to you to-day, I most sincerely ask your pardon, and hope
the anxieties I have been under will sufficiently plead my excuse. My future
conduct will be irreproachable. (*Turning to* CAELIA) Here have I placed my
happiness, and here expect it. O Caelia, if the seriousness of my behaviour
should hereafter offend you, impute it to my infirmity. It can never proceed   280
from want of affection.

> A heart like mine its *own* distress contrives,
> And feels *most* sensibly the pain it gives;
> Then even its frailties candidly approve;
> For, if it errs, it errs from too much love.   285

EPILOGUE. Spoken before the DANCE

ARAMINTA. Well, ladies, am I right, or am I not?
          Should not this foolish passion be forgot;
          This fluttering something, scarce to be exprest,
          Which pleads for coxcombs in each female breast?
          How mortified he look'd! and looks so still.   *Turning to* MODELY   5
          He really may repent. Perhaps he will.
MODELY.   Will Araminta? Ladies be so good.
          Man's made of frail materials, flesh and blood.
          We all offend at some unhappy crisis,
          Have whims, caprices, vanities, and vices.   10
          Your happier sex by Nature was designed,
          Her last best work, to perfect humankind.
          No spot, no blemish the fair frame deforms,
          No avarice taints, no naughty passion warms
          Your firmer hearts. No love of change in you   15
          E'er taught desire to stray.
ARAMINTA.   All this is true.
          Yet stay; the men, perchance, will call it sneer,
          And some few ladies think you not sincere.
          For your petition, whether wrong or right,
          Whate'er it be, withdraw it for to-night.   20
          Another time, if I should want a spouse,
          I may myself report it to the house:
          At present, let us strive to mend the age;
          Let justice reign, at least upon the stage.
          Where the fair dames, who like to live by rule,   25
          May learn two lessons from the LOVER'S SCHOOL.
          While Caelia's choice instructs them how to chuse,
          And my refusal warns them to refuse.
                         A DANCE

ELIZABETH INCHBALD

Every One Has His Fault:
A Comedy
1793

DRAMATIS PERSONAE

MEN

Lord Norland
Sir Robert Ramble
Mr. Solus
Mr. Harmony
Mr. Placid
Mr. Irwin
Hammond
Porter
Edward

Mr. Farren
Mr. Lewis
Mr. Quick
Mr. Munden
Mr. Fawcett
Mr. Pope
Mr. Powell
Mr. Thompson
Miss Grist

WOMEN

Lady Eleanor Irwin
Mrs. Placid
Mrs. Spinster
Miss Wooburn
Servants, &c.

Mrs. Pope
Mrs. Mattocks
Mrs. Webb
Mrs. Esten

SCENE, London

EVERY ONE HAS HIS FAULT

ACT I Scene I

An Apartment at Mr. PLACID's[1]
Enter Mr. PLACID and Mr. SOLUS

PLACID. You are to blame.

SOLUS. I say the same by you.

PLACID. And yet your singularity pleases me; for you are the first elderly bachelor I ever knew, who did not hug himself in the reflection, that he was not in the trammels of wedlock.

SOLUS. No; I am only the first elderly bachelor who has truth and courage enough to confess his dissatisfaction.

PLACID. And you really wish you were married?

SOLUS. I do. I wish still more, that I had been married thirty years ago. Oh! I wish a wife and half-a-score children would now start up around me, and bring along with them all that affection, which we should have had for each other by being earlier acquainted. But as it is, in my present state, there is not a person in the world I care a straw for. And the world is pretty even with me, for I don't believe there is a creature in it who cares a straw for me.

PLACID. Pshaw! You have in your time been a man of gallantry; and, consequently, must have made many attachments.

SOLUS. Yes, such as men of gallantry usually make. I have been attached to women who have purloined my fortune, and to men who have partaken of the theft: I have been in as much fear of my mistress as you are of your wife.

PLACID. Is that possible?

SOLUS. Ay; and without having one of those tender, delicate ties of a husband, as an excuse for my apprehension. I have maintained children –

PLACID. Then why do you complain for the want of a family?

SOLUS. I did not say I ever had any children. I said I had *maintained* them. But I never believed they were mine; for I could have no dependence upon the principles of their mother. And never did I take one of those tender infants in my arms, that the forehead of my Valet, the eyes of my Apothecary, or the chin of my Chaplain, did not stare me in the face, and damp all the fine feelings of the parent, which I had just called up.

[1] *Mr.* PLACID: Throughout the Larpent MS Mr. Placid is designated "the Colonel." Originally, it would seem, he was conceived as another example of the hen-pecked military man, like Sir Luke Tremor in *Such Things Are.*

PLACID. But these are accidents which may occur in the marriage state.   30
SOLUS. In that case, a man is pitied. In mine, he is only laughed at.
PLACID. I wish to Heaven I could exchange the pity which my friends bestow on me, for the merriment which your ill fate excites.
SOLUS. You want but courage to be envied.
PLACID. Does any one doubt my courage?   35
SOLUS. No. If a Prince were to offend you, you would challenge him, no doubt.
PLACID. But if my wife offend me, I am obliged to make an apology – Was not that her voice? I hope she has not overheard our conversation.
SOLUS. If she have, she'll be in an ill humour.
PLACID. That she will be, whether she have heard it or not.   40
SOLUS. Well, good-day. I don't like to be driven from my fixed plan of wedlock; and, therefore, I won't be a spectator of your mutual discontent.   (*Going*)
PLACID. But before you go, Mr. Solus, permit me to remind you of a certain concern, that, I think, would afford you much more delight, than all you can, at this time of life, propose to yourself in marriage. Make happy by your   45
beneficence, a near relation whom the truest affection has drawn into that state, but who is denied the blessing of competency to make the state supportable.
SOLUS. You mean my nephew, Irwin? But don't you acknowledge he has a wife and children? Did not he marry the woman he loved, and has he not, at this   50
moment, a large family, by whom he is beloved? And is he not, therefore, with all his poverty, much happier than I? He has often told me, when I have reproached him for his indiscreet marriage, "that in his wife he possessed kingdoms!" Do you suppose I will give any part of my fortune to a man who enjoys such extensive domains? No: Let him preserve his territories, and I will   55
keep my little estate for my own use.   (*Exit*)
PLACID. John! John! (*Enter* SERVANT) Has your mistress been enquiring for me?
JOHN. Yes, Sir: My Lady asked just now, if I knew who was with you?
PLACID. Did she seem angry?
JOHN. No, Sir; pretty well.   60
PLACID (*in anger*). You scoundrel, what do you mean by "pretty well"?
JOHN. Much as usual, Sir.
PLACID. And do you call that "pretty well"? You scoundrel, I have a great mind to –
Enter Mrs. PLACID, *speaking very loud*
MRS. PLACID. What is the matter, Mr. Placid? What is all this noise about? You   65
know I hate a noise. What is the matter?
PLACID. My dear, I was only finding fault with that blockhead.
MRS. PLACID. Pray, Sir, do not find fault with any body in this house. But I have something which I must take *you* very severely to task about, Mr. Placid.
PLACID. No, my dear, not just now, pray.   70
MRS. PLACID. Why not now?
PLACID (*looking at his watch*). Because dinner will be ready in a few minutes. I am very hungry, and it will be cruel of you to spoil my appetite. John, is the dinner on table?
MRS. PLACID (*sitting down*). No, John, don't let it be served yet. Mr. Placid, you   75
shall first hear what I have to say.   (*Exit* SERVANT)
PLACID. But then I know I sha'n't be able to eat a morsel.

MRS. PLACID. Sit down. (*He sits*) I believe, Mr. Placid, you are going to do a very silly thing. I am afraid you are going to lend some money?

PLACID. Well, my dear, and suppose I am?   80

MRS. PLACID. Then, I don't approve of people lending their money.

PLACID. But, my dear, I have known you approve of borrowing money: And, once in our lives, what should we have done, if every body had refused to lend?

MRS. PLACID. That is nothing to the purpose. And now I desire you will hear what I say, without speaking a word yourself.   85

PLACID. Well, my dear.

MRS. PLACID. Now mind you don't speak, till I have done. Our old acquaintance, Captain Irwin, and Lady Eleanor, his wife (with whom we lived upon very intimate terms, to be sure, while we were in America), are returned to London; and I find you have visited them very frequently.   90

PLACID. Not above two or three times, upon my word; for it hurts me to see them in distress, and I forbear to go.

MRS. PLACID. There! You own they are in distress. I expected as much. Now, own to me that they have asked you to lend them money.

PLACID. I do own it. I do own it. Now, are you satisfied?   95

MRS. PLACID. No: for I have no doubt but you have promised they shall have it.

PLACID. No, upon my word, I have not promised.

MRS. PLACID. Then promise me they shall not.

PLACID. Nay, my dear, you have no idea of their distress!

MRS. PLACID. Yes, I have. And it's that which makes me suspicious.   100

PLACID. His regiment is now broken. All her jewels and little bawbles are disposed of. He is in such dread of his old creditors, that, in the lodging they have taken, he passes by the name of Middleton for fear of being dunned. They have three more children, my dear, than when we left them in New England; and they have in vain sent repeated supplications, both to his uncle,   105 and her father, for the smallest bounty.

MRS. PLACID. And is not Lord Norland, her father, a remarkably wise man? And a good man too? And ought you to do for them, what he has refused?

PLACID. They have offended him, but they have never offended me.

MRS. PLACID. I think 'tis an offence to ask a friend for money, when there is no   110 certainty of returning it.

PLACID. By no means: for, if there *were* a certainty, even an enemy might lend.

MRS. PLACID. But I insist, Mr. Placid, that they shall not find a friend in you upon this occasion. What do you say, Sir?

PLACID (*after a struggle*). No, my dear, they shall not.   115

MRS. PLACID. Positively shall not?

PLACID. Positively shall not, since they have found an enemy in you.

Enter SERVANT

SERVANT. Dinner is on table.   [*Exit*]

PLACID. Ah! I am not hungry now.

MRS. PLACID. What do you mean by that, Mr. Placid? I insist on your being   120 hungry.

PLACID. Oh yes! I have a very excellent appetite. I shall eat prodigiously.

MRS. PLACID. You had best.   (*Exeunt*)

[ACT I] Scene ii

An Apartment at Mr. HARMONY'S
Enter Mr. HARMONY *followed by Miss* SPINSTER

MISS SPINSTER. Cousin, cousin Harmony, I will not forgive you for thus
continually speaking in the behalf of every servant whom you find me
offended with. Your philanthropy becomes insupportable; and, instead of
being a virtue, degenerates into a vice.

HARMONY. Dear Madam, do not upbraid me for a constitutional fault.   5

MISS SPINSTER. Very true. You had it from your infancy. I have heard your
mother say you were always foolishly tender-hearted, and never shewed one
of those discriminating passions of envy, hatred, or revenge, to which all her
other children were liable.

HARMONY. No: since I can remember, I have felt the most unbounded affection   10
for all my fellow creatures. I even protest to you, dear Madam, that, as I walk
along the streets of this large metropolis, so warm is my heart towards every
person who passes me, that I long to say, "How do you do?" and "I am glad to
see you," to them all. Some men, I should like even to stop and shake hands
with; and some women, I should like even to stop and kiss.   15

MISS SPINSTER. How can you be so ridiculous!

HARMONY. Nay, 'tis truth: And I sincerely lament that human beings should be
such strangers to one another as we are. We live in the same street, without
knowing one another's necessities; and oftentimes meet and part from each
other at church, at coffee-houses, play-houses, and all public places, without   20
ever speaking a single word, or nodding "Good bye!" though 'tis a hundred
chances to ten we never see one another again.

MISS SPINSTER. Let me tell you, kinsman, all this pretended philanthropy
renders you ridiculous. There is never a fraud, a theft, or hardly any vice
committed, that you do not take the criminal's part, shake your head, and cry,   25
"Provisions are so very scarce!" And no longer ago than last Lord-mayor's-
day,[1] when you were told, that Mr. Alderman Ravenous was ill with an
indigestion, you endeavoured to soften the matter, by exclaiming, "Provisions
are so scarce!" But, above all, I condemn that false humanity, which induces
you to say many things in conversation which deserve to stigmatize you with   30
the character of deceit.

HARMONY. This is a weakness I confess. But though my honour sometimes
reproaches me with it as a fault, my conscience never does: for it is by this very
failing that I have frequently made the bitterest enemies friends. Just by
saying a few harmless sentences, which, though a species of falsehood and   35
deceit, yet, being soothing and acceptable to the person offended, I have
immediately inspired him with lenity and forgiveness. And then, by only
repeating the self-same sentences to his opponent, I have known hearts cold
and closed to each other, warmed and expanded, as every human creature's
ought to be.   40

Lord-mayor's-day: 29 October when the newly elected lord mayor of London, in
full regalia and accompanied by the aldermen in livery, proceeds to Westminster to take
the oaths to the monarch and returns to a sumptuous banquet in the Guildhall.

Enter SERVANT

SERVANT. Mr. Solus.   (*Exit* SERVANT)

MISS SPINSTER. I cannot think, Mr. Harmony, why you keep company with
that old bachelor. He is a man, of all men on earth, I dislike. And so I am
obliged to quit the room, though I have a thousand things to say.

                                                       (*Exit angrily*)

Enter SOLUS

HARMONY. Mr. Solus, how do you do?   45

SOLUS (*yawns*). I am very lonely at home. Will you come and dine with me?

HARMONY. Now you are here, you had better stay with me: We have no
company; only my cousin Miss Spinster and myself.

SOLUS. No, I must go home: Do come to my house.

HARMONY. Nay, pray stay: What objection can you have?   50

SOLUS. Why, to tell you the truth, your Cousin, is no great favourite of mine.
And I don't like to dine with you, because I don't like her company.

HARMONY. That is, to me, surprising!

SOLUS. Why, old bachelors and old maids never agree: We are too much alike in
our habits: We know our own hearts so well, we are apt to discover every   55
foible we would wish to forget, in the symptoms displayed by the other. Your
Cousin is peevish, fretful and tiresome, and I am always in a fidget when I am
in her company.

HARMONY. How different are her sentiments of you! For one of her greatest joys
is to be in your company. (SOLUS *starts and smiles*) Poor woman! She has, to be 60
sure, an uneven temper –

SOLUS. No, perhaps I am mistaken.

HARMONY. But I will assure you, I never see her in half so much good humour as
when you are here: for I believe you are the greatest favourite she has.

SOLUS. I am very much obliged to her, and I certainly *am* mistaken about her   65
temper. Some people, if they look ever so cross, are good-natured in the main;
and I dare say she is so. Besides, she never has had a husband, poor thing, to
sooth and soften her disposition. And there should be some allowance made
for that.

HARMONY. Will you dine with us?   70

SOLUS. I don't care if I do. Yes, I think I will. I must step home first tho': but I'll
be back in a quarter of an hour. My compliments to Miss Spinster, if you
should see her before I return.   (*Exit*)

Enter SERVANT

SERVANT. My lady begs to know, Sir, if you have invited Mr. Solus to dine?
Because if you have, she will go out.   (*Exit*)   75

Enter Miss SPINSTER

HARMONY. Yes, Madam, I could not help inviting him; for, poor man, his own
house is in such a state for want of proper management, he cannot give a
comfortable dinner himself.

MISS SPINSTER. And so he must spoil the comfort of mine.

HARMONY. Poor man! Poor man! After all the praises he has been lavishing   80
upon you.

MISS SPINSTER. What praises?

HARMONY. I won't tell you; for you won't believe them.

MISS SPINSTER. Yes, I shall. Oh no, now I recollect. This is some of your
invention.   85

HARMONY. Nay, I told him it was *his* invention: For he declared you looked better the other night, than any lady at the Opera.

MISS SPINSTER. No! This sounds like truth. And, depend upon it, though I never liked the manners of Mr. Solus much, yet –

HARMONY. Nay, Mr. Solus has his faults.   90

MISS SPINSTER (*good-naturedly*). So we have all.

HARMONY. And will you leave him and me to dine by ourselves?

MISS SPINSTER. Oh no, I cannot be guilty of such ill manners, though I talked of it. Besides, poor Mr. Solus does not come so often, and it would be wrong not to shew him all the civility we can. For my part, I have no dislike to the man;   95
and, if taking a bit of dinner with us now and then can oblige either you or him, I should be to blame to make any objection. Come, let us go into the drawing-room to receive him.

HARMONY. Ay! This is right: This is as it should be.   (*Exeunt*)

[ACT I.] Scene iii

A Room at the Lodgings of Mr. IRWIN
Mr. IRWIN *and Lady* ELEANOR IRWIN *discovered*

LADY ELEANOR. My dear husband, my dear Irwin, I cannot bear to see you thus melancholy. Is this the joy of returning to our native country after a nine years banishment?

IRWIN. Yes. For I could bear my misfortunes, my wretched poverty with patience, in a land where our sorrows were shared by those about us; but here,   5
in London, where plenty and ease smile upon every face; where, by birth you claim distinction, and I by services: here to be in want, to be obliged to take another name in shame of our own, to tremble at the voice of every stranger, for fear he should be a creditor, to meet each old acquaintance with an averted eye, because we would not feel the pang of being shunned, to have no reward   10
for all this, even in a comfortable home, but there, to see our children looking up to me for that support I have not in my power to give, can I – can I love them and you, and not be miserable?

LADY ELEANOR. And yet I am not so. And I am sure you will not doubt my love to you or them.   15

IRWIN. I met uncle this morning, and was mean enough to repeat my request to him. He burst into a fit of laughter, and told me my distresses were the result of my ambition, in marrying the daughter of a nobleman, who himself was too ambitious ever to pardon us.

LADY ELEANOR. Tell me no more of what he said.   20

IRWIN. This was a day of trials: I saw your father too.

LADY ELEANOR. My father! Lord Norland! Oh Heavens!

IRWIN. He passed me in his carriage.

LADY ELEANOR. I envy you the blessing of seeing him! For – Oh! Excuse my tears – he is my father still. How did he look?   25

IRWIN. As well as he did at the time I used to watch him from his house, to steal to you. But I am sorry to acquaint you, that, to guard himself against all returning love for you, he has, I am informed, adopted a young lad, on whom he bestows every mark of that paternal affection, of which you lament the loss.

LADY ELEANOR. May the young man deserve his tenderness better than I have   30
    done. May he never disobey him. May *he* be a comfort, and cherish his
    benefactor's declining years. And when his youthful passions teach him to
    love, may they not, like mine, teach him disobedience!
                        Enter a SERVANT *with a letter*
IRWIN. What is this letter? (*Aside*) It is strange how I tremble at every letter I see,
    as if I dreaded the contents. How poverty has unmann'd me!   35
SERVANT. It comes from Mr. Placid, the servant who brought it, said, and
    requires no answer.   (*Exit*)
IRWIN (*reading the superscription*). "To Mr. Middleton." That's right. He remem-
    bers the caution I gave him. I had forgot whether I had, for my memory is not
    so good as it was. I did not even recollect this hand, though it is one I am so   40
    well acquainted with, and ought to give me joy rather than sorrow. (*Opens the
    letter hastily*) I must tell you, my dear, that finding myself left this morning
    without a guinea, I wrote to Mr. Placid to borrow a small sum and this is his
    answer. (*Reads, and drops the letter*) Now I have not a friend on earth.
LADY ELEANOR. Yes, you have me. You forget me.   45
IRWIN (*in a transport of grief*). I would forget you, you and all your children.
LADY ELEANOR. I would not lose the remembrance of you, or of them, for all my
    father's fortune.
IRWIN. What am I to do? I must leave you! I must go, I know not where! I
    cannot stay to see you perish.   (*Takes his hat, and is going.*)   50
LADY ELEANOR (*holding him*). Where would you go? 'Tis evening. 'Tis dark.
    Whither would you go at this time?
IRWIN (*distractedly*). I must consider what's to be done. And in this room
    my thoughts are too confined to reflect.
LADY ELEANOR. And are London streets calculated for reflection?   55
IRWIN. No; for action. To hurry the faint thought to resolution.
LADY ELEANOR. You are not well. Your health has been lately impaired. Your
    temper has undergone a change too: I tremble lest any accident –
IRWIN (*wildly*). What accident?
LADY ELEANOR. I know your provocations from an ungrateful world: But   60
    despise it, as that despises you.
IRWIN. But for your sake, I could.
LADY ELEANOR. Then witness, Heaven! I am happy. Though bred in all the
    delicacy, the luxury of wealth and splendour; yet I have never murmured at
    the change of fortune, while that change has made me wife to you, and mother   65
    of your children.
IRWIN. We *will* be happy, if possible. But give me this evening to consider what
    plan to fix upon. There is no time to lose. We are without friends, without
    money, without credit. Farewell for an hour. I will see Mr. Placid, if I can.
    And though he have no money to lend, he may, perhaps, give me some advice.   70
LADY ELEANOR. Suppose I call on *her*? Women are sometimes more com-
    passionate than men, and –
IRWIN. Do you for the best, and so will I. Heavens bless you!
                                            (*Exeunt separately*)

ACT II Scene i

A Coffee-room at a Tavern
Enter Sir ROBERT RAMBLE, *and Mr.* SOLUS *and Mr.* PLACID *at the opposite side*

SOLUS. Sir Robert Ramble, how do you do?

SIR ROBERT. My dear Mr. Solus, I am glad to see you. I have been dining by myself, and now come into this public room to meet with some good company.

SOLUS. Ay, Sir Robert, you are now reduced to the same necessity which I frequently am. I frequently am obliged to dine at taverns and coffee-houses, for want of company at home. Sir Robert, give me leave to introduce to you Mr. Placid: He has been many years abroad; but I believe he now means to remain in his own country for the rest of his life. This, Mr. Placid, is Sir Robert Ramble. 5

SIR ROBERT (*to Mr.* PLACID). Sir, I shall be happy in your acquaintance; and I assure you, if you will do me the honour to meet me now and then at this house, you will find every thing very pleasant. I verily believe, that since I lost my wife, which is now about five months ago, I verily believe I have dined here three days out of the seven. 10

PLACID. Have you lost your wife, Sir? And so lately? 15

SIR ROBERT (*with great indifference*). Yes, Sir; about five months ago, is it not, Mr. Solus? You keep account of such things better than I do.

SOLUS. Oh! Ask me no questions about your wife, Sir Robert. If she had been mine, I would have had her to this moment.

PLACID. What, wrested her from the gripe of death? 20

SIR ROBERT. No, Sir; only from the gripe of the Scotch lawyers.[1]

SOLUS. More shame for you, to wish to be divorced from a virtuous wife.

PLACID. Was that the case? Divorced from a virtuous wife! I never heard of such a circumstance before. Pray, Sir Robert (*very anxiously*), will you indulge me, by letting me know in what manner you were able to bring about so great an event? 25

SIR ROBERT. It may appear strange to you, Sir; but my wife and I did not live happy together.

PLACID. Not at all strange, Sir. I can conceive – I can conceive very well.

SOLUS. Yes; he can conceive that part to a nicety. 30

---

[1] *Scotch lawyers*: In England divorce could be obtained in the ecclesiastical courts on grounds of adultery only. In Scotland divorce could be obtained in the civil courts on grounds of adultery (cf. II i 33–6, below), desertion (termed "non-adherence"), or cruelty.

SIR ROBERT. And so, I was determined on a divorce.

PLACID. But then her character could not be unimpeached.

SIR ROBERT. Yes, it was, Sir. You must know, Sir, we were married in Scotland, and by the laws there, a wife can divorce her *husband* for breach of fidelity. And so, though my wife's character was unimpeached, mine was not, and she 35 divorced me.

PLACID. And is this the law in Scotland?

SIR ROBERT. It is. Blessed, blessed country! that will bind young people together before the years of discretion and, as soon as they have discretion to repent, will unbind them again! 40

PLACID. I wish I had been married in Scotland.

SOLUS. But, Sir Robert, with all this boasting, you must own that your divorce has greatly diminished your fortune.

SIR ROBERT (*taking* SOLUS *aside*). Mr. Solus, you have frequently hinted at my fortune being impaired. But I do not approve of such notions being received 45 abroad.

SOLUS. I beg your pardon. But every body knows that you have played very deep lately, and have been a great loser, and every body knows –

SIR ROBERT. No, Sir, every body does not know it, for I contradict the report wherever I go. A man of fashion does not like to be reckoned poor, no more 50 than he likes to be reckoned unhappy. We none of us endeavour to *be* happy, Sir, but merely to be *thought* so. And for my part, I had rather be in a state of misery, and envied for my supposed happiness, than in a state of happiness, and pitied for my supposed misery.

SOLUS. But consider, these misfortunes which I have just hinted at, are not of 55 any serious nature, only such as a few years oeconomy –

SIR ROBERT. But were my wife and her guardian to become acquainted with these little misfortunes, they would triumph in my embarrassments.

SOLUS. Lady Ramble triumph! (*They join Mr.* PLACID) She who was so firmly attached to you, that I believe nothing but a compliance with your repeated 60 request to be separated, caused her to take the step she did –

SIR ROBERT. Yes, I believe she did it to oblige me, and I am very much obliged to her.

SOLUS. As good a woman, Mr. Placid –

SIR ROBERT. Very good, but very ugly. 65

SOLUS. She is beautiful.

SIR ROBERT (*to* SOLUS). I tell you, Sir, she is hideous. And then she was grown so insufferably peevish.

SOLUS. I never saw her out of temper.

SIR ROBERT. Mr. Solus, it is very uncivil of you to praise her before my face. 70 Lady Ramble, at the time I parted with her, had every possible fault both of mind and person, and so I made love to other women in her presence; told her bluntly that I was tired of her; that "I was very sorry to make her uneasy, but that I could not love her any longer." And was not that frank and open?

SOLUS. Oh! that I had but such a wife as she was! 75

SIR ROBERT. I must own I loved her myself when she was young.

SOLUS. Do you call her old?

SIR ROBERT. In years I am certainly older than she. But the difference of sex makes her a great deal older than I am. For instance, Mr. Solus, you have often lamented not being married in your youth. But if you had, what would 80 you have now done with an old wife, a woman of your own age?

SOLUS. Loved and cherished her.

SIR ROBERT. What, in spite of her loss of beauty?

SOLUS. When she had lost her beauty, most likely I should have lost my eye-sight, and have been blind to the wane of her charms.   85

PLACID (*anxiously*). But, Sir Robert, you were explaining to me – Mr. Solus, give me leave to speak to Sir Robert. I feel myself particularly interested on this subject. And, Sir, you were explaining to me –

SIR ROBERT. Very true: Where did I leave off? Oh! at my ill usage of my Lady Ramble. Yes, I did use her very ill, and yet she loved me. Many a time, when   90
she has said to me, "Sir Robert, I detest your principles, your manners, and even your person," often, at that very instant, I have seen a little sparkle of a wish peep out of the corner of one eye, that has called to me, "Oh! Sir Robert, how I long to make it up with you!"

SOLUS (*to Mr.* PLACID). Do not you wish that your wife had such a sparkle at the   95
corner of one of her eyes?

SIR ROBERT (*to Mr.* PLACID). Sir, do you wish to be divorced?

PLACID. I have no such prospect. Mrs. Placid is faithful, and I was married in England.

SIR ROBERT. But if you have an unconquerable desire to part, a separate   100
maintenance will answer nearly the same end. For if your Lady and you will only lay down the plan of separation, and agree –

PLACID. But, unfortunately, we never do agree!

SIR ROBERT. Then speak of parting as a thing you dread worse than death. And make it your daily prayer to her, that she will never think of going from you.   105
She will determine upon it directly.

PLACID. I have no doubt but she will. I thank you. I'm very much obliged to you: I thank you a thousand times.

SIR ROBERT. Yes, I have studied the art of teasing a wife. And there is nothing vexes her so much as laughing at her. Can you laugh, Mr. Placid?   110

PLACID. I don't know whether I can. I have not laughed since I married. But I thank you, Sir, for your instructions. I sincerely thank you.

SOLUS. And now, Sir Robert, you have had the good nature to teach this Gentleman how to get rid of his wife, will you have the kindness to teach me how to procure one?   115

Enter Mr. IRWIN

SIR ROBERT. Hah! Sure I know that Gentleman's face?

SOLUS (*aside*). My Nephew! Let me escape his solicitations. [*Aloud*] Here, waiter!   (*Exit*)

PLACID (*starting*). Irwin! (*Aside*) Having sent him a denial, I am ashamed to see him. [*Aloud*] Here, Mr. Solus!   (*Exit, following Mr.* SOLUS)   120

IRWIN (*aside*). More cool faces! My necessitous countenance clears even a club-room.

SIR ROBERT. My dear Captain Irwin, is it you? Yes, 'faith it is. After a nine years' absence I sincerely rejoice to see you.

IRWIN. Sir Robert, you shake hands with a cordiality I have not experienced   125
these many days, and I thank you.

SIR ROBERT. But what's the matter? You seem to droop. Where have you left your usual spirits? Has absence from your country changed your manners?

IRWIN. No, Sir Robert; but I find the manners of some of my countrymen

changed. I fancy them less warm, less friendly than they were. And it is that   130
which, perhaps, has this effect upon me.

SIR ROBERT. Am I changed?

IRWIN. You appear an exception.

SIR ROBERT. And I assure you, that instead of being grown more gloomy, I am
even more gay than I was seven years ago; for then, I was upon the point of   135
matrimony, but now, I am just relieved from its cares.

IRWIN. I have heard as much. But I hope you have not taken so great an
aversion to the marriage-state, as never to marry again.

SIR ROBERT. Perhaps not: But then it must be to some rich heiress.

IRWIN. You are right to pay respect to fortune. Money is a necessary article in   140
the marriage contract.

SIR ROBERT. As to that, that would be no great object at present. No, thank
Heaven, my estates are pretty large; I have no children; I have a rich Uncle,
excellent health, admirable spirits; and it would be very strange if I did not
meet my old friends with those smiles, which never for a moment quit my   145
countenance.

IRWIN. Sir Robert, in the dispensation of the gifts of Providence, how few are
found blest like you!   (Sighing)

SIR ROBERT. And I assure you, my dear Mr. Irwin, it gives me the most serious
reflections, and the most sincere concern, that they are not.   150

IRWIN. I thank you, Sir, most heartily: I thank you for mankind in general, and
for myself in particular. For after this generous declaration (with less scruple
than I should to any man in the world) I will own to you, that I am at this very
time in the utmost want of an act of friendship.

SIR ROBERT (aside). And so am I. Now must I confess myself a poor man; or pass   155
for an unfeeling one; and I will choose the latter. (Bowing with great
ceremony and coldness) Any thing that I can command, is at your service.

IRWIN (confounded and hesitating). Why then, Sir Robert – I am almost ashamed to
say it – But circumstances have been rather unfavourable. My wife's father
(affecting to smile) is not reconciled to us yet. My regiment is broke. My Uncle   160
will not part with a farthing. Lady Eleanor, my wife, (wipes his eyes) has been
supported as yet, with some little degree of tenderness and elegance; and – In
short, I owe a small sum which I am afraid of being troubled for. I want a trifle
also for our immediate use, and if you would lend me a hundred pounds –
Though, upon my honour, I am not in a situation to fix the exact time when I   165
can pay it.

SIR ROBERT. My dear Sir, never trouble yourself about the time of paying it,
because it happens not to be in my power to lend it you.

IRWIN. Not in your power? I beg your pardon; but have not you this moment
been saying you are rich?   170

SIR ROBERT. And is it not very common to be rich without money? Are not half
the town rich? And yet half the town has no money. I speak for this end of the
town, the West end. The Squares, for instance, part of Piccadilly, down St.
James's-street, and so home by Pall Mall. We have all, estates, bonds, drafts,
and notes of hand without number; but as for money, we have no such thing   175
belonging to us.

IRWIN. I sincerely beg your pardon. And be assured, Sir, nothing should have
induced me to have taken the liberty I have done, but the necessities of my

unhappy family, and having understood by your own words, that you were in
affluence.   180
SIR ROBERT. I *am* in affluence, I am, I am; but not in so much, perhaps, as my
hasty, inconsiderate account may have given you reason to believe. I forgot to
mention several heavy incumbrances, which you will perceive are great
drawbacks on my fortune. As my wife sued for the divorce, I have her fortune
to return. I have also two sisters to portion off, a circumstance I totally forgot.   185
But, my good friend, though I am not in circumstances to do what you
require, I will do something that shall be better. I'll wait upon your
father-in-law, (Lord Norland) and entreat him to forgive his daughter: And I
am sure he will if I ask him.
IRWIN. Impossible.   190
SIR ROBERT. And so it is, now I recollect: For he is no other than the guardian of
my late wife, and a request from me, will be received worse than from any
other person. However, Mr. Irwin, depend upon it, that whenever I have an
opportunity of serving you, I will. And whenever you shall do me the favour to
call upon me, I shall be heartily glad to see you. If I am not at home, you can   195
leave your card, which, you know, is all the same, and depend upon it, I shall
be extremely glad to see you or that, at any time.   (*Exit*)
IRWIN. Is this my native country? Is this the hospitable land which we describe
to strangers? No. We are savages to each other. Nay worse. The savage makes
his fellow-savage welcome; divides with him his homely fare; gives him the   200
best apartment his hut affords, and tries to hush those griefs that are confided
in his bosom. While in this civilized city, among my own countrymen, even
among my brother officers in the army, and many of my nearest relations, so
very civilized they are, I could not take the liberty to enter under one roof,
without a ceremonious invitation, and that they will not give me. I may leave   205
my card at their door, but as for me, or any one of mine, they would not give us
a dinner; unless, indeed, it was in such a style, that we might behold with
admiration their grandeur, and return still more depressed, to our own
poverty. Can I bear this treatment longer? No, not even for you, my Eleanor.
And this (*takes out a pistol*) shall now be the only friend to whom I will apply.   210
And yet I want the courage to be a villain.
                    Enter Mr. HARMONY, *speaking as he enters.*
                    IRWIN *conceals the pistol instantly*
HARMONY. Let me see half a dozen newspapers, every paper of the
day.
                            Enter WAITER
WAITER. That is about three dozen, Sir.
HARMONY. Get a couple of porters, and bring them all.   215
            (*He sits down. They bring him papers, and he reads.*
IRWIN *starts, sits down, leans his head on one of the tables, and shews various signs of
                    uneasiness; then comes forward*)
IRWIN. Am I a man, a soldier? And a coward? Yes, I run away. I turn my back
on life. I forsake the post, which my commander, Providence, has allotted me,
and fly before a banditti of rude misfortunes. Rally me, love, connubial and
parental love, rally me back to the charge! No, it is those very affections which
sound the retreat.   220
            (*Sits down with the same emotions of distraction as before*)

HARMONY (*aside*). That gentleman does not seem happy. I wish I had an opportunity of speaking to him.

IRWIN (*comes forward and speaks again*). But Oh! my wife, what will be your sufferings when I am brought home to your wretched habitation! And by my own hand!   225

HARMONY (*holding up the papers*). I am afraid, Sir, I engross all the news here.

IRWIN (*still apart*). Poor soul, how her heart will be torn!

HARMONY (*after looking steadfastly on him*). Captain Irwin, till this moment I had not the pleasure of recollecting you! It is Mr. Irwin, is it not?

IRWIN (*his mind deranged by his misfortunes*). Yes, Sir: But what have you to say to   230
him more than to a stranger?

HARMONY. Nothing more, Sir, than to apologize to you, for having addressed you just now in so familiar a manner, before I knew who you were; and to assure you, that although I have no other knowledge of you, than from report, and having been once, I believe, in your company at this very house before   235
you left England; yet, any services of mine, as far as my abilities can reach, you may freely command.

IRWIN. Pray, Sir, do you live at the West end of the town?

HARMONY. I do, Sir.

IRWIN. Then, Sir, your services can be of no use to me.   240

HARMONY. Here is the place where I live. Here is my card, Sir.

                                                                                        (*Gives it to him*)

IRWIN. And here is mine, Sir. And now I presume we have exchanged every act of friendship, which the strict forms of etiquette, in this town, will admit of.

HARMONY. By no means, Sir. I assure you my professions never go beyond my intentions. And if there is any thing that I can serve you in –   245

IRWIN. Have you no sisters to portion off? No lady's fortune to return? Or, perhaps, you will speak to my wife's father, and entreat him to forgive his child.

HARMONY. On that subject you may command me; for I have the honour to be intimately acquainted with Lord Norland.   250

IRWIN. But is there no reason you can recollect, "why you would be the most unfit person in the world to apply to him?"

HARMONY. None. I have been honoured with marks of his friendship for many years past. And I do not know any one who could, with less hazard of his resentment, venture to name his daughter to him.   255

IRWIN. Well, Sir, if you should see him two or three days hence, when I am set out on a journey I am going, if you will then say a kind word to him for my wife and children, I'll thank you.

HARMONY. I will go to him instantly.   (*Going*)

IRWIN. No, do not see him yet. Stay till I am gone. He will do nothing till I am   260
gone.

HARMONY. May I ask where you are going?

IRWIN. No very tedious journey. But it is a country, to those who go without a proper passport, always fatal.

HARMONY. I'll see Lord Norland to-night: Perhaps I may persuade him to   265
prevent your journey. I'll see him to-night, or early in the morning, depend upon it. I am a man of my word, Sir; though I must own I do live at the West end of the town.   (*Exit*)

IRWIN. 'Sdeath, am I become the ridicule of my fellow-creatures? Or am I not in
my senses? I'll try. I know this is London, this house a tavern. I know I have a   270
wife. Oh! 'twere better to be mad than to remember her! She has a father too.
He is rich and proud. That I will not forget. But I will pass his house, and send
a malediction as I pass it (*furiously*). No; breathe out my last sigh at his
inhospitable door, and that sigh shall breathe – forgiveness.   (*Exit*)

[ACT II] Scene ii

The Lodgings of Mr. IRWIN
Enter Mrs. PLACID, *followed by Lady* ELEANOR IRWIN

LADY ELEANOR. I am ashamed of this trouble I have given you, Mrs. Placid. It
had been sufficient to have sent me home in your carriage; to attend me
yourself was ceremonious.

MRS. PLACID. My dear Lady Eleanor, I was resolved to come home with you, as
soon as Mr. Placid desired I would not.   5

LADY ELEANOR. Was that the cause of your politeness? I am sorry it should.

MRS. PLACID. Why sorry? It is not proper he should have his way in every thing.

LADY ELEANOR. But I am afraid you seldom let him have it at all.

MRS. PLACID. Yes, I do. But where, my dear, is Mr Irwin?

LADY ELEANOR (*weeping*). I cannot hear the name of Mr. Irwin without   10
shedding tears: His health has been so much impaired of late, and his spirits
so bad. Sometimes I even fear for a failure in his mind.   (*Weeps again*)

MRS. PLACID. Is not he at home?

LADY ELEANOR. I hope he is. (*Goes to the side of the scenes*) Tell your master, Mrs.
Placid is here.   15

Enter SERVANT

SERVANT. My master is not come in yet, Madam.

LADY ELEANOR. Not yet? I am very sorry for it. It's a wet evening, and –

MRS. PLACID. Bless me, my dear, don't look thus pale. Come sit down, and I'll
stay with you till he returns.   (*Sits down herself*)

LADY ELEANOR. My dear Mrs. Placid, you forget that Mr. Placid is in the   20
carriage at the door all this time.

MRS. PLACID. No, I don't. Come, let us sit and have half an hour's conversation.

LADY ELEANOR. Nay, I insist upon your going to him, or desiring him to walk
in.

MRS. PLACID. Now I think of it, they may as well drive him home, and come   25
back for me.

Enter Mr. PLACID

MRS. PLACID. Why surely, Mr. Placid, you were very impatient! I think you
might have waited a few minutes longer.

PLACID. I would have waited, my dear, but the night is so damp.

LADY ELEANOR. Ah! 'tis that damp I fear for Mr. Irwin.   30

PLACID. Lady Eleanor, you are one of the most tender, anxious, and affectionate
wives I ever knew.

MRS. PLACID. There! Now he wishes he was your husband. He admires the

conduct of every wife but his own, and envies every married man of his
acquaintance. But it is very ungenerous of you.   35

PLACID. So it is, my dear; and not at all consistent with the law of retaliation.
For I am sure there is not one of my acquaintance who envies me.

MRS. PLACID. Mr. Placid, your behaviour throughout this whole day has been
so totally different to what it ever was before, that I am half resolved to live no
longer with you.   40

PLACID (*aside*). It will do.

LADY ELEANOR. Oh, my dear friends, do not talk of parting; how can you, while
every blessing smiles on your union? Even I, who have reason to regret mine,
yet, while that load of grief, a separation from Mr. Irwin, is but averted, I will
think every other affliction supportable. (*A loud rapping at the door*) That is he.   45

MRS. PLACID. Why, you seem in raptures at his return.

LADY ELEANOR. I know no greater rapture.

Enter IRWIN *pale, trembling, and disordered*

LADY ELEANOR. My dear, you are not well, I see.

IRWIN. Yes. (*Aside to her in anger*) Why do you speak of it?

PLACID. How do you do, Irwin?   50

IRWIN. I am glad to see you.   (*Bows*)

MRS. PLACID. But I am sorry to see you look so ill.

IRWIN. I have only been taking a glass too much.   (*Lady* ELEANOR *weeps*)

PLACID. Pshaw! Don't I know you never drink?

IRWIN. You are mistaken: I do when my wife is not by. I am afraid of her.   55

PLACID. Impossible.

IRWIN. What! To be afraid of one's wife?

PLACID. No; I think that very possible.

MRS. PLACID. But it does not look well when it is so. It makes a man appear
contemptible, and a woman a termagant. Come, Mr. Placid, I cannot stay   60
another moment. Good night. (*To Lady* ELEANOR) Heaven bless you! Good
night, my dear Mr. Irwin; and now, pray take my advice and keep up your
spirits.

IRWIN. I will, Madam. (*Shaking hands with* PLACID) And do you keep up your
spirits.   (*Exeunt Mr. and Mrs.* PLACID)   65

(IRWIN *shuts the door with care after them, and looks round the room as if he feared to be seen
or overheard*)

IRWIN. I am glad they are gone. I spoke unkindly to you just now, did I not? My
temper is altered lately; and yet I love you.

LADY ELEANOR. I never doubted it, nor ever will.

IRWIN. If you did, you would wrong me. For there is not a danger I would not
risk for your sake; there is not an infamy I would not be branded with to make   70
you happy, nor a punishment I would not undergo, with joy, for your welfare.
But there is a bar to this. We are unfortunately so entwined together, so
linked, so rivetted, so cruelly, painfully fettered to each other, you could not
be happy unless I shared the self same happiness with you. But you will learn
better, now you are in London, and amongst fashionable wives. You must   75
learn better.

(*Walks about and smiles, with a ghastly countenance*)

LADY ELEANOR. Do not talk, do not look thus wildly. Indeed, you make me very
uneasy.

IRWIN. What! Uneasy when I come to bring you comfort; and such comfort as
you have not experienced for many a day? (*He pulls out a pocket-book*) Here is a   80
friend in our necessity, a friend that brings a thousand friends; plenty and –
no, not always – peace. (*He takes several papers from the book, and puts them into her
hands. She looks at them, then screams*)
LADY ELEANOR. Ah! 'Tis money. (*Trembling*) These are Bank notes.
IRWIN. Hush! For heaven's sake, hush! We shall be discovered. (*Trembling and in
great perturbation*) What alarms you thus?   85
LADY ELEANOR. What alarms you?
IRWIN. Do you say I am frightened?
LADY ELEANOR. A sight so new has frightened me.
IRWIN. Nay, they are your own: by heaven, they are! No one on earth has a
better, or a fairer right than you have. It was a laudable act by which I   90
obtained them. The parent-bird had forsook its young and I forced it back to
perform the rites of nature.
LADY ELEANOR. You are insane, I fear. No, no, I do not *fear*, I *hope* you are.
(*A loud rapping at the street-door. He starts, takes the notes from her, and puts them hastily
into his pocket*)
IRWIN. Go to the door yourself. And if 'tis any one who asks for me, say I am not
come home yet. (*She goes out, then returns*)   95
LADY ELEANOR. It is the person belonging to the house: no one to us.
IRWIN. My dear Eleanor, are you willing to quit London with me in about two
hours time?
LADY ELEANOR. Instantly.
IRWIN. Nay, not only London, but England.   100
LADY ELEANOR. This world, if you desire it. To go in company with you, would
make the journey pleasant; and all I loved on earth would still be with me.
IRWIN. You can, then, leave your father without regret, *never, never* to see him
more?
LADY ELEANOR. Why should I think on him, who will not think of me?   105
                                                        (*Weeps*)
IRWIN. But our children –
LADY ELEANOR. We are not to leave them behind?
IRWIN. One of them we must; but do not let that give you uneasiness. You know
he has never lived with us since his infancy, and cannot pine for the loss of
parents whom he has never known.   110
LADY ELEANOR. But I have *known him*. He was my first; and, sometimes, I think
more closely wound around my heart, than all the rest. The pangs I felt on
being forced to leave him when we went abroad, and the constant anxiety I
have since experienced lest he should not be kindly treated, have augmented,
I think, my tenderness.   115
IRWIN. All my endeavours to-day, as well as every other day, have been in vain
to find into what part of the country his nurse has taken him. Nay, be not thus
overcome with tears. We will (in spite of all my haste to be gone) stay one
more miserable day here, in hopes to procure intelligence, so as to take him
with us; and then smile with contempt on all we leave behind.   (*Exeunt*)   120

ACT III Scene i
A Library at Lord NORLAND's

Enter Lord NORLAND, *followed by Mr.* HARMONY

LORD NORLAND (*in anger*). I tell you, Mr. Harmony, that if an indifferent
person, one on whom I had never bestowed a favour in my life, were to offend
me, it is in my nature never to forgive. Can I then forgive my own daughter,
my only child,[1] on whom I have heaped continual marks of the most
affectionate fondness? Shall she dare to offend me in the tenderest point, and   5
you dare to suppose I will pardon her?

HARMONY. Your child, consider.

LORD NORLAND. The weakest argument you can use. As my child, was she not
most bound to obey me? As my child, ought she not to have sacrificed her own
happiness to mine? Instead of which, mine has been yielded up for a whim, a   10
fancy, a fancy to marry a beggar. And as such is her choice, let her beg with
him.

HARMONY. She does by me; pleads hard for your forgiveness.

LORD NORLAND. If I thought she dared to send a message to me, though
dictated on her knees, she should find that she had not yet felt the full force of   15
my resentment.

HARMONY. What could you do more?

LORD NORLAND. I have done nothing yet. At present, I have only abandoned
her; but I can persecute.

HARMONY. I have no doubt of it: And, that I may not be the means of   20
aggravating your displeasure, I assure you, that what I have now said has
been entirely from myself, without any desire of hers; and, at the same time, I
give you my promise, I will never presume to intrude the subject again.

LORD NORLAND. On this condition (but on no other) I forgive you now.

HARMONY. And now then, my Lord, let us pass from those who have forfeited   25
your love, to those who possess it. I heard some time ago, but I never
presumed to mention it to you, that you had adopted a young man as your
son?

---

[1] *only child*: Lord Norland disinheriting his only child and heiress in place of his
grandson recapitulates *A Simple Story* (III i) in which Lord Elmwood disinherits his
only child and heiress in place of a nephew. The violence and intransigence of Lord
Norland's character also recalls Lord Elmwood.

LORD NORLAND. "A young man!" Pshaw!' No; a boy, a mere child, who fell in
my way by accident.

HARMONY. A chance child! O! ho! I understand you.   30

LORD NORLAND. Do not jest with me, Sir. Do I look –

HARMONY. I can't say you do, but you look as if you would be ashamed to own
it, if you had one.

LORD NORLAND. But this boy I am not ashamed of: He is rather a favourite. I   35
did not like him so well at first; but custom, and having a poor creature
entirely at one's mercy, one begins to love it merely from the idea of – what
would be its fate if one did not?

HARMONY. Is he an orphan then?

LORD NORLAND. No.
                                                                     40
HARMONY. You have a friendship for his parents?

LORD NORLAND. I never saw the father; His mother I had a friendship for
once.   (*Sighing*)

HARMONY. Ay, while the husband was away?

LORD NORLAND (*violently*). I tell you, no. But ask no more questions. Who his   45
parents are, is a secret, which neither he, nor any one (that is now living)
knows, except myself; nor ever shall.

HARMONY. Well, my Lord, since 'tis your pleasure to consider him as your child,
I sincerely wish you may experience more duty from him that you have done
from your daughter.   50

LORD NORLAND. Thank Heaven, his disposition is not in the least like her's. No:
(*very much impassioned*) I have the joy to say, that never child was so unlike its
mother.

HARMONY (*starting*). How! His mother!

LORD NORLAND. Confusion! What have I said? I am ashamed –   55

HARMONY. No, be proud.

LORD NORLAND. Of what?

HARMONY. That you have a lawful heir to all your riches; proud that you have a
grandson.

LORD NORLAND. I would have concealed it from all the world. I wished it even   60
unknown to myself. And let me tell you, Sir, (as not by my design, but through
my inadvertency, you are become acquainted with this secret) that, if ever you
breathe it to a single creature, the boy shall answer for it; for, were he known
to be her's, though he were dearer to me than ever *she* was, I would turn him
from my house, and cast him from my heart, as I have done her.   65

HARMONY. I believe you; and in compassion to the child, give you my *solemn
promise* never to reveal who he is. I have heard that those unfortunate parents
left an infant behind when they went abroad, and that they now lament him as
lost. Will you satisfy my curiosity, in what manner you sought and found him
out?
                                                                     70
LORD NORLAND. Do you suppose I searched for him? No; he was forced upon
me. A woman followed me, about eight years ago, in the fields adjoining to my
country seat, with a half-starved boy in her hand, and asked my charity for my
grand-child: The impression of the word, made me turn round involuntarily;
and casting my eyes upon him, I was glad not to find a feature of his mother's   75
in all his face; and I began to feel something like pity for him. In short, he
caught such fast hold by one of my fingers, that I asked him carelessly "if he'd

go home and live with me?" on which, he answered me so willingly "Yes," I
took him at his word.

HARMONY. And did your regard for him never plead in his mother's behalf?   80

LORD NORLAND. Never. For, by Heaven, I would as soon forgive the robber
who met me last night at my own door, and, holding a pistol to my breast,
took from me a sum to a considerable amount, as I would pardon her.

HARMONY. Did such an accident happen to you?

LORD NORLAND. Have you not heard of it?   85

HARMONY. No.

LORD NORLAND. It is amazing we cannot put a stop to such depredations.

HARMONY. Provisions are so scarce!

LORD NORLAND. How! Do you take the part of public ruffians?

HARMONY. No. I wish them all extirpated. But if there are persons who, by their   90
oppression provoke these outrages, I wish them punished first.

Enter SERVANT

SERVANT. Miss Wooburn, my Lord, if you are not engaged, will come and sit an
hour with you.

LORD NORLAND. I have no company but what she is perfectly acquainted with,
and shall be glad of her visit.   (*Exit* SERVANT)   95

HARMONY. You forget I am a stranger, and my presence may not be welcome.

LORD NORLAND. A stranger! What, to my ward? To Lady Ramble? For that is
the name which custom would authorise her to keep. But such courtesy she
disdains, in contempt of the unworthy giver of the title.

HARMONY. I am intimate with Sir Robert, my Lord; and though I acknowledge   100
that both you and his lady have cause for complaint, yet Sir Robert has still
many virtues.

LORD NORLAND. Not one. He is the most vile, the most detestable of characters.
He not only contradicted my will in the whole of his conduct, but he seldom
met me that he did not give me some personal affront.   105

HARMONY. It is, however, generally held better to be uncivil in a person's
presence, than in his absence.

LORD NORLAND. He was uncivil to me in every respect.

HARMONY. That I will deny; for I have heard Sir Robert, in your absence, say
such things in your praise –   110

LORD NORLAND. Indeed!

HARMONY. Most assuredly.

LORD NORLAND. I wish he had sometimes done me the honour to have spoken
politely to my face.

HARMONY. That is not Sir Robert's way. He is no flatterer. But then, no sooner   115
has your back been turned, than I have heard him lavish in your praise.

LORD NORLAND. I must own, Mr. Harmony, that I never looked upon Sir
Robert as incorrigible. I could always discern a ray of understanding, and a
beam of virtue through all his foibles. Nor would I have urged the divorce, but
that I found his wife's sensibility could not bear his neglect. And even now,   120
notwithstanding her endeavour to conceal it, she pines in secret, and laments
her hard fortune. All my hopes of restoring her health rest on one prospect,
that of finding a man worthy my recommendation for her second husband,
and, by creating a second passion, expel the first. Mr. Harmony, you and I
have been long acquainted. I have known your disposition from your   125

infancy.[1] Now, if such a man as you were to offer –

HARMONY. You flatter me.

LORD NORLAND. I do not. Would you venture to become her husband?

HARMONY. I can't say I have any particular desire; but if it will oblige either you or her – For my part, I think the short time we live in this world, we should do   130
all we can to oblige each other.

LORD NORLAND. I should rejoice at such a union myself, and I think I can answer for her. You permit me then to make overtures to her in your name?

HARMONY (considering). This is rather a serious piece of business – However, I never did make a difficulty when I wished to oblige a friend. But   135
there is one proviso, my Lord. I must first mention it to Sir Robert.

LORD NORLAND. Why so?

HARMONY. Because he and I have always been very intimate friends. And to marry his wife, without even telling him of it, will appear very uncivil!

LORD NORLAND. Do you mean then to ask his consent?   140

HARMONY. Not absolutely his consent. But I will insinuate the subject to him, and obtain his approbation in a manner suitable to my own satisfaction.

LORD NORLAND. You will oblige me then if you will see him as early as possible; for it is reported he is going abroad.

HARMONY. I will go to him immediately. And, my Lord, I will do all in my   145
power to oblige you, Sir Robert and the Lady. (Aside) But as to obliging myself, that was never one of my considerations.   (Exit)

Enter Miss WOOBURN

LORD NORLAND. I am sorry to see you thus. You have been weeping? Surely your pride should teach you to overcome this continual sorrow. You appear to lament your separation from a cruel husband, as if you had followed a kind   150
one to the grave?

MISS WOOBURN. By no means, my Lord. Tears from our sex are not always the result of grief; they are frequently no more than little sympathetic tributes which we pay to our fellow-beings, while the mind and the heart are steeled against the weakness which our eyes indicate.   155

LORD NORLAND. Can you say, your mind and heart are so steeled?

MISS WOOBURN. I can: My mind is as firmly fixed against Sir Robert Ramble, as at our first acquaintance it was fixed upon him. I despise his dissipation, his vain boasting, all his vices and all his follies, and were we again together, I should weep for a separation, but being separated, I weep for the necessity   160
which caused our parting.

LORD NORLAND. He hears and triumphs in the uneasiness which your appearance betrays to the world.

MISS WOOBURN. Then my appearance deceives the world. For I here solemnly protest –   165

LORD NORLAND. To a man of my age and observation, protestations are vain. Give me a proof that you have rooted him from your heart.

MISS WOOBURN. Any proofs you require.

LORD NORLAND. I ask but one.

MISS WOOBURN. Whatever it is then, my Lord, I will give it you without a   170
moment's hesitation.

[1] *disposition from ... infancy*: cf. I ii 6–9, above.

LORD NORLAND. I take you at your word; and desire you to accept a Gentleman, whom I shall recommend for your second husband. (*Miss* WOOBURN *starts*) You said you would not hesitate a moment.

MISS WOOBURN. I thought I should not. But this is something so unexpected – 175

LORD NORLAND. You break your word then, and still give cause for this ungrateful man, to ridicule your fondness for him.

MISS WOOBURN. No, I will put an end to that humiliation. And whoever the Gentleman is whom you mean to propose – Yet, do not name him at present, but give me the satisfaction of keeping the promise I have made to you (at 180 least for a little time) without exactly knowing how far it extends. For, in return, I have a promise to ask from you before I acquaint you with the nature of your engagement.

LORD NORLAND. I give my promise. Now name your request.

MISS WOOBURN. Then, my Lord (*hesitating and confused*), the law gave me back, 185 upon my divorce from Sir Robert, the very large fortune which I brought to him. I am afraid, that in his present circumstances, to enforce the strict payment of this debt, would very much embarrass him.

LORD NORLAND. What if it did?

MISS WOOBURN. It is my entreaty to you (in whose hands is invested the power 190 to demand this right of law) to lay my claim aside for the present. (*Lord* NORLAND *offers to speak*) I know, my Lord, what you are going to say. I know Sir Robert is not *now*, but I never can forget that he *has been* my husband.

LORD NORLAND. To shew my gratitude for your compliance with my request, I will go as far as possible in granting yours. (*Goes to a table in the library*) Here is 195 the bond by which I am impowered to seize on the greatest part of his estates in right of you: Take the bond into your own possession till your next husband demands it of you. And by the time you have called him husband for a few weeks, this tenderness, or delicacy to Sir Robert, will be worn away.

Enter HARMONY, *hastily*

HARMONY. My Lord, I beg pardon; but I forgot to mention –   200

MISS WOOBURN. Oh, Mr. Harmony, I have not seen you before I know not when: I am particularly happy at your calling just now, for I have (*hesitating*) a little favour to ask of you.

HARMONY. If it were a great favour, Madam, you might command me.

LORD NORLAND. That I am sure you might.   205

MISS WOOBURN. But – My Lord I beg your pardon, but the favour I have to ask of Mr. Harmony must be told to him in private.

LORD NORLAND. Oh! I am sure I have not the least objection to you and Mr. Harmony having a private conference. I'll leave you together. (HARMONY *appears embarrassed*) You do not derange my business. I'll be back in a short 210 time.   (*Exit*)

MISS WOOBURN. Mr. Harmony, you are the very man on earth I most wanted to see. (HARMONY *bows*) I know the kindness of your heart, the liberality of your sentiments, and I wish to repose a charge to your trust, very near to me indeed, but you must be secret.   215

HARMONY. When a Lady reposes a trust in me, I should not be a man if I were not.

MISS WOOBURN. I must first inform you, that Lord Norland has just drawn from me a promise, that I will once more enter into the marriage-state; and without knowing to whom he intends to give me, I will keep my promise. But it is in 220

vain to say, that, though I mean all duty and fidelity to my second husband, I
shall not experience moments when my thoughts – will wander on my first.

HARMONY (*starting*). Hem! Hem! (*To her*) Indeed?

MISS WOOBURN. I must always rejoice in Sir Robert's successes, and lament his
misfortunes.   225

HARMONY. If that is all –

MISS WOOBURN. No, I would go one step further: (HARMONY *starts again*) I would
secure him from those misfortunes, which to hear of, would disturb my peace
of mind. I know his fortune has suffered very much, and I cannot, *will not*,
place it in the power of the man, whom my Lord Norland may point out for   230
my next marriage, to distress him farther. This is the writing, by which that
Gentleman may claim the part of my fortune from Sir Robert Ramble, which
is in landed property. Carry it, my dear Mr. Harmony, to Sir Robert
instantly; and tell him, that in separating from him, I meant only to give him
liberty, not make him the debtor, perhaps the prisoner of my future husband.   235

HARMONY. Madam, I will most undoubtedly take this bond to my friend, Sir
Robert. But will you give me leave to suggest to you, that the person on whom
you bestow your hand, may be a little surprised to find, that while he is in
possession of you, Sir Robert is in the possession of your fortune?

MISS WOOBURN. Do not imagine, Sir, that I shall marry any man, without first   240
declaring what I have done. I only wish at present it should be concealed from
Lord Norland. When this paper is given to Sir Robert, it cannot be recalled.
And when that is past, I shall divulge my conduct to whom I please; and first
of all, to him, who shall offer me his addresses.

HARMONY. And if he be a man of my feelings, his addresses will be doubly   245
importunate for this proof of liberality to your former husband. But are you
sure, that in the return of this bond, there is no secret affection, no latent spark
of love?

MISS WOOBURN. None. I know my heart. And if there was, I could not ask you,
Mr. Harmony (nor any one like you), to be the messenger of an imprudent   250
passion. Sir Robert's vanity, I know, may cause him to judge otherwise; but
undeceive him; let him know, that this is a sacrifice to the golden principles of
duty, and not an offering to the tinselled shrine of love.

Enter Lord NORLAND

Put up the bond. (HARMONY *conceals it*)

LORD NORLAND. Well, my dear, have you asked the favour?   255

MISS WOOBURN. Yes, my Lord.

LORD NORLAND. And has he granted it.

HARMONY. Yes, my Lord. I am going to grant it?

LORD NORLAND. I sincerely wish you both joy of this good understanding
between you. But, Mr. Harmony (*in a whisper*), are not you going to Sir   260
Robert?

HARMONY. Yes, my Lord, I am going this moment.

LORD NORLAND. Make haste then, and do not forget your errand.

HARMONY. No, my Lord, I sha'n't forget my errand. It won't slip my memory.
Good morning, my Lord. Good morning, Madam.   (*Exit*)   265

LORD NORLAND. Now, my dear Miss Wooburn, as you and Mr. Harmony seem
to be on such excellent terms, I think I may venture to tell you (if he has not
yet told you himself), that he is the man, who is to be your husband.

MISS WOOBURN. He! Mr. Harmony! No, my Lord, he has not told me; and I am
confident he never will.   270

LORD NORLAND. What makes you think so?

MISS WOOBURN. Because – Because he must be sensible he would not be the
man I should choose.

LORD NORLAND. And where is the woman who marries the man she would
choose? You are reversing the order of society. Men, only, have the right of   275
choice in marriage. Were women permitted theirs, we should have handsome
beggars allied to our noblest families, and no such object in our whole island
as an old maid.

MISS WOOBURN. But being denied that choice, why am I forbid to remain as I
am?   280

LORD NORLAND. What are you now? Neither a widow, a maid, nor a wife. If I
could fix a term to your present state, I should not be this anxious to place you
in another.

MISS WOOBURN. I am perfectly acquainted with your friendly motives, and feel
the full force of your advice. I therefore renew my promise. And although Mr.   285
Harmony (in respect to the marriage state) is as little to my wishes as any man
on earth, I will nevertheless endeavour – whatever struggles it may cost me –
to be to him, if he prefers his suit, a dutiful, an obedient – but, a loving wife,
that I can never be again.   (*Exeunt severally*)

[ACT III Scene ii]

An apartment at Sir ROBERT RAMBLE*'s*
Enter Sir ROBERT *and Mr.* HARMONY

SIR ROBERT. I thank you for this visit. I was undetermined what to do with
myself. Your company has determined me to stay at home.

HARMONY. I was with a Gentleman just now, Sir Robert, and you were the
subject of our conversation.

SIR ROBERT. Had it been a Lady, I should be anxious to know what she said.   5

HARMONY. I have been with a Lady likewise. And she made you the subject of
her discourse.

SIR ROBERT. But was she handsome?

HARMONY. Very handsome.

SIR ROBERT. My dear fellow, what is her name? What did she say, and where   10
may I meet with her?

HARMONY. Her name is Wooburn.

SIR ROBERT. That is the name of my late wife.

HARMONY. It is her I mean.

SIR ROBERT. Zounds, you had just put my spirits into a flame, and now you   15
throw a bucket of cold water all over me.

HARMONY. I am sorry to hear you say so, for I came from her this moment; and
what do you think is the present she has given me to deliver to you?

SIR ROBERT. Pshaw! I want no presents. Some of my old love-letters returned, I
suppose, to remind me of my inconstancy?   20

HARMONY. Do not undervalue her generosity: This is her present; this bond,
which has the power to take from you three thousand a year, her right.

SIR ROBERT. Ah! this is a present indeed. Are you sure you speak truth? Let me
look at it: Sure my eyes deceive me! No, by Heaven it is true! (*Reads*) "Estate
entail" – The very thing I wanted, and will make me perfectly happy. Now I'll   25
be generous again. My bills shall be paid, my gaming debts cancelled, poor
Irwin shall find a friend; and I'll send her as pretty a copy of verses as ever I
wrote in my life.

HARMONY. Take care how you treat with levity a woman of her elevated mind.
She charged me to assure you, "that love had no share whatever in this act, but   30
merely compassion to the embarrassed state of your affairs."

SIR ROBERT. Zounds, Sir, I am no object of compassion. However, a Lady's
favour one cannot return. And so, I'll keep this thing.   (*Puts it in his pocket*)

HARMONY. Nay, if your circumstances are different from what she imagines,
give it me back and I will return it to her.   35

SIR ROBERT. No, poor thing! It would break her heart to send it back. No, I'll
keep it. She would never forgive me, were I to send it back. I'll keep it. And
she is welcome to attribute her concern for me to what she pleases. But surely
you can understand – But Heaven bless her for her love! And I would love her
in return – if I could.   40

HARMONY. You would not talk thus, if you had seen the firm dignity with which
she gave me that paper. "Assure him," said she, "no remaining affection
comes along with it, but merely a duty which I owe him, to protect him from
the humiliation of being a debtor to the man whom I am going to marry."

SIR ROBERT (*with the utmost emotion*). Why, she is not going to be married again!   45

HARMONY. I believe so.

SIR ROBERT. But are you sure of it, Sir?

HARMONY. Both she and her guardian told me so.

SIR ROBERT. That guardian, my Lord Norland, is one of the vilest of men. I tell
you what, Sir, I'll resent this usage.   50

HARMONY. Wherefore? As to his being the means of bringing about your
separation from your Lady, in that he obliged you.

SIR ROBERT. Yes, Sir, he certainly did. But though I am not the least offended
with him on that head (for at that I rejoice), yet I will resent his disposing of
her a second time.   55

HARMONY. And why?

SIR ROBERT. Because, little regard as I have for her myself, yet no other man
shall dare to treat her so ill, as I have done.

HARMONY. Do not fear it. Her next husband will be a man, who, I can safely
say, will never insult, or even offend her; but sooth, indulge, and make her   60
happy.

SIR ROBERT. And do you dare to tell me, Sir, that her next husband shall make
her happy? Now, curse me, if that is not worse than the other. No, Sir, no man
shall ever have it to say "he has made her either happy or miserable," but
myself.   65

HARMONY. I know of but one way to prevent it.

SIR ROBERT. And what is that?

HARMONY. Pay your addresses to her, and marry her again yourself.

SIR ROBERT. And I would, rather than she should be happy with any body else.
Curse me if I would not.   70

HARMONY. To shew that I am wholly disinterested in this affair, I will carry her
a letter from you if you like, and say all I can in your behalf.

SIR ROBERT. Ha, ha, ha! Now, my dear Harmony, you carry your good-natured simplicity too far. However, I thank you, I sincerely thank you. But do you imagine I should be such a blockhead, as to make love to the same woman I 75 made love to seven years ago, and who for the last six years I totally neglected?

HARMONY. Yes: For if you have neglected her six years, she will now be a novelty.

SIR ROBERT. Egad, and so she will. You are right.

HARMONY. But being in possession of her fortune, you can be very happy 80 without her.

SIR ROBERT. Take her fortune back, Sir. (*Taking the bond from his pocket and offering it to* HARMONY) I would starve, I would perish, die in poverty and infamy, rather than owe an obligation to a vile, perfidious, inconstant woman.

HARMONY. Consider, Sir Robert, if you insist on my taking this bond back, it 85 may fall into the husband's hands.

SIR ROBERT. Take it back. I insist upon it. (*Gives it him, and* HARMONY *puts it up*) But, Mr. Harmony, depend on it, Lord Norland shall hear from me, in the most serious manner, for his interference. I repeat, he is the vilest, the most villanous of men. 90

HARMONY. How can you speak with such rancour of a nobleman who speaks of *you* in the highest terms?

SIR ROBERT. Does he, 'faith?

HARMONY. He owns you have some faults.

SIR ROBERT. I know I have. 95

HARMONY. But he thinks your good qualities are numberless.

SIR ROBERT. Now dam'me, if ever I thought so ill of *him*, as I have appear'd to do! But who is the intended husband, my dear friend? Tell me, that I may laugh at him, and make you laugh at him.

HARMONY. No, I am not inclined to laugh at him. 100

SIR ROBERT. Is it old Solus?

HARMONY. No.

SIR ROBERT. But I will bet you a wager it is somebody equally ridiculous.

HARMONY. I never bet.

SIR ROBERT. Solus is mad for a wife, and has been praising mine up to the 105 heavens. You need say no more; I know it is he.

HARMONY. Upon my honour, it is not. However, I cannot disclose to you at present the person's name. I must first ask Lord Norland's permission.

SIR ROBERT. I shall ask you no more. I'll write to her. She will tell me. Or, I'll pay her a visit, and ask her boldly myself. Do you think (*anxiously*) – Do you 110 think she would see me?

HARMONY. You can but try.

Enter SERVANT

SERVANT. Mr. Solus.

SIR ROBERT. Now I will find out the secret immediately. I'll charge him with being the intended husband. 115

HARMONY. I'll not stay to hear you.

Enter SOLUS

Mr. Solus, how do you do? I am extremely sorry that my engagements take me away as soon as you enter. (*Exit* HARMONY *running, to avoid an explanation*)

SOLUS. Sir Robert, what is the matter? Has any thing ruffled you? Why, I never saw you look more out of temper, even while you were married. 120

SIR ROBERT. Ah! that I had never married! Never known what marriage was! For, even at this moment, I feel its torments in my heart.

SOLUS. I have often heard of the torments of matrimony; but I conceive, that at the worst, they are nothing more than a kind of violent tickling, which will force the tears into your eyes, though at the same time you are bursting your sides with laughter.   125

SIR ROBERT. You have defined marriage too favourably. There is no laughter in the state: All is melancholy, all gloom.

SOLUS. Now I think marriage is an excellent remedy for the spleen. I have known a Gentleman at a feast receive an affront, disguise his rage, step home, vent it all upon his wife, return to his companions, and be as good company as if nothing had happened.   130

SIR ROBERT. But even the necessary expences of a wife should alarm you.

SOLUS. I can then retrench some of my own. Oh! my dear Sir, a married man has so many delightful privileges to what a bachelor has! An old Lady will introduce her daughters to you in a dishabille, "It does not signify, my dears, it's a married man." One Lady will suffer you to draw on her glove, "Never mind, it's a married man." Another will permit you to pull on her slipper; a third will even take you into her bed-chamber, "Pshaw, it's *nothing* but a married man."   135

   140

SIR ROBERT. But the weight of your fetters will overbalance all these joys.

SOLUS. And yet I cannot say, notwithstanding you are relieved from the bond, that I see much joy or brightness here.

SIR ROBERT. I am not very well at present; I have the head-ach. And, if ever a wife can be of comfort to her husband, it must be when he is indisposed. A wife, then, binds up your head, mixes your powders, bathes your temples, and hovers about you, in a way that is most endearing.   145

SOLUS. Don't speak of it. I long to have one hover about me. But I will. I am determined I will, before I am a week older. Your description has renewed my eagerness. Don't attempt to persuade me not. I *will* be married.   150

SIR ROBERT. And without pretending not to know whom you mean to make your wife, I tell you plainly, it is Miss Wooburn. It is my late wife. I know you have made overtures to my Lord Norland, and that he has given his consent.

SOLUS. You tell me a great piece of news. I'll go ask my Lord if it be true. And if he says it is, I shall be very glad to find it so.   155

SIR ROBERT. That is right, Sir; marry her, marry her. I give you joy; that's all. Ha, ha, ha! I think I should know her temper. But if you will venture to marry her, I sincerely wish you happy.

SOLUS. And if we are not, you know we can be divorced.

SIR ROBERT. Not always. Take my advice, and live as you are.   160

SOLUS. You almost stagger my resolution. I had painted such bright prospects in marriage: Good day to you. (*Going, returns*) You think I had better not marry?

SIR ROBERT. You are undone if you do.

SOLUS (*sighing*). *You* ought to know from experience.   165

SIR ROBERT. From that I speak.

SOLUS (*going to the door, and returning once or twice, as unstable in his resolution*). But then, what a poor disconsolate object shall I live, without a wife to hover about me; to bind up my head, and bathe my temples! Oh! I am impatient for all the chartered rights, privileges, and immunities of a married man. (*Exit*)   170

SIR ROBERT. Furies, racks, torments. I cannot bear what I feel, and yet I am
ashamed to own I feel any thing!

Enter Mr. PLACID

PLACID. My dear Sir Robert, give me joy. Mrs. Placid and I are come to the very
point you advised. Matters are in the fairest way for a separation.

SIR ROBERT. I do give you joy, and most sincerely. You are right; you'll soon be   175
as happy as I am. (*Sighing*) But would you suppose it? That deluded woman,
my wife, is going to be married again! I thought she had had enough of me!

PLACID. You are hurt, I see, lest the world should say she has forgot you.

SIR ROBERT. She cannot forget me. I defy her to forget me.

PLACID. Who is her intended husband?   180

SIR ROBERT. Solus. An old man, an ugly man. He left me this moment, and
owned it! Go after him, will you, and persuade him not to have her.

PLACID. My advice will have no effect, for you know he is bent upon matrimony.

SIR ROBERT. Then could not you, my dear Sir (as you are going to be
separated), could you not recommend him to marry your wife? It will be all   185
the same to him, I dare say, and I should like it much better.

PLACID. Ours will not be a divorce, consider, but merely a separate maintenance. But were it otherwise, I wish no man so ill, as to wish him married to
Mrs. Placid.

SIR ROBERT. That is my case exactly. I wish no man so ill, as to wish him   190
married to my Lady Ramble; and poor old Solus in particular, poor old man!
A very good sort of man. I have a great friendship for Solus. I can't stay a
moment in the house. I must go somewhere. I'll go to Solus. No, I'll go to
Lord Norland. No, I'll go to Harmony; and then I'll call on you, and we'll take
a bottle together. And when we are both free (*takes his hand*) we'll join – From 195
that moment we'll join, to laugh at, to contemn, to despise all those who boast
of the joys of conjugal love.   (*Exeunt*)

ACT IV Scene i

An Apartment at Mr. HARMONY'*s*
Enter Mr. HARMONY

HARMONY. And now, for one of the most painful tasks that brotherly love ever
draws upon me; to tell another, the suit, of which I gave him hope, has failed.
Yet, if I can but overcome Captain Irwin's delicacy so far, as to prevail on him
to accept one proof more of my good wishes towards him – But to a man of his
nice sense of obligations, the offer must be made with caution.   5

Enter Lord NORLAND

LORD NORLAND. Mr. Harmony, I beg your pardon: I come in thus abruptly,
from the anxiety I feel concerning what passed between us this morning in
respect to Miss Wooburn. You have not changed your mind, I hope?

HARMONY. Indeed, my Lord, I am very sorry that it will not be in my power to
oblige you.   10

LORD NORLAND (*in anger*). How, Sir? Did not you give me your word?

HARMONY. Only conditionally, my Lord.

LORD NORLAND. And what were the conditions?

HARMONY. Have you forgot them? Her former husband.

Enter SERVANT

SERVANT. Sir Robert Ramble is in his carriage at the door, and, if you are at   15
leisure, will come in.

HARMONY. Desire him to walk up. I have your leave, I suppose, my Lord?

(*Exit* SERVANT)

LORD NORLAND. Yes; but let me get out of the house without meeting him.
(*Going to the opposite door*) Can I go this way?

HARMONY. Why should you shun him?   20

LORD NORLAND. Because he used his wife ill.

HARMONY. He did. But I believe he is sorry for it. And as for you, he said to me
only a few hours ago – But no matter.

LORD NORLAND. What did he say? I insist upon hearing.

HARMONY. Why then he said, "that if he had a sacred trust to repose in any one,   25
you should be the man on earth, to whom he would confide it."

LORD NORLAND. Well, I am in no hurry. I can sit a few minutes.

Enter Sir ROBERT RAMBLE

SIR ROBERT. Oh! Harmony! I am in such a distracted state of mind.

(*Seeing Lord* NORLAND, *he starts, and bows with the most humble respect*)

LORD NORLAND. Sir Robert, how do you do?

203

SIR ROBERT. My Lord, I am pretty well. I hope I have the happiness of seeing   30
your Lordship in perfect health.

LORD NORLAND. Very well, Sir Robert, I thank you.

SIR ROBERT. Indeed, my Lord, I think I never saw you look better.

LORD NORLAND. Mr. Harmony, you and Sir Robert may have some business.
I'll wish you a good morning.   35

HARMONY. No, no, my Lord. I fancy Sir Robert has nothing particular.

SIR ROBERT. Nothing, nothing, I assure you, my Lord.

LORD NORLAND. However, I have business myself in another place, and so you
will excuse me.   (*Going*)

SIR ROBERT (*following him*). My Lord – Lord Norland, I trust you will excuse my   40
enquiries. I hope, my Lord, all your family are well?

LORD NORLAND. All very well, Sir.

SIR ROBERT. Your little Elève, Master Edward, the young Gentleman you have
adopted, I hope he is well. (*Hesitating and confused*) And your Ward, Sir, Miss
Wooburn, I hope, my Lord, she is well?   45

LORD NORLAND. Yes, Sir Robert, Miss Wooburn is tolerably well.

SIR ROBERT. Only tolerably, my Lord? I am sorry for that.

HARMONY. I hope, my Lord, you will excuse my mentioning the subject; but I
was telling Sir Robert just now, of your intentions respecting a second
marriage for that Lady. But Sir Robert does not appear to approve of the   50
design.

LORD NORLAND. What objection can *he* have?

SIR ROBERT. My Lord, there are such a number of bad husbands. There are
such a number of dissipated, unthinking, unprincipled men! And – I should
be extremely sorry to see any Lady, whom I have had the honour to be so   55
closely allied to, united to one who would undervalue her worth.

LORD NORLAND. Pray, Sir Robert, were you not then extremely sorry for her,
while she was united to you?

SIR ROBERT. Very sorry for her indeed, my Lord. But, at that time, my mind
was so taken up with other cares, I own I did not feel the compassion which   60
was her due. But, now that I am single, I shall have leisure to pay her more
attention. And should I find her unhappy, it must, inevitably, make me so.

LORD NORLAND. Sir Robert, depend upon it, that on the present occasion, I
shall take infinite care in the choice of her husband.

SIR ROBERT. Might I, my Lord, presume to recommend any one sort of man, it   65
should be a reformed Rake.

HARMONY. I have a notion Sir Robert could point out the exact person.

SIR ROBERT. If your Lordship would permit me to have an interview with Miss
Wooburn, I think I should be able at least –

LORD NORLAND. You would not sure insult her by your presence?   70

SIR ROBERT. Never, if you will promise not to dispose of her without my
consent.

LORD NORLAND. Why your consent?

SIR ROBERT. Because I know her taste. I know what she will like better than any
body in the world.   75

LORD NORLAND. Her request has been, that I will point her out a husband just
the reverse of you.

SIR ROBERT. Then, upon my honour, my Lord, she won't like him.

LORD NORLAND. Have not you liked women the reverse of her?

SIR ROBERT. But I don't think I ever shall again. For, Oh! let me confess to you,   80
my Lord – (*Aside*) though it goes damnably against me to do so – [*To him*] Let
me declare to you, that from the moment our marriage has been dissolved,
from that very moment, I have been languishing in the most torturing, though
concealed desire, to become her husband again. I know I have neglected her
for others; but I now find I could neglect all the world for her. I have treated   85
you, my Lord, oftentimes, with an unwarrantable liberty, but I am at present,
ready to implore your pardon, and to acknowledge my gratitude in the highest
degree, that with all my vices, you have nevertheless allowed, my virtues are
numberless. (*Lord* NORLAND *shews surprise.*)

HARMONY (*aside to Sir* ROBERT). Hush! Don't talk of your virtues now.   90

LORD NORLAND. Sir Robert, to all this incoherent, frantic language, this is my
answer, this is my will: The Lady, to whom I have had the honour to be
guardian, shall never (while she calls me friend) see you more. (*Sir* ROBERT, *at
this sentence, stands silent for some time, then, suddenly recollecting himself*)

SIR ROBERT. Lord Norland, I am too well acquainted with the truth of your
word, and the firmness of your temper, to press my suit one sentence farther.   95

LORD NORLAND. I commend your discernment.

SIR ROBERT. My Lord, I feel myself a little embarrassed. I am afraid I have
made myself a little ridiculous upon this occasion. Will your Lordship do me
the favour to forget it?

LORD NORLAND. I will forget whatever you please.   100

SIR ROBERT. My Lord, I take my leave.

HARMONY (*following him, whispers*). I am sorry to see you going away in despair.

SIR ROBERT. I never did despair in my *life*, Sir; and while a woman is the object
of my wishes, I never will.   (*Exit*)

LORD NORLAND. What did he say?   105

HARMONY. That he thought your conduct that of a just and an upright man.

LORD NORLAND. To say the truth, he has gone away with better manners than I
could have imagined, considering his jealousy is provoked.

HARMONY. I always knew he loved his wife, notwithstanding his behaviour to
her; for, if you remember, he always spoke well of her behind her back.   110

LORD NORLAND. No, I do not remember it.

HARMONY. Yes, he did. And that is the only criterion of a man's love, or of
his friendship.

Enter SERVANT

SERVANT. A young gentleman is at the door, Sir, enquiring for Lord Norland.

LORD NORLAND. Who can it be?   115

HARMONY. Your young gentleman from home, I dare say. Desire him to walk
in. Bring him here.   (*Exit* SERVANT)

LORD NORLAND. What business can he have to follow me?

Enter EDWARD

EDWARD. Oh, my Lord, I beg your pardon for coming hither; but I come to tell
you something you will be glad to hear.   120

HARMONY. Good Heaven! how like his mother!

LORD NORLAND (*taking him by the hand*). I begin to think he is, but he was not so
when I first took him. No, no, if he had, he would not have been thus near me
now. But to turn him away because his countenance is a little changed, I think
would not be right.   125

EDWARD (*to* HARMONY). Pray, Sir, did you know my mother?

HARMONY. I have seen her.

EDWARD. Did you ever see her, my Lord?

LORD NORLAND. I thought you had orders never to enquire about your parents?
Have you forgot those orders?   130

EDWARD. No, my Lord. But when this gentleman said I was like my mother, it
put me in mind of her.

HARMONY. You do not remember your mother, do you?

EDWARD. Sometimes I think I do. I think sometimes I remember her kissing
me, when she and my father went on board of a ship. And so hard she pressed   135
me, I think I feel it now.

HARMONY. Perhaps she was the only Lady that ever saluted you?

EDWARD. No, Sir; not by many.

LORD NORLAND. But pray, young man (to have done with this subject), what
brought you here? You seem to have forgot your errand?   140

EDWARD. And so I had, upon my word. Speaking of my mother, put it quite out
of my head. But, my Lord, I came to let you know, the robber who stopped
you last night is taken.

LORD NORLAND. I am glad to hear it.

EDWARD. I knew you would; and therefore I begged to be the first to tell you.   145

HARMONY (*to Lord* NORLAND). Should you know the person again?

LORD NORLAND. I cannot say I should. His face seemed so much distorted.

HARMONY. Ay, wretched man! I suppose with terror.

LORD NORLAND. No; it appeared a different passion from fear.

EDWARD. Perhaps, my Lord, it was *your* fear that made you think so.   150

LORD NORLAND. No, Sir, I was not frightened.

EDWARD. Then why did you give him your money?

LORD NORLAND. It was surprise caused me to do that.

EDWARD. I wondered what it was! You said it was not fear, and I was sure it
could not be love.   155

HARMONY. How has he been taken?

EDWARD. A person came to our steward, and informed against him. And, Oh!
my Lord, his poor wife told the officers who took him, they had met with
misfortunes, which she feared had caused a fever in her husband's head. And,
indeed, they found him too ill to be removed. And so, she hoped, she said,   160
"that as a man, not in his perfect mind, you would be merciful to him."

LORD NORLAND. I will be just.

EDWARD. And that is being merciful, is it not, my Lord?

LORD NORLAND. Not always.

EDWARD. I thought it had been. It is not *just* to be unmerciful, is it?   165

LORD NORLAND. Certainly not.

EDWARD. Then it must be *just*, to have mercy.

LORD NORLAND. You draw a false conclusion. Great as is the virtue of *mercy*,
justice[1] is greater still. *Justice* holds its place among those cardinal virtues
which include all the lesser. Come, Mr. Harmony, will you go home with me?   170

---

[1] *justice*: Françoise Moreux cites a similar scene in *Nature and Art* (ed. Janice M.
Cauwels, [Ann Arbor, Michigan: Xerox University Microfilms, 1976], 34–36) as
evidence that "Mrs Inchbald penche, comme l'enfant, pour la compassion et non vers
une justice qui appliquée de manière trop stricte, deviendrait la pire des injustices"
(*Elizabeth Inchbald et la comédie "sentimentale" au XVIIIe siècle*, 102).

And before I attend to this business, let me persuade you to forget there is
such a person in the world as Sir Robert, and suffer me to introduce you to
Miss Wooburn, as the man who –

HARMONY. I beg to be excused. Besides the consideration of Sir Robert, I have
another reason why I cannot go home with you. The melancholy tale which   175
this young gentleman has been telling, has cast a gloom on my spirits which
renders me unfit for the society of a Lady.

LORD NORLAND. Now I should not be surprised were you to go in search of this
culprit and his family, and come to me to intreat me to forgo the prosecution.
But, before you ask me, I tell you it is in vain. I will not.   180

HARMONY. Lord Norland, I have lately been so unsuccessful in my petitions to
you, I shall never presume to interpose between your rigour and a weak
sufferer more.

LORD NORLAND. Plead the cause of the good, and I will listen. But you find
none but the wicked for your compassion.   185

HARMONY. The good in all states, even in the very jaws of death, are objects of
envy. It is the bad who are the only real sufferers: There, where no internal
consolation cheers, who can refuse a little external comfort? (*Speaking with
unaffected compassion*) And let me tell you, my Lord, that amidst all your
authority, your state, your grandeur, I often pity you.   190

LORD NORLAND. Good-day, Mr. Harmony. And when you have apologised for
what you have said, we may be friends again.   (*Exit, leading off* EDWARD)

HARMONY. Nay, hear my apology now. I cannot – No, it is not in my nature to
live in resentment, nor under the resentment of any creature in the world.

(*Exit, following Lord* NORLAND)

[ACT IV] Scene ii

An Apartment at Lord NORLAND's
Enter Sir ROBERT RAMBLE, *followed by a servant*

SIR ROBERT. Do not say who it is, but say a Gentleman who has some very
particular business with her.

SERVANT. Yes, Sir.
                                                              (*Going*)

SIR ROBERT. Pray (SERVANT *returns*), you are but lately come into this service, I
believe?
                                                                            5
SERVANT. Only a few days, Sir.

SIR ROBERT. You don't know me, then?

SERVANT. No, Sir.

SIR ROBERT. I am very glad of it. So much the better. Go then to Miss
Wooburn, with a Stranger's compliments who is waiting, and who begs to   10
speak with her upon an affair of importance.

SERVANT. Yes, Sir.
                                                              (*Exit*)

SIR ROBERT. I wish I may die if I don't feel very unaccountably! How different
are our sensations towards our wives, and all other women! This is the very
first time she has given me a palpitation since the honey-moon.   15

Enter Miss WOOBURN, *who starts on seeing Sir* ROBERT; *he bows in great confusion*

MISS WOOBURN (*aside*). Support me, Heaven!

SIR ROBERT (*bows repeatedly, and does not speak till after many efforts, aside*). Was
ever man in such confusion before his wife!

MISS WOOBURN. Sir Robert, having recovered in some measure, from the
surprise into which this intrusion first threw me, I have only to say, that   20
whatever pretence may have induced you to offer me this insult, there are
none to oblige me to bear with it.   (*Going*)

SIR ROBERT. Lady Ramb – (*recalling himself*) Miss Woo – (*she turns*) Lady
Ramble – (*recalling himself again*) Miss Wooburn – Madam – You wrong me. I
have in my time, insulted you, I confess; but it is impossible that time should   25
ever return.

MISS WOOBURN. While I stay with you, I incur the danger.   (*Going*)

SIR ROBERT (*holding her*). Nay, listen to me as a friend, whom you have so often
heard as an enemy. You offered me a favour by the hands of Mr. Harmony –

MISS WOOBURN. And is this the motive of your visit, this the return –   30

SIR ROBERT. No, Madam, that obligation was not the motive which drew me
hither. The real cause of this seeming intrusion is – You are going to be
married once more, and I come to warn you of your danger.

MISS WOOBURN. That you did sufficiently in the marriage-state.

SIR ROBERT. But now I come to offer you advice that may be of the most   35
material consequence, should you really be determined to yield yourself again
into the power of a husband.

MISS WOOBURN. Which I most assuredly am.

SIR ROBERT. Happy man! How much is he the object of my envy! None so well
as I, know how to envy him, because none so well as I, know how to value you.   40
(*She offers to go*) Nay, by Heaven you shall not go till you have heard all that I
came to say!

MISS WOOBURN. Speak it then instantly.

SIR ROBERT. No, it would take ages to speak. And should we live together, as
long as we *have* lived together, still I should not find time to tell you – how   45
much I love you.   (*A loud rapping at the street-door*)

MISS WOOBURN. That, I hope, is Lord Norland.

SIR ROBERT. And what has Lord Norland to do with souls free as ours? Let us go
to Scotland again; and bid defiance to his stern commands.

MISS WOOBURN. Be assured, that through him only, will I ever listen to a   50
syllable you have to utter.

SIR ROBERT. One syllable only, and I am gone that instant.

MISS WOOBURN. Well, Sir?

(*He hesitates, trembles, seems to struggle with himself; then approaching her slowly, timidly,
and as if ashamed of his humiliation, kneels to her. She turns away*)

SIR ROBERT (*kneeling*). Maria, Maria, look at me! Look at me in this humble
state. Could you have suspected this, Maria?   55

MISS WOOBURN. No: Nor can I conceive what this mockery means.

SIR ROBERT. It means, that now you are no longer my wife, you are my
Goddess. And thus I offer you my supplication, that (if you are resolved not to
live single) amongst the numerous train who prefer their suit, you will once
more select me.   60

MISS WOOBURN. You! You who have treated me with cruelty; who made no
secret of your love for others, but gloried, boasted of your gallantries?

SIR ROBERT. I did, I did. But here I swear – Only trust me again, and I swear by

all I hold most sacred, that I will for the future carefully conceal all my
gallantries from your knowledge, though they were ten times more frequent   65
than before.

Enter EDWARD

EDWARD. Oh, my dear Miss Wooburn. What! Sir Robert here too! (*Goes to Sir*
ROBERT *and shakes hands*) How do you do, Sir Robert? Who would have thought
of seeing you here? I am glad to see you though, with all my heart. And so I
dare say is Miss Wooburn, though she may not like to say so.   70

MISS WOOBURN. You are impertinent, Sir.

EDWARD. What, for coming in? I will go away then.

SIR ROBERT. Do, do. There's a good boy. Do.

EDWARD (*going, returns*). I cannot help laughing, though, to see you two
together! For you know you never were together when you lived in the same   75
house.

SIR ROBERT. Leave the room instantly, Sir, or I shall call Lord Norland.

EDWARD. Oh, don't take that trouble, I will call him myself. (*Runs to the door*) My
Lord, my Lord, pray come here this moment. Here is Sir Robert Ramble
along with Lady Ramble!   80

Enter Lord NORLAND

Sir ROBERT *looks confounded, Lord* NORLAND *points to* EDWARD *to leave the room*

(*Exit* EDWARD)

LORD NORLAND. Sir Robert, on what pretence do you come hither?

SIR ROBERT. On the same pretence, as when I was first admitted into your
house; to solicit this Lady's hand. And, after having had it once, no force shall
compel me to take a refusal.

LORD NORLAND. I will try however. Madam, quit the room instantly.   85

SIR ROBERT. My Lord, she shall not quit it.

LORD NORLAND. I command her to go.

SIR ROBERT. And I command her to stay.

LORD NORLAND. Which of us will you obey?

MISS WOOBURN. My inclination, my Lord, disposes me to obey you. But I have   90
so lately been accustomed to obey him, that *custom* inclines me to obey him
still.

SIR ROBERT. There! my Lord! Now I hope you will understand better for the
future, and not attempt to interfere between a man and his wife.

LORD NORLAND (*to her*). Be explicit in your answer to this question. Will you 95
consent to be his wife?

MISS WOOBURN. No, never.[1]

SIR ROBERT. Zounds, my Lord, now you are hurrying matters. You should do it
by gentle means. Let me ask her gently. (*With a most soft voice*) Maria, Maria,
will you be my wife once again?   100

MISS WOOBURN. Never.

SIR ROBERT. So you said seven years ago when I asked you, and yet you
consented.

LORD NORLAND. And now, Sir Robert, you have had your answer. Leave my
house.

(*Going up to him*) 105

---

[1] *No, never*: The ward's equivocal replies to her guardian's questions, here and below,
recapitulate similar scenes in *A Simple Story* (I xiv, xvi).

SIR ROBERT. Yes, Sir; but not without my other half.

LORD NORLAND. "Your other half"?

SIR ROBERT. Yes, Sir, the wife of my bosom, the wife, whom I swore at the altar "to love and to cherish, and, forsaking all others, cleave only to her as long as we both should live." 110

LORD NORLAND. You broke your oath, and made the contract void.

SIR ROBERT. But I am ready to take another oath; and another after that. Oh, my dear Maria, be propitious to my vows, and give me leave to hope you will again be mine.

(He goes to her, and kneels in the most supplicating attitude. Enter EDWARD, *shewing in Mr.* SOLUS *and Mr.* PLACID; EDWARD *points to Sir* ROBERT *(who has his back to them) and goes off)*

SIR ROBERT *(still on his knees, and not perceiving their entrance)*. I cannot live without 115 you. Receive your penitent husband, thus humbly acknowledging his faults, and imploring you to accept him once again.

SOLUS *(going up to Sir Robert)*. Now, is it wonderful that I should want a wife?

PLACID. And is it to be wondered at, that I should hesitate about parting with mine? 120

SIR ROBERT *(starts up in great confusion)*. Mr. Solus, Mr. Placid, I am highly displeased that my private actions should be thus inspected.

SOLUS. No one shall persuade me now, to live a day without a wife.

PLACID. No one shall persuade me now, not to be content with my own.

SOLUS. I will procure a special licence, and marry the first woman I meet. 125

SIR ROBERT. Mr. Solus, you are, I believe, particularly interested about the marriage of this Lady.

SOLUS. And, poor man, you are sick, and want somebody to "bathe your temples," and to "hover about you."

MISS WOOBURN. You come in most opportunely, my dear Mr. Solus, to be a 130 witness –

SIR ROBERT. "My dear Mr. Solus"!

SOLUS. To be a witness, Madam, that a man is miserable without a wife. I have been a fatal instance of that, for some time.

MISS WOOBURN. Come to me then, and receive a lesson. 135

SIR ROBERT. No, Madam, he shall not come to you; nor shall he receive a lesson. No one shall receive a lesson from you, but me.

LORD NORLAND. Sir Robert, one would suppose by this extraordinary behaviour, you were jealous.

SIR ROBERT. And so I am, my Lord. I have cause to be so. 140

LORD NORLAND. No cause to be jealous of Mr. Solus. He is not Miss Wooburn's lover, I assure you.

SIR ROBERT. Then, my Lord, I verily believe it is yourself. Yes, I can see it is by her eyes, and by every feature in your face.

MISS WOOBURN. Oh! my good friend, Mr. Placid, only listen to him. 145

SIR ROBERT. And why "my good friend, Mr. Placid"? *(To* PLACID) By Heavens, Sir, I believe that you only wished to get rid of your own wife, in order to marry mine.

PLACID. I do not wish to part with my own wife, Sir Robert, since what I have just seen. 150

SIR ROBERT *(going up to* SOLUS *and Lord* NORLAND). Then, pray, gentlemen, be so

good as to tell me, which of you two is the happy man, that I may know how to
conduct myself towards him?

MISS WOOBURN. Ha, ha, ha!

SIR ROBERT. Do you insult me, Maria? Oh! have pity on my sufferings.   155

SOLUS. If you have a mind to kneel down again, we will go out of the room.

PLACID. Just as I was comforting myself with the prospect of a divorce, I find my
instructor and director pleading on his knees to be remarried.

Enter Mrs. PLACID, who steals upon Mr. PLACID unperceived

MRS. PLACID. What were you saying about a divorce?

SIR ROBERT. Now, down on your knees, and beg pardon.   160

MISS WOOBURN. My dear Mrs. Placid, if this visit is to me, I take it very kind.

MRS. PLACID. Not absolutely to you, my dear. I saw Mr. Placid's carriage at the
door, and so I stepped in to desire him to go home. Go home directly.

PLACID. Presently, my dear; I will go presently.

MRS. PLACID. Presently won't do. I say directly. There is a lady at my house in   165
the greatest possible distress (*whispers him*), Lady Eleanor. I never saw a
creature in such distraction. (*Raising her voice*) Therefore go home this
moment. You sha'n't stay an instant longer.

SOLUS. Egad, I don't know whether I will marry or no.

MRS. PLACID. Why don't you go, Mr. Placid, when I bid you?   170

SOLUS. No; I think I won't marry.

PLACID. But, my dear, will not you go home with me?

MRS. PLACID. Did not I tell you to go by yourself?   (PLACID *bows, and goes off*)

SOLUS. No; I am sure I won't marry.

LORD NORLAND. And now, Mr. Solus and Sir Robert, these ladies may have   175
some private conversation. Do me the favour to leave them alone.

MISS WOOBURN. My Lord, with your leave *we* will retire. (*Turns when she gets to the
door*) Sir Robert, I have remained in your company, and compelled myself to
the painful task of hearing all you have to say, merely for the satisfaction of
exposing your love, and then enjoying the triumph of bidding you farewell for   180
ever.   (*Exit with Mrs. PLACID*)

SOLUS (*looking steadfastly at SIR ROBERT*). He turns pale at the thought of losing
her. Yes, I think I'll marry.

LORD NORLAND. Come, Sir Robert, it is in vain to loiter here. Your doom is
fixed.   185

SIR ROBERT (*in a melancholy musing tone*). Shall I then never again know what it is
to have a heart like her's, to repose my troubles on –

SOLUS. Yes, I am pretty sure I'll marry.

SIR ROBERT. – A friend in all my anxieties, a companion in all my pleasures, a
physician in all my sicknesses –   190

SOLUS. Yes, I *will* marry.

LORD NORLAND. Come, come, Sir Robert, do not let you and I have a dispute.
                                            (*Leading him towards the door*)

SIR ROBERT. Senseless man, not to value those blessings, not to know how to
estimate them, till they were lost.   (*Lord NORLAND leads him off*)

SOLUS (*following*). Yes, I am determined; nothing shall prevent me. I will be   195
married.

ACT V Scene i

An Apartment at Lord NORLAND'*s*
Enter HAMMOND, *followed by Lady* ELEANOR

HAMMOND. My Lord is busily engaged, Madam. I do not suppose he would see
any one, much less a stranger.

LADY ELEANOR. I am no stranger.

HAMMOND. Your name then, Madam?

LADY ELEANOR. That, I cannot send in. But tell him, Sir, I am the afflicted wife   5
of a man, who for some weeks past has given many fatal proofs of a disordered
mind. In one of those fits of phrensy, he held an instrument of death, meant for
his own destruction, to the breast of your Lord (who by accident that moment
passed), and took from him, what he vainly hoped might preserve his own life,
and relieve the wants of his family. But his paroxysm over, he shrunk from   10
what he had done, and gave the whole he had thus unwarrantably taken, into
a servant's hands to be returned to its lawful owner. The man, admitted to
this confidence, betrayed his trust, and instead of giving up what was so
sacredly delivered to him, secreted it; and, to obtain the promised reward,
came to this house, but to inform against the wretched offender; who now,   15
only resting on your Lord's clemency, can escape the direful fate[1] he has
incurred.

HAMMOND. Madam, the account you give, makes me interested in your behalf,
and you may depend, I will repeat it all with the greatest exactness.

(Exit HAMMOND*)*

LADY ELEANOR *(looking around her)*. This is my father's house! It is only   20
through two rooms and one short passage, and there he is sitting in his study.
Oh! in that study, where I have been so often welcome; where I have urged
the suit of many an unhappy person, nor ever urged in vain. Now I am not
permitted[2] to speak for myself, nor have one friendly voice to do that office for
me, which I have so often undertaken for others.   25

Re-enter HAMMOND, EDWARD *following*

HAMMOND. My Lord says, that any petition concerning the person you come

---

[1] *fate*: execution by hanging.

[2] *only through two rooms ... not permitted*: Here the parallel with *A Simple Story* (III vi) is
verbal as well as situational: "My father within a few rooms of me, and yet I am
debarred from seeing him!"

212

about, is in vain. His respect for the laws of his country demands an example
such as he means to make.

LADY ELEANOR. Am I – Am I to despair then? (*To* HAMMOND) Dear Sir, would
you go once more to him, and humbly represent –   30

HAMMOND. I should be happy to oblige you, but I dare not take any more
messages to my Lord. He has given me my answer. If you will give me leave,
Madam, I'll see you to the door.   (*Crosses to the other side, and exit*)

LADY ELEANOR. Misery! Distraction! Oh, Mr. Placid! Oh, Mr. Harmony! Are
these the hopes you gave me, could I have the boldness to enter this house?   35
But you would neither of you undertake to bring me here, neither of you
undertake to speak for me!

(*She is following the Servant;* EDWARD *walks softly after her, till she gets near the door;*
he then takes hold of her gown, and gently pulls it; she turns and looks at him)

EDWARD. Shall I speak for you, Madam?

LADY ELEANOR. Who are you, pray, young Gentleman? Is it you, whom Lord
Norland has adopted for his son?   40

EDWARD. I believe he has, Madam; but he has never told me so yet.

LADY ELEANOR. I am obliged to you for your offer; but my suit is of too much
consequence for *you* to undertake.

EDWARD. I know what your suit is, Madam, because I was with my Lord when
Hammond brought in your message. And I was so sorry for you, I came out   45
on purpose to see you. And, without speaking to my Lord, I could do you a
great kindness, if I durst.

LADY ELEANOR. What kindness?

EDWARD. But I durst not. No, do not ask me.

LADY ELEANOR. I do not. But you have raised my curiosity. And in a mind so   50
distracted as mine, it is cruel to excite one additional pain.

EDWARD. I am sure I would not add to your grief for the world. But then, pray
do not speak of what I am going to say. I heard my Lord's lawyer tell him just
now, "that as he said he should not know the person again, who committed
the offence about which you came, and as the man who informed against him   55
is gone off, there could be no evidence that he did the action, but from a book,
a particular pocket-book of my Lord's, which he forgot to deliver to his
servant with the notes and money he returned, and which was found upon
him at your house." And this, Lord Norland will affirm to be his. Now, if I did
not think I was doing wrong – This is the very book. (*Takes a pocket-book from his*   60
pocket) I took it from my Lord's table. But it would be doing wrong, or I am
sure I wish you had it.   (*Looking wishfully at her*)

LADY ELEANOR. It will save my life, my husband's and my children's.

EDWARD (*trembling*). But what is to become of me?

LADY ELEANOR. That Providence, who never punishes the deed, without[1] the   65
will be an accomplice, shall protect you for saving one, who has only erred in a
moment of distraction.

EDWARD. I never did any thing to offend my Lord in my life; and I am in such

---

[1] *without*: "Without" used as a conjunction meaning "unless" was "Formerly common in
literary use," but was put down in Johnson's *Dictionary* (1755) as colloquial and is "now
chiefly *illiterate*" (*OED*). All of the printed editions read "unless."

fear of him, I did not think I ever should. Yet, I cannot refuse *you*. Take it.
(*Gives her the book*) But pity me, when my Lord shall know of it.   70

LADY ELEANOR. Oh! should he discard you for what you have done, it will
embitter every moment of my remaining life.

EDWARD. Do not frighten yourself about that. I think he loves me too well to
discard me quite.

LADY ELEANOR. Does he indeed?   75

EDWARD. I think he does. For often, when we are alone, he presses me to his
bosom so fondly, you would not suppose. And, when my poor nurse died, she
called me to her bed-side, and told me (but pray keep it a secret), she told me I
was – his grand-child.

LADY ELEANOR. You are. You are his grand-child. I see, I feel you are. For I feel   80
that I am your mother. (*Embraces him*) Oh! take this evidence back. (*Returning
the book*) I cannot receive it from thee, my child. No, let us all perish, rather
than my boy, my only boy, should do an act to stain his conscience, or to lose
his grand-father's love.

EDWARD. What do you mean?   85

LADY ELEANOR. The name of the person with whom you lived in your infancy,
was Heyland?

EDWARD. It was.

LADY ELEANOR. I am your mother; Lord Norland's only child, (EDWARD *kneels*)
who, for one act of disobedience, have been driven to another part of the globe   90
in poverty, and forced to leave you, my life, behind. (*She embraces and raises
him*) Your father, in his struggles to support us all, has fallen a victim. But
Heaven, which has preserved my child, will save my husband, restore his
senses, and once more –

EDWARD (*starting*). I hear my Lord's step. He is coming this way: Begone,   95
mother, or we are all undone.

LADY ELEANOR. No, let him come. For though his frown should kill me, yet
must I thank him for his care of thee.

                              (*She advances towards the door to meet him*)
                           Enter Lord NORLAND

(*Falling on her knees*) You love me. 'Tis in vain to say you do not: You love my
child. And with whatever hardships you have dealt, or still mean to deal by   100
me, I will never cease to think you love me, nor ever cease my gratitude for
your goodness.

LORD NORLAND. Where are my servants? Who let this woman in?

                              (*She rises, and retreats from him alarmed and confused*)

EDWARD. Oh, my Lord, pity her. Do not let me see her hardly treated. Indeed
I cannot bear it.   105

                           Enter HAMMOND

LORD NORLAND (*to* LADY ELEANOR). What was your errand here? If to see your
child, take him away with you.

LADY ELEANOR. I came to see my father. I have a house too full of such as he
already.

LORD NORLAND. How did she gain admittance?   110

HAMMOND. With a petition, which I repeated to your Lordship.

                              (*Exit* HAMMOND)

LORD NORLAND. Her husband then it was, who – (*To Lady* ELEANOR) But let
him know, for this boy's sake, I will not farther pursue him.

LADY ELEANOR. For that boy's sake you will not pursue his father; but for whose sake are you so tender of that boy? 'Tis for mine, for my sake; and by 115 that I conjure you – (*Offers to kneel*)

LORD NORLAND. Your prayers are vain. (*To* EDWARD) Go, take leave of your mother *for ever*, and instantly follow me; or shake hands with me for the last time, and instantly begone with her.

(EDWARD *stands between them in doubt for some little time: looks alternately at each with emotions of affection; at last goes to his grandfather, and takes hold of his hand*)

EDWARD. Farewell, my Lord. It almost breaks my heart to part from you. But, if 120 I have my choice, I must go with my mother.

(*Exit Lord* NORLAND *instantly. Lady* ELEANOR *and her Son go off on the opposite side*)

[ACT V] Scene ii

Another Apartment at Lord NORLAND*'s*
Enter Miss WOOBURN *and Mrs.* PLACID

MRS. PLACID. Well, my dear, farewell. I have staid a great while longer than I intended. I certainly forgot to tell Mr. Placid to come back after he had spoken with Lady Eleanor, or he would not have taken the liberty not to have come.

MISS WOOBURN. How often have I lamented the fate of Lord Norland's daughter! But, luckily, I have no personal acquaintance with her, or I should 5 probably feel a great deal more on her account than I do at present. She had quitted her father's house before I came to it.

Enter Mr. HARMONY

HARMONY. My whole life is passed in endeavouring to make people happy, and yet they won't let me. I flattered myself, that after I had resigned all pretensions to you, Miss Wooburn, in order to accommodate Sir Robert, that, 10 after I had told both my Lord and him, in what high estimation they stood in each other's opinion, they would of course be friends; or, at least, not have come to any desperate quarrel: Instead of which, what have they done, but, within this hour, had a duel![1] And poor Sir Robert –

MISS WOOBURN. For Heaven's sake, tell me of Sir Robert. 15

HARMONY. You were the only person he mentioned after he received his wound. And such encomiums as he uttered –

MISS WOOBURN. Good Heavens! If he is in danger, it will be vain to endeavour to conceal what I shall suffer.   (*Retires a few paces to conceal her emotions*)

MRS. PLACID. Was my husband there? 20

HARMONY. He was one of the seconds.

MRS. PLACID. Then he shall not stir out of his house this month, for it.

HARMONY. He is not likely; for he is hurt too.

MRS. PLACID. A great deal hurt?

HARMONY. Don't alarm yourself. 25

MRS PLACID. I don't.

HARMONY. Nay, if you had heard what he said!

MRS PLACID. What did he say?

---

[1] *duel*: Mr. Harmony is building upon Sir Robert's threats (III ii 49, 54, 88), but the duel is purely notional.

HARMONY. How tenderly he spoke of you to all his friends –

MRS. PLACID. But what did he say?   30

HARMONY. He said you had imperfections.

MRS. PLACID. Then he told a falsehood.

HARMONY. But he acknowledged they were such as only evinced a superior understanding to the rest of your sex; and that your heart –   35

MRS. PLACID (*bursting into tears*). I am sure I am sorry that any misfortune has happened to him, poor, silly man! But I don't suppose (*drying up her tears at once*) he'll die.

HARMONY. If you behave kind to him, I should suppose not.

MRS. PLACID. Mr. Harmony, if Mr. Placid is either dying or dead, I shall behave with very great tenderness. But if I find him alive and likely to live, I   40 will lead him such a life as he has not led a long time.

HARMONY. Then you mean to be kind? But, my dear Miss Wooburn, (*going to her*) why this seeming grief? Sir Robert is still living; and should he die of his wounds, you may at least console yourself, that it was not your cruelty which killed him.   45

MISS WOOBURN. Rather than have such a weight on my conscience, I would comply with the most extravagant of his desires, and suffer *his* cruelty to be the death of me.

HARMONY. If those are your sentiments, it is my advice that you pay him a visit in his affliction.   50

MISS WOOBURN. Oh no, Mr. Harmony, I would not for the universe. Mrs. Placid, do you think it would be proper?

MRS. PLACID. No, I think it would not. Consider, my dear, you are no longer a wife, but a single Lady, and would you run into the clutches of a man?

HARMONY. He has no clutches, Madam; he is ill in bed, and totally helpless.   55 But, upon recollection, it would, perhaps, be needless to go; for he may be too ill to admit you.

MISS WOOBURN. If that is the case, all respect to my situation, my character, sinks before the strong desire of seeing him once more. Oh! were I even married to another, I feel, that in spite of all my private declarations, or public   60 vows, I should fly from him, to pay my duty where it was first plighted.

HARMONY. My coach is at the door. Shall I take you to his house? Come, Mrs. Placid, wave all ceremonious motives on the present melancholy occasion, and go along with Miss Woodburn and me.

MISS WOOBURN. But, Mrs. Placid, perhaps Mr. Placid is in want of your   65 attendance at home.

HARMONY. No, they were both carried in the same carriage to Sir Robert's.

MISS WOOBURN (*as* HARMONY *leads her to the door*). Oh! how I long to see my dear husband, that I may console him!

MRS. PLACID. Oh! how I long to see my dear husband, that I may quarrel with   70 him!   (*Exeunt*)

[ACT V] Scene iii

The Hall at Sir ROBERT RAMBLE's
The PORTER *discovered asleep. Enter a* FOOTMAN

FOOTMAN. Porter, porter, how can you sleep at this time of the day? It is only
  eight o'clock.
PORTER. What did you want, Mr. William?
FOOTMAN. To tell you my master must not be disturbed, and so you must not let
  in a single creature.   5
PORTER. Mr. William, this is no less than the third time I have received those
  orders within this half hour: First, from the butler, then from the valet, and
  now from the footman. Do you all suppose I am stupid?
FOOTMAN. I was bid to tell you. I have only done what I was desired. And mind
  you do the same.   (*Exit*)   10
PORTER. I'll do my duty, I warrant you. I'll do my duty. (*A loud rapping at the
  door*) And there's a rap to put my duty to the trial.   (*Opens the door*)
          Enter HARMONY, *Miss* WOOBURN, *and Mrs.* PLACID
HARMONY. These ladies come on a visit to Sir Robert. Desire one of the servants
  to conduct them to him instantly.
PORTER. Indeed, Sir, that is impossible. My master is not —   15
HARMONY. We know he is at home, and therefore we can take no denial.
PORTER. I own he is at home, Sir; but indeed he is not to be seen.
MRS. PLACID. But let him know who we are.
PORTER. Indeed, Madam, my master is not in a situation —
MISS WOOBURN. We know his situation.   20
PORTER. Then, Madam, you must know he is not to be disturbed. I have strict
  orders not to let in a single soul.
HARMONY. This Lady, you must be certain, is an exception.
PORTER. No Lady can be an exception in my master's present state. For I
  believe, Sir, but perhaps I should not speak of it, I believe my master is nearly 25
  gone.
MISS WOOBURN. Oh! support me, Heaven!
MRS. PLACID. But has he his senses?
PORTER. Not very clearly, I believe.
MISS WOOBURN. Oh! Mr. Harmony, let me see him before they are quite lost.   30
PORTER. I cannot let you go to him indeed, Madam. He must not be disturbed.
  It is as much as my place is worth, to let a creature farther than this hall; for
  my master is but in the next room.
MRS. PLACID. That is the dining-room. Is not he in bed?
HARMONY (*aside to the ladies*). In cases of wounds, the patient is oftentimes 35
  propped up in his chair.
MISS WOOBURN. Does he talk at all?
PORTER. Yes, Madam, I heard him just now very loud.
MISS WOOBURN (*listening*). I think I hear him rave.
HARMONY. No, that murmuring is the voice of other persons.   40
MRS. PLACID. The Doctors in consultation, I apprehend. Has he taken any
  thing?
PORTER. A great deal, I believe, Madam.
MRS. PLACID. No amputation, I hope?

PORTER. What, Madam?   45

HARMONY. He does not understand you. (*To Miss* WOOBURN) Come, will you go
   back?

PORTER. Do, my Lady, and call in the morning.

MISS WOOBURN. By that time he may be totally insensible, and die without
   knowing how much I am attached to him.   50

MRS. PLACID. And my husband may die without knowing how much I am
   enraged with him. Mr. Harmony, never mind this foolish man, but force your
   way into the next room.

PORTER. Indeed, Sir, you must not. Pray, Mr. Harmony, pray, Ladies, go
   away.   55

MISS WOOBURN. Yes, I must go from my husband's house for ever; never to see
   that, or him again.   (*Faints on Mr.* HARMONY)

MRS. PLACID. She is fainting. Open the windows. Give her air.

PORTER. Pray go away: There is plenty of air in the streets, Ma'am.

HARMONY. Scoundrel! Your impertinence is insupportable. Open these doors.   60
   I insist upon their being opened.

   (*He thrusts at a door in the centre of the stage; it opens and discovers Sir* ROBERT *and*
   Mr. PLACID *at a table surrounded by a company of Gentlemen*)

SIR ROBERT. A song, a song, another song! (*Miss* WOOBURN, *all astonishment, is*
   supported by Mr. HARMONY *and Mrs.* PLACID. *The* PORTER *runs off*) Oh! what do I
   see! Women! Ladies! Celestial beings we were talking of.[1] Can this be real?
   (*Sir* ROBERT *and Mr.* PLACID *come forward. Sir* ROBERT *perceiving it is Miss*
   WOOBURN, *turns himself to the company*) Gentlemen, Gentlemen, married men   65
   and single men, hear me thus publicly renounce every woman on earth but
   this; and swear henceforward to be devoted to none but my own wife.
                                                        (*Goes to her in raptures*)

PLACID (*looking at Mrs.* PLACID, *then turning to the company*). Gentlemen,
   Gentlemen, married men and single men, hear me thus publicly declare, I will
   henceforth be master; and from this time forward, will be obeyed by my   70
   own wife.

   (*Sir* ROBERT *waves his hand, and the door is closed on the company of Gentlemen*)

MRS. PLACID. Mr. Placid, Mr. Placid, an't you afraid?

PLACID. No, Madam. I have consulted my friends, I have drank two bottles of
   wine, and I never intend to be afraid again.

MISS WOOBURN (*to Sir* ROBERT). Can it be, that I see you without a wound?   75

SIR ROBERT. No, my life, that you do not. For I have a wound through my heart,
   which none but you can cure. But in despair of your aid, I have flown to wine,
   to give me a temporary relief by the loss of reflection.

MRS. PLACID. Mr. Placid, you will be sober in the morning.

PLACID. Yes, my dear. And I will take care that you shall be dutiful in the   80
   morning. Sir Robert, come hither, and see me laugh at her. Ha, ha, ha!

HARMONY. For shame, Mr. Placid! How can you treat Mrs. Placid thus? You
   would not, if you knew what kind things she has been saying of you; and how
   anxious she was when I told her you were wounded in a duel.

MRS. PLACID. Was not I, Mr. Harmony?   (*Bursting into tears*) 85

---

[1] *Ladies! Celestial beings we were talking of*: This is particularly ironical since the
drinkers have assembled to make fun of "the joys of conjugal love" (III ii 197).

PLACID (*aside to* HARMONY *and Sir* ROBERT). I did not know she could cry. I never saw it before, and it has made me sober in an instant.

SIR ROBERT. I have been perfectly myself, from the moment I saw my beloved Lady Ramble.

MISS WOOBURN. Mr. Placid, I rely on you to conduct me immediately from this house.   90

SIR ROBERT. That I protest against; and will use even violent measures to prevent it.

Enter SERVANT

SERVANT. Lord Norland.   (*Exit* SERVANT)

Enter Lord NORLAND

MISS WOOBURN. He will protect me.   95

SIR ROBERT. Who shall protect you in my house but I? My Lord, she is under my protection; and if you offer to take her from me, I'll exercise the authority of a husband, and lock her up.

LORD NORLAND (*to Miss* WOOBURN). Have you been deluded hither, and wish to leave the place with me? Tell me instantly, that I may know how to act.   100

MISS WOOBURN. My Lord, I am ready to go with you, but –

HARMONY. But you find she is inclined to stay. And do have some compassion upon two people that are so fond of you.

Enter Mr. SOLUS, *drest in a suit of white clothes*

SOLUS. I am married! Wish me joy! I am married!

SIR ROBERT. I cannot give you joy, for envy.   105

SOLUS. Nay, I do not know that you will envy me so much when you see my spouse. I cannot say she was exactly my choice. However, she is my wife now. And that is a name so engaging, that I think I love her better since the ceremony has been performed.

MRS. PLACID. And pray, when did the ceremony take place?   110

SOLUS. This moment. We are now returning from a friend's house, where we have been joined by a special licence; and I felt myself so happy, I could not pass Sir Robert's door, without calling to tell him my good fortune. And, as I see your Lady here, Sir Robert, I guess you are just married too. And so I'll hand my wife out of the carriage, and introduce the two Brides to each other.   115

(*Exit* SOLUS)

SIR ROBERT. You see, my Lord, what construction Mr. Solus has put on this Lady's visit to me. And by Heaven, if you take her away, it will be said, that she came and offered herself to me, and that I rejected her!

MISS WOOBURN. Such a report would kill me.

Enter SOLUS, *leading on Miss* SPINSTER

SOLUS. Mistress Solus.   (*Introducing her*)   120

HARMONY (*starting*). My Relation! Dear Madam, by what strange turn of fortune do I see you become a wife?

MRS. SOLUS. Cousin, it is a weakness I acknowledge. But you can never want an excuse for me, when you call to mind "the scarcity of provisions."

SOLUS. Mr. Harmony, I have loved her ever since you told me she spoke so well   125
of me behind my back.

Enter SERVANT, *and whispers Mr.* HARMONY, *who follows him off*

LORD NORLAND. I agree with you, Mr. Solus, that this is a most excellent proof of a person's disposition. And in consideration, Sir Robert, that, throughout

all our many disagreements, you have still preserved a respect for my
character in my absence, I do at last say to that Lady, she has my consent to   130
trust you again.

SIR ROBERT. And she will trust me. I see it in her smiles. Oh! unexpected
ecstasy!

Enter Mr. HARMONY

HARMONY (*holding a letter in his hand*). Amidst those bright prospects of joy which
this company are contemplating, I come to announce an event that ought to   135
cloud the splendour of the horizon. A worthy, but an ill-fated man, whom ye
were all acquainted with, has just breathed his last.

LORD NORLAND. Do you mean the husband of my daughter?

SOLUS. Do you mean my nephew?

PLACID. Is it my friend?   140

SIR ROBERT. And my old acquaintance?

HARMONY. Did Mr. Irwin possess all those titles you have given him,
Gentlemen? (*To Lord* NORLAND) Was he your son? (*To* SOLUS) Your nephew?
(*To Mr.* PLACID) Your friend? (*To Sir* ROBERT) And your old acquaintance?
How strange he did not know it!   145

PLACID. He did know it.

HARMONY. Still more strange that he should die for want, and not apply to one
of you!

SOLUS. What! Die for want in London! Starve in the midst of plenty!

HARMONY. No; but he seized that plenty, where law, where honour, where every   150
social and religious tie forbad the trespass; and in punishment of the guilt, has
become his own executioner.

LORD NORLAND. Then my daughter is wretched, and her boy involved in his
father's infamy.

SOLUS. The fear of his ghost haunting me, will disturb the joys of my married   155
life.

PLACID. Mrs. Placid, Mrs. Placid, my complying with your injunctions in
respect of Mr. Irwin, will make me miserable for ever.

MISS WOOBURN. I wish he had applied to me.

SIR ROBERT. And as I refused him his request, I would give half my estate he   160
had *not* applied to me.

HARMONY. And a man who always spoke so well of you all behind your backs! I
dare say, that, in his dying moments, there was not one of you whom he did
not praise for some virtue.

SOLUS. No, no. When he was dying he would be more careful of what he said.   165

LORD NORLAND. Sir Robert, good-day to you. Settle your marriage as you and
your Lady shall approve. You have my good wishes. But my spirits have
received too great a shock to be capable of any other impression at present.

MISS WOOBURN (*holding him*). Nay, stay, my Lord.

SOLUS. And, Mrs. Solus, let me hand you into your carriage to your company.   170
But excuse my going home with you. *My* spirits have received too great a
shock, for me to be capable of any other impression at present.

HARMONY (*stopping* SOLUS). Now, so loth am I to see any of you, only for a
moment, in grief, while I have the power to relieve you, that I cannot help –
Yes, my philanthropy will get the better of my justice.   175

(*Goes to the door, and leads on Lady* ELEANOR, IRWIN, *and* EDWARD)

LORD NORLAND (*runs to* IRWIN, *and embraces him*). My son! (IRWIN *falls on his knees*) I take a share in all your offences,[1] the worst of accomplices, while I impelled you to them.

IRWIN (*on his knees*). I come to offer my returning reason; to offer my vows, that while *that* reason continue, so long will I be penitent for the phrensy which put your life in danger.   180

LADY ELEANOR (*moving timidly to her father, leading* EDWARD *by the hand*). I come to offer you this child, this affectionate child; who, in the midst of our caresses, droops his head and pines for your forgiveness.

LORD NORLAND. Ah! there is a corner of my heart[1] left to receive him. (*Embraces*   185
him)

EDWARD. Then, pray, my Lord, suffer the corner to be wide. Let it be large enough to hold my mother.

LORD NORLAND. It is. My heart is softened, and receives you all. (*Embraces Lady* ELEANOR, *who falls on her knees; he then turns to* HARMONY) Mr. Harmony, I thank you, I most sincerely thank you for this, the joyfullest moment of my   190
life. I not only experience release from misery, but a return to happiness.

HARMONY (*goes hastily to* SOLUS, *and leads him to* IRWIN; *then turns to Mr. and Mrs.* PLACID). And now, that I see you all reconciled, I can say, there are not two enemies in the whole circle of my acquaintance, that I have not within these three days made friends.

SIR ROBERT. Very true, Harmony. For we should never have known half how   195
well we all love one another, if you had not told us.

HARMONY. And yet, my good friends, I must own to you, that with all the merit you attribute to me, I have one most tremendous fault. And it weighs so heavy on my conscience, I would confess what it is, but that you might hereafter call my veracity in question.   200

SIR ROBERT. My dear Harmony, without a fault, you would not be a proper companion for any of us.

LORD NORLAND. And while a man like you, may have (among so many virtues) some faults; let us hope there may be found in each of us, (among all our faults) some virtues.   205

HARMONY. Yes, my Lord. And notwithstanding all our faults, it is my sincere wish, that the world may speak well of us – behind our backs.

THE END

---

[1] *I take a share in* ... *your offences*: Lord Norland tacitly admits that he is one of those "persons who, by their oppressions provoke ... outrages" (III i 90). But since he was the *victim* of the outrage he provoked, poetic justice requires no further punishment for him.

[2] *corner of my heart*: cf. *King Lear*, III ii 73. Similar Shakespearean echoes that fail to be quotations occur at II i 263 and II ii 92, above.

Index